The Suspension
of Henry Adams

*The Augustus St. Gaudens statue (1891) over the
graves of Henry Adams and his wife, Rock Creek
Cemetery, Washington, D.C.*

—Photograph by W. Sprague Holden

The Suspension
of Henry Adams

A Study of Manner and Matter

by Vern Wagner

WAYNE STATE UNIVERSITY

Wayne State University Press   *Detroit, 1969*

124821

Winner of the Hilberry Publication Prize for 1966

Contents

Chapter 1

Preliminaries

I. Introduction

Many of the finest books we know cannot be readily classified. In America *Moby Dick, Huckleberry Finn* and *Walden* defy categories because each is unique. In one sense all of them are prose but looked at otherwise they are at least poetic if they are not poetry. *Moby Dick* and *Huckleberry Finn* are novels but they exceed normal lines. *Walden* is an autobiography but much more too. So is this true of Henry Adams' best-known books, *The Education of Henry Adams* and *Mont-Saint-Michel and Chartres*. It is easily seen that the former is much more than an autobiography, and the latter, while it is history, is art appreciation, and it is—but here is the difficulty.

Great works baffle and above all beguile because they break new paths. In his *Education* Henry Adams offers a possible explanation of this phenomenon in words that themselves baffle and beguile. He calls the new paths "labyrinths":

> In . . . labyrinths, the staff is a force almost more necessary than the legs; the pen becomes a sort of blind-man's dog, to keep him from falling into the gutters. The pen works for itself, and acts like a hand, modelling the plastic material over and over again to the form that suits it best. The form is never arbitrary, but is a sort of growth like crystallization, as any artist knows too well; for often

the pencil or pen runs into side-paths and shapelessness, loses its relations, stops or is bogged. Then it has to return on its trail, and recover, if it can, its line of force. The result of a year's work depends more on what is struck out than on what is left in; on the sequence of the main lines of thought, than on their play or variety.[1]

The passage is not easily clear, but I think Adams means the "pen" is the literary artist trying to convey genuine and original matter to a reader. Everyone understands that an artist's manner conveys his meaning, but how matter calls forth a particular manner is not easy to see. In what proportions is each influential? Adams implies matter is the primary consideration, the basic force. Yet the major emphasis in the quotation is on the manner, on the form which is "never arbitrary." And manner was a principal consideration of Adams as a literary artist.

In an 1874 letter to Henry Cabot Lodge, Adams wrote about a rule that seemed to him essential to good prose:

> . . . the reader ought to be as little conscious of the style as may be. It should fit the matter so closely that one should never be quite able to say that the style is above the matter—nor below it. . . . The higher you pitch the key, the harder it is to sing up to it, and the effect no greater.[2]

Whoever has read Adams very much before finding this remark, made early in his writing career, discovers in it a usual paradox. Applying the pieces of the statement to that short, quizzical man behind a veil, I find (1) in all of his great works—*History of the United States, Mont-Saint-Michel and Chartres,* the *Education* and his final two essays, "The Rule of Phase Applied to History" plus "A Letter to American Teachers of History"—a reader usually is "conscious of the style as may be"; (2) still, in few pages of all the hundreds does the style fail to fit the matter so closely that one is able to say it is above or below it. What complicates the paradox is that, despite Adams' warning against keys pitched too high, the increased height of his own style in the final essays leads most readers to think he did fail to sing up to it at the last and ended shrill and flat. Or if not that, if it was not a failure in style finally, his "matter" was simply wrong.

In any event, to join manner successfully to matter is the fundamental problem an artist faces. Adams noted in *Chartres* that some schoolmen in the middle ages sought to establish logical explanation for the scheme of things by assuming a universe; others began with the atom. So "once having started, they necessarily came into collision at some point between the two" (291).* What is that point? Similarly, in discussing manner and matter in literature the worrisome problem is the point where they collide. Adams wrote in *Chartres:* "When one is not a professor, one has not the right to make inept guesses, and, when one is not a critic, one should not risk confusing a difficult question by baseless assumptions" (230).[3] As a professor I will claim the right to guess; and assuming the role of critic I will risk confusing difficult questions— in this case the relation of Henry Adams' manner to his matter—by making assumptions admittedly baseless in any final sense. To overstate a case as Adams nearly always did provokes livelier thought. Any reader is free to cut mine back. I preface my study of Henry Adams with this disclaimer: I would be foolishly disloyal to what I have learned from studying him if I were less than tentative about conclusions.

A most troublesome puzzle to readers of Henry Adams' works is that after presenting great numbers of conflicts and opposites he failed to conclude anything. Yvor Winters subtitled his resentful Adams essay in *The Anatomy of Nonsense* (1943) "Or the Creation of Confusion." [4] Bernard DeVoto read *The Education of Henry Adams* more than a dozen times (by 1947) only to see how "superhumanly absurd much of his reasoning is." [5] Newton Arvin (1951) wrote that Adams had "a first-rate mind" generally, but "he has obstinately shut his eyes to every manifestation of new life that he does not wish to consider, and allowed his prophetic catastrophism to waste and weaken itself in senile hysteria." [6] William Jordy revealed in his detailed study *Henry Adams: Scientific Historian* (1952) a growing annoyance with the indecision and restless tension Adams died with—or of. One recent writer has forced a solution after all: "The Virgin and the dynamo are not opposing principles permeating the universe: they are allies" who somehow produced "the growth of medieval power technology, which escaped Adams' attention." He concluded, "Man is a bit cosmic; the cosmos is a bit humane; and the free man may worship without despair." [7]

* Numbers in parentheses indicate page numbers in *Mont-Saint-Michel and Chartres* or, hereafter, in the particular work being discussed.

11

Adams is assailed for desiring a universe while almost convinced of a multiverse—and leaving it at that. Most critics and ordinary readers deplore the state of mind that produced as final work the wrong-headed "The Rule of Phase Applied to History" (1909) and "A Letter to American Teachers of History" (1910) in which Adams suggested historians scientifically accept as a fundamental basis the second law of thermodynamics which leads to entropy, and extend Comtean positivism to order the chaos of contrary learnings. Adams never stopped crying for unity and complaining about multiplicity; he talked from both sides of his mouth at once; he refused both faith and despair. Henry Adams gravely called for good temper but he is treated to a considerable quantity of bad because he settled nowhere. He assumed no position of rest. The Augustus St. Gaudens statue sitting above the grave of Henry Adams and his wife in Rock Creek Cemetery in Washington ought rightly to be labeled "Grief," which is definite and conclusive and is its popular name. But it is rather a representation of questioning "Silence" —this Adams meant it to be.[8] But then of course a Ptolemaic universe is easier than a Copernican, and that in turn is comparatively more comfortable than Einstein's with time flying apart.

R. P. Blackmur is the rare critic who met Adams on his own ground. Discussing Adams as a symbolist he wrote: "True symbols, in the sense that the term is here used, are the means by which we express our understanding, or our helplessness in understanding, of what we cannot articulate verbally or by any other intellectual means."[9] The definition parallels Adams' own though he used the word "images"; he wrote in the *Education:* "Images are not arguments, rarely even lead to proof, but the mind craves them, and, of late more than ever, the keenest experimenters find twenty images better than one, especially if contradictory" (489).

Adams used more than twenty contradictory images—Boston and Quincy, action and thought, freedom and discipline, the Virgin and the dynamo, Mont-Saint-Michel and Chartres, justice and mercy, physics and metaphysics, the comet and the mind. I think his use of them explains the increased "confusion," "nonsense," and "fantastic effort" of his late works—if we consider these images as verbal articulations for inconclusiveness. We err if in craving certainty we mistake them for fact or when we read Adams otherwise than as the historian of an education that was a continual quest. Beneath Adams' search for education was his appraisal early in the *Education* of his own set of mind, his "tendency to regard every question as open" (6).[10] Again Blackmur: "Education has no term and if arrested at all is only arrested by impassable failure." [11]

Symbols or images are but two among many words that label what are almost amorphous elements in prose writing in that they are sometimes stylistic, elements of form and manner, sometimes substance itself, elements in the matter of the writing. Like them are hyperbole, wit, satire, irony, paradox, comedy and humor, and all are bridges, junctures between form and content. Together in various mixtures they give the peculiar tones, general characters, and totalities to a piece of prose. Charting components of prose writing like vocabulary, sentence forms, punctuation, paragraph order, figure patterns, abstractions and concrete terminology is necessary for beginning a style analysis. But the analyst who stops with them does not find out what marks the unique quality of a style. And such analysis leaves the matter largely untouched. An analyst must advance to appraise hyperbole, images, wit, symbol, satire, irony, paradox, comedy and humor. Often manner, often matter, they are what I think of as the hermaphroditic aspects of writing. They are also the centrality of literature as art. Considering these mediating qualities helps clarify the proportionate influence of manner and matter, for one concentrates on the vital points of juncture that like any point exists not at all in time or in space—but paradoxically does. This juncture is thus both a distinct element in writing along with form and meaning and is yet non-existent and permanently problematical because it is embedded in both.[12]

One such juncture particularly prominent in Adams' writings is hyperbole. Adams used it in the *History* as a literary device in single statements. In *Chartres* hyperbole is a matter of substance. In the *Education* it is the basis of wit. In the "Rule" and the "Letter" it became so extreme it created grotesquerie. And throughout his works the opposed images forming the paradoxes he increasingly delighted in reveal Adams' recognition of the incongruous elements of the world that forced him to inconclusive thought that became what I think is humor. In his final style, in "A Letter to American Teachers of History" in 1910, Adams wrote:

13

The most ardent lover of paradox,—the most inveterate humorist,
—would hardly think it worth his while to follow a train of reasoning which would surely immolate physics and metaphysics together.
Such amusements seem to be reserved for astronomers (232).

Adams not only emphasized here the opposition between physics and
metaphysics, one of his commonest pairs of conflicting images (one
representing the concrete and the other the abstract, man's double inventions that are in constant conflict), but offhandedly he paralleled paradox with humor. He suggested fine distinctions in his word choice, for
to "immolate" physics and metaphysics not only sacrifices them but also
kills them. The additional remark about astronomers served to fix the
problem by introducing an absurdity—cautiously modified by the word
"seems." The statements leave the reader like Adams himself in a state
of inconclusion. Only good temper can contain the confusion, what we
more usually call a sense of humor, and of all the junctures I have listed
that blend manner and matter, it is this one that I think is most important in Henry Adams' major works. But what humor is puzzles thought,
more so, I think, than does satire or irony, but not less than wit,
laughter or the comic, all subtle divisions of the larger term.

II. Humor

In trying to explain humor one is tempted to agree with E. B. White
that "essentially, it is a complete mystery." [13] This is pretty conclusively
proved by seeking to explain a joke as, for example, Freud tried to do,
with helpless results. Contemplating the meaning of the term introduces
a consideration of wit (if that is verbal play, what is play?), of laughter
(if it is only physiological spasms, why?), of the funny (what is so
funny? If it is incongruity, what is that precisely?), of comedy (if it is
pleasant reconciliation, what is reconciling and to what?), of the comic
(we are back at funny), and of satire and irony. In the last two terms
everyone agrees humor is essential, but quite how or why is elusive. Yet
like speculation about the intricate meanings of art, beauty, goodness or
tragedy, the temptation to define humor is naggingly present.

I think one can best meet the term by considering it a metaphysical
problem. This is to reach the ground immediately that grants the mys-

tery, admits the difficulty, but claims reality. One further move brings up a consideration of the *sense* of humor, and this is what can perhaps be called a problem of attitude. This sense I think Henry Adams exhibited beyond all else.

One thing is admissible in searching through the term humor. As several writers have pointed out or implied—Schiller, Bergson, Meredith and Baudelaire—the exercise of intelligent consciousness, of mind, is essential to it. One other thing is also admissible, I think, and that is that humor is founded on suspicion. Max Beerbohm in his wry little essay on laughter explains this when he declared that he suffered "from a strong suspicion that things in general cannot be accounted for through any formula or set of formulae, and that any one philosophy, howsoever new, is no better than another." He added, "That is in itself a sort of philosophy," and then provided the key to an explanation of humor by further adding, "and I suspect it accordingly." [14] Beerbohm thus supplied a neat capsule explanation of ultimate humor: to suspect any settled position must include a suspicion of the suspicion.

Henry Adams' final lesson teaches humor as I understand the term so far. In the *Education* he said in two places, once at the beginning of his book and again at the end, "silence next to good-temper was the mark of sense." (first Preface, viii; repeated, 501) Elsewhere he spoke of his "aching consciousness of religious void." (352) Together these two short passages provide a basis for understanding Adams' humor. The alternative to faith or to outright denial is a balance between them, the void itself; but the void "aches" because of a double pull between affirmation, acceptance and belief on the one hand, and denial, refusal and rejection on the other. Is there God? Is there no God? In the *History* he had said "Scientific habits of thought would provide control over destiny," then asked what destiny was. He said quickness of mind is an advantage, then wondered how it is this when man is confronted with insoluble questions. All dilemmas Henry Adams encountered left him inconclusive, irresolute, uncertain, doubtful. They left him in transition. He ended with tentative silence which is an image of non-commitment, of balance between all positions, in suspension. Such a position was Adams' ideal, and though he failed to realize it completely he did come closer to it than most.[15]

For Adams the greater wisdom lay in "good temper" since bad

temper is outright rejection. Henry Adams rejected no possibility. To him human beings triumph only through seeking the deepest harmony the world allows, and this is the sense of flux. This is to seek the elusive point between dreams of stable unity in a universe and the anarchic flow of forces in the multiverse. Only a sense of humor provides this suspension, a third position to be maintained at all costs between the probing horns of all dilemmas. This is why humor is ultimately not very "funny"; the sense of it provokes little outright laughter at all, for it stares incongruity full in the face, seeing opposites as probably irreconcilable, realizing conflict and confusion as constantly present. It knows truth plays tricks, assumes guises, and swings unpredictably only to pause or hover occasionally. Such thorough incongruity is the only absolute Adams accepted. In the face of it silence is therefore the only philosophical position to take while good temper is the only attitude.

To have a sense of humor is to possess a rare ability to watch the clash of immovable walls and unstoppable forces without rushing to some solid and comforting corner. The true man of humor stoutly quivers among choices, calling plagues on all our houses.[16] But this does not imply that the man of humor exhibits a sense of superiority. He exhibits a brave humility in that he only observes, seeking to recognize as best he may, choosing no sides by giving judgment. He knows irony, of course; he plays the gadfly, but he remains as coldly selfless as mind can make him. Through mind he sets himself apart, separate, to appraise but not to judge. He deeply suspects positions, attitudes, decisions and dogmas of every kind. He believes nothing because he finds nothing worthy of belief. To him every man's weakest point is that closed spot where he is convinced. Nor does he disbelieve, realizing that to do so exhibits belief by being anti-belief, like the religious man who adopts atheism as a creed. He teeters. The true man of humor therefore distrusts in all respects. He keeps proportion by suspecting with as good temper as he can muster the profundity of his distrust. Thus he has no firm attitude that regards all questions as open; smarter than this, he has a chastening "tendency" to regard all questions as open. This is Henry Adams.

The true man of humor only records, only recognizes. He fully registers no things he sees, mistrusting his sight. He hovers perpetually, something like Meredith's Comic Spirit, but unlike it he does not hover above all things but in the free space among them. He does do what Meredith says the Comic Spirit does, "eyes but does not touch." [17] Decision alone dams the living stream of his continuous looking. A confirmed gambler in ideas, speculation is his game. Nothing is sacred, nothing whatever is certain including uncertainty. Though he contemplates all things "for fun," this is not to say his game is not serious or is foolish. The much-quoted maxim applies here: "The wise man never laughs but he trembles." And in Henry Adams' case, the reverse was also true for Adams never trembled but he sought to laugh.

We can see what humor is by indirection, considering satire in a kind of negative contrast. In Henry Adams' major works satire is not important. Alan D. McKillop in speaking of the eighteenth century in his *Eighteenth Century Poetry & Prose* talks of "the satiric spirit of the age, the impulse to pass genial or bitter judgment on the failings of mankind in the light of an absolute standard of virtue and reason." [18] Edgar Johnson writes of satire as it has generally appeared on much the same basis in his *A Treasury of Satire:* "The essential trick of satire is a dexterous stripping away of false fronts"; it is a "kind of *unmasking.*" "It is criticism getting around or overcoming an obstacle"—this is "what satire really is." [19] Both writers indicate that the satirist founds his efforts on firm belief in trustworthy, even "moral" reality. McKillop speaks of "judiciousness" and "moralizing commentary" (xxi, xxii). Johnson says serious satire is "born of bitter earnest," adding that the satirist is "a licensed teller of unpleasant truths" (17, 23). Since Adams grew to hold no absolute standards of truth, or of virtue or of reason, satire was of little use to him in his late works.

Satire aims at fools among human beings and foolishness in human institutions; it is not directed at the universe itself because that remains a mystery criticism cannot alter. The satirist assumes possible correction. Johnson says:

> It is no easy job to tidy up our intellectual and spiritual universe. But to live in chaos is to accept defeat. We all want order in our lives and meaning in our world . . . so we have to hew a path through the absurdities and empty-headed mouthings of conventional formulas, through old and new fanaticisms, through muddle and deliberate misrepresentations, through cruelty and suffering (36).

At first one thinks that to live in chaos is to accept defeat. But if one finds good temper while realizing all things change, all are in transition, he can repel defeat. If one sees chaos constitutes reality, it is wrong to deny it for the sake of desired order. That would be pretension.[20] Thus satire is directed here below. The satirist trusts man's reason will achieve order eventually. It is therefore only a joke when Adams quotes Clarence King's remark that "Except for two mistakes, the earth would have been a success": the changes of the seasons and the division of the sexes (*Education*, 269). Anyone can deride things he cannot change. Derision is not satire though it may be a part of humor.

Satire proved no use to Adams in his late works for he did not seek to amend anything. His 1880 political novel *Democracy* is satirical as a result of disappointment when Adams discovered what he had thought was real American democracy was being defeated by real corrupt people. When he looked at democracy again in the *Education* in 1905 he found he did not have enough basic faith in it to provide him with a basis for satire. The satirical passages that occur in this book ridiculed people who willfully failed to appreciate unreality. Thus the fine story Adams tells about Victor Hugo. The poet sat throned at the end of a large room with men and women seated along the walls. He declared after a long silence that he believed in God. Another silence ensued. Then came the worshipful comment of an idolator, "Chose sublime! un Dieu qui croit en Dieu!" With criticism, he treated the "Eccentricity" of the British ruling class, the thick-headedness of the German university system, and in a long and curious description, that supposed genius of the late Victorian age Charles Algernon Swinburne, in which he finally and shortly after many paragraphs of awed praise showed his final doubt of Swinburne's complete genius because, like Hugo probably, Swinburne was too complete a mind to admit uncertain possibilities. (*Education*, 143)

In the religious novel *Esther* (1884) and in *Chartres* (1904) Adams dealt with uncertainties and confusions too great for satire. A case can be made for satire in the "Rule" and the "Letter," in which Adams' fellow historians are held up to ridicule, though I do not see it easily. These essays are, rather, examples of Adams' richest humor; they can be read as satire only if satire includes multiversal situations as fit subjects for reform by man which they clearly are not. The satire present strikes human beings, but it is a minor element. Adams' large interest was in the Mighty All, not the minuscular human.

Humor is then a larger term than satire. Satirists do employ their wits to evoke laughter, usually as a key device, but they shoot their arrows at mankind. They do not aim at God. The great humorists are not fundamentally satirical. They do deal with God. In my sense of the term satire does not stem from a sense of humor at all because it is founded on a relatively stable position from which the satirist judges, criticizes and deplores other positions. The humorist, I repeat, has no position. We can see from the rich display of their work in Johnson's anthology *A Treasury of Satire*, which only samples the great mass of satirical literature throughout the ages, that satirists abound. Most of these satirists are writers whose work also appears in collections of "humor." Those from our century whom Johnson includes are people like James Thurber, Ogden Nash, Dorothy Parker, Ring Lardner, Aldous Huxley, Saki and Anatole France. But "humorous" though the writings of these people are in that they draw laughter, only when they deal with man's relationships to forces beyond the edges of his physical world, only when they deal with ideas themselves and not with the people who hold them, only when they show a full suspension of mind, are they humorists also. Plato's Socrates was a humorist because he was serious in his claim of ignorance and reveals non-position. Cervantes was another because though most obviously satirizing chivalry and courteous love in *Don Quixote* more basically he really settled nowhere in suspending his reader between the Noble Knight who threw his bonnet over the windmill and his lowly squire who kept his firmly tied on his head. Shakespeare was probably a humorist beyond everything else. The world has produced few real humorists because the bigness of mind that will permit vast tolerance is too difficult to have. I sometimes think, of Americans, that Benjamin Franklin was a humorist. Nathaniel Hawthorne certainly was, and Herman Melville was truly one at the last as "Billy Budd" shows, for here Melville quietly reveals the irreconcilable conflicts between Billy and Captain Vere and Claggart and does not resolve them. Mark Twain recognized the humorist's necessary behavior when he says at the end of "The Mysterious Stranger" that only laughter, a refusal to be committed, is man's final defense; but he did not, finally, laugh himself for he was too grimly bitter. Emily Dickinson, Gertrude Stein, George Santayana and Robert Frost frequently reveal humor, although I do not think they are basically humorists. But Henry Adams was a humorist par excellence.[21]

The humorist mocks. He exasperates. He lacks reverence entirely. Max Eastman rightly says religion and humor are antithetical.[22] Conviction of any kind exhibits man's frailty of mind since conviction is conclusion and a prop against chaos. The declaration of the devout that "God is love" is therefore as lacking in humor as the Preacher's cry in Ecclesiastes that "All is vanity." Humorists only add. They do not do sums. This distinguishes them from the satirists since the latter imply a basic summation of what ought to be. Finally, humorists do not rest because in refusing any kind of definition they preserve movement.

To most people a true humorist is a threat of Satanic proportions since he doubts all serious positions by being essentially silent and not-committed. Outright pessimism is virtue in contrast since pessimists, at least, evince a kind of conviction.

Henry Adams distinguished the true man of humor by implication through another approach, one that "conclusively" points up the humorist's suspension. Toward the end of *Mont-Saint-Michel and Chartres* he described "three kinds of skeptics: the disbelievers in human reason; the passive agnostics; and the skeptics proper, who would have been atheists had they dared." Saint Francis was of the first. John of Salisbury, Bishop of Chartres in 1176, was of the second—"I prefer to doubt," he said, "rather than rashly define what is hidden." The last class is the one to look at, and it is Adams' own. It contains the true man of humor, those who would be atheists "had they dared" but who did not dare because they were what John of Salisbury himself called them, "Cornificci": "as though they made a practice of inventing horns of dilemma on which to fix their opponents" (318–319). Adams followed this definition with a perfect illustration that leaves the reader at last in empty air.[23] The Cornificci asked "whether a pig which was led to market was led by the man or the cord. One asks instantly: What cord?—whether Grace, for instance, or Free Will?" (319) The perfect end to the joke is the fact that no reader can fully understand just what the problem became. It is magicianship in which the humorist even fools himself, for he is after all puzzled and uncertain before a mystery that, though embodied in a ridiculous example, demonstrates the unknown and requires suspension of mind as the only answer. And it is suspension of mind that lies beneath humor.[24]

III. Biography

Before proceeding with a closer study of Henry Adams' writings, some preliminary orientation is necessary to have in mind more clearly who Henry Adams was, what his world was like generally as best we can recapture it, and what part he played in it. It is helpful to realize certain basic facts that provide a frame for the man.

Henry Adams' eighty years covered remarkable history in his own country, in the rest of the world, and in what he came to think it was, in the multiverse at large. Born in Boston, Massachusetts, in 1838, his boyhood witnessed the Mexican War, his young manhood the Civil War, and his late middle age the Spanish American War. He died in Washington, D.C. in 1918, just before the end of the First World War. More important was the fact that during these eighty years he saw the industrial revolution flower, capitalism develop and world communism begin. Material inventions in his lifetime developed in spectacular fashion every important tool man has devised including the lever, the wheel, the compass, gunpowder, the printing press and the magnifying glass. At his birth the world was vegetable, animal and perhaps spiritual. At his death it was mineral, mechanical and probably material. At his birth the world was unified and God-willing. Man was primate. Progress upward was the assumption of nearly the entire western world. Science was hardly more than a cozy corner in metaphysics. In his lifetime Adams considered Comte, Darwin, and Marx, and he was even aware of Freudian thought and Einsteinian physics. He lived to see the first three discredited in part but did not live to observe the full impact of the last two.

His best-known work is the book wrongfully called his "autobiography," *The Education of Henry Adams*. Written mostly in 1905–1906 it was originally published privately in a hundred copies in 1907. Adams was nearly seventy years old when he finished it, a seventy years that saw him develop in the eyes of the world as a successful college professor, as an editor, and especially as an historian—his nine-volume *His-*

tory of the United States (1891) is a definitive study of American politics and diplomacy in the first two decades of the nineteenth century. The *Education* is intriguing for several reasons, one of which is that throughout its 500 pages Adams makes constant claims of failure. This is a puzzle, especially because the notion is linked to this fact: the *Education* is an important key to understanding the development of American intellectual thought as it came out of the nineteenth century. It is a necessary textbook for any student of the nineteenth century. But this does not say that Adams was a representative nineteenth-century American in any usual sense.

The external facts of Adams' life show no spectacular adventure. Born the son of one of our greatest American diplomats (Charles Francis Adams, Minister to the Court of St. James's during the difficult years of the Civil War) he was the grandson of one President of the United States, John Quincy Adams, and the great-grandson of another, John Adams. In his youth he thought of the White House as the family's Washington home. Few American families can present such distinction. Unlike millions of his fellow Americans, he was deeply dyed with ancestral inheritance and weighted with a great tradition and the drag of past ages. Unlike so many of us who cannot name our four grandparents, Henry Adams knew minute details about his great-grandparents. The burden implied that he was genuinely a child of the past, what he called repeatedly "an eighteenth century child," not of the present. That he became so markedly a man of the future as well is a significant aspect of his genius though it is a paradox of his career.

As a boy he spent his summers in the free country air of Quincy, Massachusetts, and his winters pent in Boston schools. He entered Harvard with his Boston Latin School mates in 1854 in a class of 100 students, only three or four of whom were outsiders, one the son of Robert E. Lee. He was graduated in 1858 with the distinction of being elected class orator. But he complained that Harvard had taught him nothing. He went to Berlin to study civil law. But he found to his chagrin that to study civil law there required a knowledge of German he did not have. For nearly three months, at the age of twenty, he attended a German junior high school with boys of fourteen—a fact that either belies the carefully established pose in the *Education* of his shyness, sense of propriety and family dignity, or supports the view that as an

Adams he knew what he did was above criticism. He spent two years in Germany, learning, he claimed, nothing of value but the appreciation of a Beethoven symphony accidentally acquired in a German beer hall. He traveled to Rome, saw Garibaldi, wrote a few letters back to Boston that appeared in one of the local newspapers, stopped in Paris, and after completing what amounted to the grand tour of eighteenth-century young gentlemen, in November of 1860 he returned to his father's house in Boston intending to read law.

The Civil War interfered. Lincoln appointed his father Minister to England and Mr. Adams enlisted young Henry's services as private secretary. The Adamses were in London seven years, all through the Civil War and for three years following. When Henry again returned to the United States in 1868 he was thirty years old, untrained for any profession, unfitted for any business but the lesser tasks of diplomacy— as under secretary, perhaps to some obscure legation, a career his friend John Hay picked up. Unsure what to do in the bustling, post-Civil War American world, he decided to go to Washington, a town that was in large part his as much as anyone's, considering the number of years his family had lived in it.

During his years in London he had written two articles the influential *North American Review* printed, one the real story of Captain John Smith and Pocahontas (January, 1867), the other a "review" of Sir Charles Lyell's *Principles of Geology* (October, 1868), a scientific volume in the Darwinian strain. The success of these pieces and of his earlier letters from Italy encouraged him to hope he could become at Washington a magazinist and newspaperman, a political pundit writing commentaries on the national government in action. This career did not continue. In 1870 he accepted two other jobs.

President Eliot invited Adams to Harvard to teach medieval history as an assistant professor. Adams disclaimed knowledge in the field, but he accepted the appointment—and the editorship of the *North American Review* itself. He stayed at Cambridge for seven years, until 1877, when he resigned both his positions to move to Washington once again, this time with a very clear purpose: to write on American history. Until 1891 he worked at this chore, and that year he finished publishing his *History*. He had also published a number of articles and essays, two volumes of biography, and two novels, one entitled *Democracy* (1880), a harsh satire on the workings of American democracy as corruption (like Twain's *The Gilded Age*), and the other *Esther* (1884), a study of religious faith in the modern age.

After 1891 Adams devoted himself to travel and study—or as he put it to the pursuit of the "education" he had interrupted in 1870 to take up "active life" like his neighbors. During the following three decades, with a yearly income of some $25,000 that rose to $50,000,[25] he saw most of the world—Japan, the South Seas, Mexico, India, the Mediterranean area, Scandinavia, and more thoroughly England and France. He even visited Russia. But during these seemingly idle years he continued to write: letters by the score; a biography of the last queen of Tahiti (1893), another of his young poet friend George Cabot Lodge (1911). But, most important, he wrote his *Education* and the book to which it was a sequel, *Mont-Saint-Michel and Chartres* (1904) a study of the architecture, history, poetry, song, and especially the theology of the late medieval period in France from 1100 to 1300. In 1909 he wrote but did not publish an extended essay called "The Rule of Phase Applied to History" (which he called the third of a trilogy along with the *Education* and *Chartres* [Cater, lxxxvii]). In 1910 he published a longer essay, "A Letter to American Teachers of History."

What drama existed in Adams' life beyond his mind, study and writing desk occurred during what has since become famous as "the silent twenty years," the period from 1870–1890 when he was most active in the usual pursuits of man, in his case as teacher, editor and historian. These years are particularly intriguing because the "autobiography" he wrote in his old age ignores them. The reader of the *Education* learns with surprise that Henry Adams married a suitable Boston girl in 1872. The marriage was a happy one, all observers agreed, and Mrs. Adams died in 1884 after twelve years of marriage. The reader is shocked to learn that one December Sunday morning Mrs. Adams went to her room, swallowed potassium cyanide and died a suicide. The existence of Mrs. Adams is ignored in the *Education*. Readers of books like the *Education* whose attention immediately strays to the writer—those who have a strong biographical bias in interpreting literature—find the grim nature of the book explained when they learn this fact of Mrs. Adams' death. To date no one knows the full explanation of her action, and her husband tried to obscure it by recalling letters, burning diaries and refusing to discuss it. But this drama brands Adams' life as different from most.

To the present day the more obvious facts about Henry Adams add up to this: Henry Adams was a poseur and a dilettante, a cynic and a pessimist, an atheist and an aristocrat. They also show that he was a student, a humanist and a free thinker. A closer study reveals that he is a paradox and a contradiction. And this closer study compels a realization that he is among the greatest students, thinkers and writers America has produced. I suggest a careful reading of Adams' major works with —and this is my thesis—special attention to their manner will help to clarify the real Henry Adams. Even without resolving the paradox he was—though that too should result in part—it will show these things:

1. Henry Adams is a great stylist in American English.
2. Henry Adams is a protestant in the fullest sense.
3. Henry Adams' major works deal with the deepest American thought. And finally,
4. Henry Adams is one of the few genuine humorists of our literary history.

Henry Adams' outward life was so largely without drama that his wife's suicide is incongruous because it unbalances an appreciation of his career. The outward life is important only as it surrounds "the life within." As the years increase past his death, as the years have separated us from Emerson, Franklin—and Shakespeare and Plato—what will increasingly remain is his "artistic product." Adams wrote in the second Preface to the *Education* that the "garment of education" should be the object of study, but admittedly the "figure" necessarily gets attention too. Most of us, however much we are attracted to the figure, are discontent to remain with it finally. Example we look for, but precept we cling to. Likewise an examination of specific subject matter regardless of its manner of presentation is not a fully rewarding study. What literature teaches us most in the long run as beauty, as goodness, and eventually as truth, comes from a concentrated examination of its art, of the form that contains the matter, or the form that may be called forth by it.

My attempt here is to expose the art of Henry Adams, but an art that is inseparable from the thought; I seek to reveal the manner whereby Henry Adams conveyed his matter.

Studying Adams' letters, the many books he read in his lifetime, the facts of his life, does help to explain the major works, as many fine Adams scholars have amply demonstrated. But too much attention devoted to these contributory matters detract importance from the formal works. The major formal works are the artistic product requiring emphasis. I have therefore concentrated my study on them, the four major ones consisting of the *History* (1891), *Chartres* (1904), the *Education* (1907) and the final two essays considered together, the "Rule" (1909) and the "Letter" (1910).

Chapter 2

The Historical Critic

I. The Histories

Adams' *Historical Essays* printed in 1891 contain his earliest formal work, essays written between 1867 and 1884. They are careful, factual and flowing, in a style a modern reader is little conscious of, barring his sensitivity to the formality and stiffness here as in most late nineteenth-century non-fiction prose. Blocks in the sentences, half-veiled allusions and aphoristic statements, so common later in Adams' writings, are missing. The accounts are straightforward, employing lengthy quotations from documents. But recognizable signs of the Adams of the later years do appear in a few places.

A first example is a long sentence describing President Grant (the "caveman" of the *Education*) in "The Session. 1869–1870" (first printed in *North American Review* in July 1870). It has a touch of acid, negative words, inversion, mild over-statement, abstract vocabulary, and it ends with the live and sharply concrete word "brains":

Nothing could be more interesting to any person who has been perplexed with the doubts which President Grant's character never fails to raise in every one who approaches him, than to have these doubts met and explained by some competent authority,—by some old associate like General Sherman, with an active mind ever eager to grapple with puzzles; by some civil subordinate such as a civil subordinate ought to be, quick at measuring influences and at unravelling the tangled skein of ideas which runs through the brains of an Administration.[1]

A second example is in "Primitive Rights of Women," a lecture read before the Lowell Institute in 1876, but revised when reprinted in 1891. Adams tells with relish the story of the Icelandic *Njalsaga* and its heroine Hallgerda who paid off slaps in the face from two of her three husbands by having one murdered and by refusing to help the other when he was pressed towards death by his enemies. The note here is typical Adams: admiration for that early feminist in Iceland linked with a quiet exposure of woman's less soft and feminine qualities:

> Then Gunnar said to Hallgerda: "Give me two locks of thy hair; and ye two, thy mother and thou, twist them together into a bowstring for me."
> "Does aught lie on it?" said she.
> "My life lies on it," he said; "for they will never come close quarters with me if I can keep them off with my bow."
> "Well," she said, "now I will call to thy mind that slap on the face which thou gavest me; and I care never a whit whether thou holdest out a long while or a short."
> She sat by, all that night, and saw her husband slowly exhausted by one wound after another, until at last his enemies could come near enough to kill him; but he did not turn his hand against her, and Hallgerda lived to enjoy the wealth acquired from her three murdered husbands, and to bring more misery and death on her friends (*Historical Essays*, 30–31).

The relish is in the telling as well as the told—and we are at one of those points where manner and matter coincide, the crucial juncture to be considered in appraising literary style.

Another early work, *The Life of Albert Gallatin* (1879) is of small consequence in a study of Henry Adams' style since it consists largely of a compilation of the papers of the great Secretary of the Treasury, a man who had Adams' admiration.[2] Like most darkly suspicious thinkers and most novelists Adams wrote with greater color of people he disliked. John Randolph was such a figure. Adams' biography of him (*John Randolph*, 1882) is a short study (304 small pages) of the sorry politician from Virginia who described himself, so Adams was pleased to quote him in the last sentence of the book, as a man of "Time misspent, and faculties misemployed, and senses jaded by labor or impaired by excess" (304). Adams exhibited no sympathy for this confession. Throughout the book he condemned the "brutality or bitterness" of Randolph and his lamentable lack of self-restraint.[3] Again, the matter overlaps the manner and they are not quite separable.

This book is clear, lively, and almost casually written: "John Thomson, one of Randolph's intimates, the author of Gracchus, Cassius, Curtius, and Heaven knows how many more classical effusions . . ." (45–46). But a common Adams' manner, balance in the sentences with the heaviest weight on the final swing, occasionally occurs:

> These principles implied a policy of peace abroad and of loose ties at home, leaned rather towards a confederation than towards a consolidated union, and placed the good of the human race before the glory of a mere nationality (34).

> Avoiding all discussion of impeachment as a theory, and leaving untouched the political meaning of his eighth article, he [Randolph] deliberately tangled his limbs in the meshes of law, and offered himself a willing victim to the beak and claws of the eagles who were marking him for their sport (142).

Adams wrote Henry Cabot Lodge in 1879, "The most difficult thing to me is to vary the length of my sentences so as to relieve the attention" (Ford, I, 318). He achieved and did not achieve the goal here. Generally he is readable. But he failed frequently, as in the two sentences I have quoted, by calling attention to a style which distracts the reader. I think the explanation for the looseness of style is that *Randolph* was a secondary product, a volume Adams tossed off while composing his major early work, the nine-volume *History*.[4]

In taking up now the great *History* for consideration one finds that the matter of the nine volumes has been thoroughly dealt with in the books of such able scholars as Ernest Samuels, William Jordy, J. C. Levenson and Elizabeth Stevenson and in many periodical articles by others. As a history it remains one of the "universally acknowledged historical masterworks"; Ferdinand Schevill has written:

Foremost of these in the English language is by general consent Gibbon's *Decline and Fall of the Roman Empire*. . . . However, because of merits different from those of the older work but of equal importance, Adams' *History* presses it close.[5]

Even Yvor Winters in his *Anatomy of Nonsense* says the same: the *History* is "the greatest historical work in English, with the probable exception of *The Decline and Fall of the Roman Empire*" (415). One sees much reason for these declarations. Like Gibbon, Adams exhausted sources in his dogged insistence on documenting all facts, the spoil from years of digging in family papers at the Adams home place at Quincy, and documents in Washington, Madrid, London and Paris. Nearly eight decades after its publication it stands as definitive as any historical work we have.

Adams published the work as a tetralogy, dividing it into parts of two volumes each except for the last which was in three volumes. Levenson, however, presents a division of the material that better marks it as a series of three trilogies:

Domestic Problems:
    Vol. I—Jefferson's experiment in negative government.
    Vol. II—The Louisiana Purchase: the basis of American policy is national sovereignty.
    Vol. III—Burr; the nation's ability to withstand him.

International Problems:
    Vol. IV—The Embargo as a test of pacific national policy.
    Vol. V—American government, borrowing from Europe, stumbles.
    Vol. VI—Germination of popular energy at the cost of war.

The War of 1812:
    Vol. VII—Account of the War of 1812.
    Vol. VIII—Account of the War of 1812.
    Vol. IX—Account of the War of 1812.[6]

Each of the nine volumes contains from 385 to 474 pages, averaging 440-odd, and from fourteen to twenty-five chapters, usually twenty-odd, except for Vol. IX which has only 242 pages but includes 125 pages of index. Each chapter is about twenty-five or twenty-six pages in length, and the paragraphs are about half a page long, regularly, although the quotations and the documentation do not allow an easy count.

This kind of examination reveals the *History* as regular, measured and controlled. But it is only when one gets beyond this easy count and digs into the paragraphs themselves to see what the sentences are like, those smallest units of writing that communicate to most of us a complete or nearly complete idea, that we can approach closest to understanding Adams' unique style.

What does this style provide? Does it condition such diapasons of praise as Professor Schevill's and Mr. Winters'? Does it fit the matter so closely that, as Adams had written Henry Cabot Lodge in 1874, "one should never be quite able to say that the style is above the matter—nor below it"? Henry Steele Commager thinks so:

> . . . the limpid clarity and beauty, the classic restraint, the flashing brilliance of the prose; the lofty and tranquil impartiality, rigidly judicious without being abstract or impersonal; the serene philosophic approach which permeates the grave unhurried pages of the volumes; the fine sense of balance and form that distinguishes the work of art from the mere compilation of historical facts; the splendid devotion to, the rigorous regard for, truth as the ultimate end of history.[7]

Mr. Commager sees the *History* written as well as one could ever expect. But I think he does not appraise it accurately. "Limpid clarity" is often missing. Vast stretches of the work are dull. "Classic restraint" is often violated for the sake of telling sentences and phrases—for the sake of the "flashing brilliance" Commager praises. Frequently a reverse of lofty impartiality and serenity occur. But these things distinguish the writing, and, ironically, point up Adams' grand goal: truth. But it is ironic this is so, and thus we come to a gnarliness inseparable from Adams' matter and his thought.

A different point of view is expressed by Ernest Samuels. Commenting on Adams' revisions of his essays for publication in 1891, Samuels says

> A glance at the alterations made . . . indicates how rigorously he applied to his own writing the Spartan advice he gave to others.

The historical present which had annoyed him in Nicolay's sections of the *Lincoln* was regularly changed to the simple past tense. The editorial *we* similarly went by the board. So also vanished the vague moralizing at the end of "The Legal Tender Act." Relentlessly he hunted down adjectives and intensives whose force was already implicit in the narrative. Why "a series of disasters"? Why not simply "disasters"? He slashed away at "which" clauses and verbal crutches like "but," "however," "It seems," and all the parenthetical reservations of the scholar.

Samuels concludes:

One result of this zeal for a completely functional style, void of adornment like a runner or prize fighter, impersonal as fate—or science, was to give to some reviewers of the *History* an impression of coldness and inhuman detachment. He was called a "brilliant and somewhat cold-blooded truth teller . . . [whose writing] approaches nearer the standard of science than any extended historical work yet written on this side of the Atlantic." [8]

The style is functional, right enough. But it is not void of adornment; nor does it produce an impression of inhuman detachment. At the end of the third chapter of the first volume, "Intellect of New England," Adams concluded:

Evidently an intellectual condition like that of New England could not long continue. The thoughts and methods of the eighteenth century held possession of men's minds only because the movement of society was delayed by political passions. Massachusetts, and especially Boston, already contained a younger generation eager to strike into new paths, while forcibly held in the old ones. The more decidedly the college graduates of 1800 disliked democracy and its habits of thought, the more certain they were to compensate for political narrowness by freedom in fields not political. The future direction of the New England intellect seemed already suggested by the impossibility of going further in the line of President Dwight and Fisher Ames. Met by a barren negation on that side, thought was driven to some new channel; and the United States were the more concerned in the result because, with the training and literary habits of New Englanders and the new models already established in Europe for their guidance, they were likely again to produce something that would command respect (I, III, 106–107).

The most evident quality of this prose is structural balance in the sentences. But balance is also the substance of the paragraph, reflecting the scale-like attitude of Adams' mind. New England intellect in 1800 faced oppositional attractions between the fixed past and the fluid future; both stimulated an unknowable mixture. Throughout the *History* Adams constantly dealt with oppositions that resulted in change, the only conclusive result. Thus the eight open questions in the final paragraph of the *History* pointed to the future of Americans after 1815 but all were worded as balances, indicating uncertain possibilities: "They were mild, but what corruptions would their relaxations bring? They were peaceful, but by what machinery were their corruptions to be purged? . . . What object, besides physical content, must a democratic continent aspire to attain?" (IX, X, 242)

Balance occurred so frequently it is the most notable characteristic of the sentences. Often it was achieved by sentence inversion. In Volume III, Chapter XI, within the space of a few pages these occur:

Had Burr . . . they would. . . . (254)

Furnished with these . . . Ogden. . . . (255)

Owing chiefly to . . . the town. . . . (258)

Leaving his wife . . . Blennerhassett. . . . (260)

To communicate . . . Burr. . . . (261)

More usually the balance is correlative, as these scattered examples occur:

[No] diplomatist was so fortunate as Livingston for the immensity of his results compared with the paucity of his means (II, II, 48).

[Congress] showed little energy except for debate, and no genius except for obedience (IV, IX, 200).

. . . if Stanford's speech was exasperating in its candor, Randolph's was stinging in its sarcasm (IV, IX, 215).

The army, already mutinous, submitted with what philosophy it could command to the necessity it could not escape (VI, XV, 334).

[Chapter beginning:] In such a war the people of the U. S. had only themselves to fear; but their dangers were all the more formidable (VI, XVIII, 388).

Occasionally the balance doubles back on itself:

Madison would have been glad to secure for Gallatin the succession; he had no special love or admiration for Monroe, while his regard for Gallatin was strong and constant; but Pennsylvania cared more for interests than for men, while Virginia cared so much for men that she became prodigal of interests (VII, II, 39).

Such a sentence distorts acceptable fact; it is doubtful Pennsylvania and Virginia were so opposite. Virginia and Pennsylvania must then be read as symbols (Blackmur's word) or images (Adams'). Specious perhaps, the sentence does satisfy what Adams called the craving of the mind for images. (*Education,* 489)

More noticeable than sentences of balance are those appearing throughout all nine volumes in which exaggeration predominates. Thus:

That an insane man could be guilty . . . punished . . . [etc.] seemed such a perversion of justice that the precedent fell dead on the spot (II, VII, 158).

. . . Europe, gorged as for fifteen years she had been with varied horrors, shuddered from St. Petersburg to Cadiz (IV, III, 66).

The American people pardoned everything except an empty Treasury (IV, VI, 148–149).

History has nothing to do with law except to record the development of legal principles (IV, XI, 265).

. . . not an American could be found, between Canada and Texas, who avowed the wish to fight [in 1809] (IV, XVIII, 424).

. . . every mind was intent on profiting (IV, XX, 473).

Madison flung himself into Canning's arms (V, V, 88).

The navy was a sink of money. [New paragraph:]
The army was something worse (V, VIII, 168).

Although no one doubted that the year 1812 was to witness a new
convulsion of society . . . (VI, IV, 67).

. . . a child could calculate . . . (VI, VI, 123).

[Congress went home.] At home they found chaos (VI, X, 210).

The government was ruined in credit and character [1813]; bankrupt, broken, and powerless, it continued to exist merely because of
habit, and must succumb to the first shock (VII, III, 68).

Any reader of the *Education* will find such a series of quotations
familiar. But the *History* has a reputation for being impartial, judicious,
serene and tranquil, as Professor Commager described it, as well as
having flashing brilliance and cold-bloodedness. The exaggerations,
however, and the absoluteness in such statements I have quoted, do not
show Adams' style in the *History* was always one of classic restraint.
The explanation for this lack of restraint stems, I think, from Adams'
use of balance in sentence structure. He always sought a counterpart for
an initial statement to create a more definite image—chiaroscuro. Not
"shuddered all over Europe," or even "shuddered in St. Petersburg,
Cadiz and elsewhere," but the sharper though overdone "shuddered
from St. Petersburg to Cadiz." Literal sense was distorted; the figurative
was enhanced; and the visible sign of the idea is much clearer. Such an
explanation accounts for the exaggeration of "The American people
pardoned everything except an empty Treasury." Exaggeration became
for Adams a natural habit of expression to achieve readability, extending to full *hyperbole* which becomes, finally, the single word best describing what is unique in the style of the *History*. Thus:

Most picturesque of all figures in modern history, Napoleon
Bonaparte, like Milton's Satan on his throne of state, although
surrounded by a group of figures little less striking than himself,
sat unapproachable on his bad eminence; or, when he moved, the
dusky air felt an unusual weight (I, XIII, 334).

The death of Hamilton and the Vice-President's flight, with their
accessories of summer-morning sunlight on rocky and wooded

heights, tranquil river, and distant city, and behind all, their dark background of moral gloom, double treason, and political despair, still stand as the most dramatic moment in the early politics of the Union (II, VIII, 190–191).

. . . the earthen pot of Spanish dominion. . . . the iron energy of American democracy (III, III, 58).

The brand seethed and hissed like the glowing olive-stake of Ulysses in the Cyclops' eye, until the whole American people, like Cyclops, roared with pain and stood frantic on the shore, hurling abuse at their enemy, who taunted them from his safe ships (IV, II, 27).

[John Randolph] alone shone among this mass of mediocrities, and like the water-snakes in Coleridge's silent ocean his every track was a flash of golden fire (IV, XVI, 379).

While Napoleon labored to reconstruct his system mutilated by American legislation, the Government of Great Britain sank lower and lower toward disappearance, while the star of Spencer Perceval shone alone with dull lustre on the British horizon (V, XIII, 262).

Spain had little reason to draw distinctions between friends, allies, and enemies. She could hardly stop to remember that the United States were filching a petty sand-heap in a remote corner of the world, at a time when England was "wresting" not one but all the splendid American provinces from their parent country, and when France was kneeling on the victim's breast and aiming stab after stab at her heart (V, XIV, 315).

[Monroe,] Secretary of State, acting Secretary of War, general-in-chief by a double guarantee, and President thereafter, what more could the witches promise on the blasted heath of politics that could tempt ambition? (VI, XIX, 423–424)

The troops remained till October 14 in their transports in the bay, and then set sail for Jamaica, leaving Virginia and Maryland to a long repose, which the vexed shores sorely needed (VIII, VI, 173).

Such hyperbole is also what Adams' critic "Housatonic" called it as early as 1890, *"tropical,"* [9] in that Adams thought in terms tinged with terror and horror, not sanguinary but "sanguinolent." [10] This accounts for the cold-bloodedness.

Elizabeth Stevenson says Adams' "most pervasive manner was that of wit. . . . Yet it was not incompatible with pity or with passion." [11] Most of the quotations I have given so far are witty—that is, they reveal Adams' facility in verbal play—but only Gallatin escapes censure.[12] Another series of passages more fully exemplify the wit peculiar to Adams in that they have as ingredients balance, exaggeration, hyperbole, and often a sanguinolent touch. The *History* as a whole is not a witty work except that it is intelligently written. It is a serious, weighty, scholarly production. But one of its great virtues is that seriousness is relieved as it is in Gibbon by touches of wit that give special point to situations, people or happenstance. So:

> The sentiments in which Paine gloried [in a letter to Jefferson in 1801] "to have steadily labored," so far as they were recent, chiefly consisted in applause of the French Revolution, in libels on President Washington and his successor, and in assaults on the Christian religion (I, XII, 316).

A few pages later appears a more excessive comment:

> The clergy had always hated Jefferson, and believed him not only to be untruthful, but to be also a demagogue, a backbiter, and a sensualist. When they found him, as they imagined, actually at work stripping not only the rags from their religion, but the very coats from their backs, and setting Paine to bait them, they were beside themselves with rage and contempt (I, XII, 321).

Some other largely built sentences are these:

> To leave Bonaparte "under apprehensions" was to be the object of Madison's diplomacy at Paris,—a task which several European governments were then employing half a million men to accomplish, hitherto without success, but which Madison hoped to effect by civilities to Merry [the British Minister to Washington] (III, III, 71).

> The most aristocratic American of the twentieth century will probably agree with the most extreme socialist in admitting that Congress, in 1808, might with advantage have doubled its propor-

tion of tailors, butchers, and swindlers, if by doing so it could have lessened the number of its conspirators (IV, VIII, 184).

Before midnight the flames of three great conflagrations [the Capitol, the White House, and the navy-yard on the Eastern Branch] made the whole country light, and from the distant hills of Maryland and Virginia the flying President and Cabinet caught glimpses of the ruin their incompetence had caused (VIII, V, 145).

More frequently the witticism is abrupt:

No man in American history left a better name than [Nathaniel] Macon; but the name was all he left (I, X, 267).

If the Prince of Peace [Godoy of Spain] was a man of no morals, the ex-Bishop of Autun was one of no morality (I, XIV, 352).

[A quotation from Madison which read "we flatter ourselves. . . ." Adams' comment:] He flattered himself in vain (III, II, 34–35).

. . . they had every sense except the sense of proportion (III, XV, 366).

Erskine, the British minister, . . hurried from one to another of the officials at Washington, trying to penetrate their thought,—an easy task,—and to . . . (IV, XVII, 384).

[Canning] lost more habitually than ever the thread of his own labyrinth (V, VII, 133).

[A quotation from a London newspaper sneering at] "a few fir-built frigates, manned by a handful of bastards and outlaws,"—a phrase which had great success in America (VII, I, 2).

Monroe's character . . . was transparent; no one could mistake his motives, except by supposing them to be complex (VII, II, 35).

[On the Thirteenth Congress, 1813:] Otherwise the members varied little from the usual type, and showed more than their usual faculty for discussing topics no longer worth discussion (VII, III, 53).

All these examples can be grasped in a rapid reading. Others, however, fewer in number, are considerably more subtle, intriguing remarks preceding the rich profusion in the *Education* that go so far to make of that book one to be read with great care. These witticisms ripple in the mind after they are first noted:

[If Talleyrand had attached himself to Moreau and not to Bonaparte] some millions of men would have gone more quietly to their graves (I, XIII, 335).

They still would have died.

To sum up the story in a single word, Spain had immense influence over the United States; but it was the influence of the whale over its captors,—the charm of a huge, helpless, and profitable victim (I, XIII, 340).

These have a more sophisticated double direction:

. . . a formidable list of articles, which if not, like Jamaica rum, necessary to America, were essential to civilized existence (III, VII, 155).

Or—Congress had passed a measure to spend a large sum on equipping naval vessels in 1808, a measure which

threatened to take from the Treasury and throw into the ocean all the money reserved to support the first year of hostilities (IV, XVIII, 426).

Or:

They could not believe that a government would fling itself headlong out of the window in order to oblige the people to save it from breaking its neck (V, XVI, 356).

And another doubled remark is:

. . . but the true story proved more modern, if not less amusing, than the conspiracies of Greece and Rome (VI, VIII, 175).

Another variety of witticisms in the sentences of the *History* points up a larger and less easily recognized fact about the work:

> No one who saw the quickness of this revolution could doubt that whatever evils war might cause, it was a potent force to sweep nations forward on their destined way of development or decline (VI, XX, 436).

> [A comparison of the South's use, in 1812, of "commercial deprivations" of their goods from Europe—assuming their "necessity to Europe"—with that of a later "experiment":] and their second experiment had results still more striking than those which attended their first (VII, XV, 379).

The reference here to the Civil War—which is nowhere named—and the implication in the preceding quotation that "wars cause changes—somehow" both reveal the mind of an historian not so much dispassionate as acid, not cool but cold, not impartial but grim, not certain but distrustful. He described his *History* in the *Education* thus:

> Historians undertake to arrange sequences,—called stories, or histories—assuming in silence a relation of cause and effect. . . . [Adams] had even published a dozen volumes of American history for no other purpose than to satisfy himself whether, by the severest process of stating, with the least possible comment, such facts as seemed sure, in such order as seemed rigorously consequent, he could fix for a familiar moment [the United States, 1800–1817] a necessary sequence of human movement.

But he concluded:

> Satisfied that the sequence of men led to nothing and that the sequence of their society could lead no further, while the mere sequence of time was artificial, and the sequence of thought was chaos, he turned at last to the sequence of force (382).

The "severest process of stating, with the least possible comment" was Adams' ideal. But his hyperbole and wit demonstrate one way he failed to achieve it. His conviction of inconclusion shows it another. He appraised in the *History* itself some of the documents he had to use:

The expressions of newspapers, like those of orators, could not be accepted without allowance, for they aimed at producing some desired effect, and said either more or less than the truth; as a rule, they represented the cool opinion neither of the person who uttered nor of the audience who heard them; but in the absence of other records, public opinion was given only in the press, and the London newspapers alone furnished evidence of its character (VII, XIV, 356).

The final musings in the last volume on "American Character" and Adams' explanation that his *History* was a diplomatic and political story whereas the future America must be studied as a race or a society all amount to this:

The result had satisfied him as little as at Harvard College (*Education*, 382).

Why?

. . . all opinion founded on fact must be error, because the facts can never be complete, and their relations must be always infinite (410).

Therefore:

History is a tangled skein that one may take up at any point, and break when one has unravelled enough (302).

The *History* shows Adams felt in his bones history is conflict, confusion and ignorance.[13] Such an attitude required a style to match. Thus his use of balance, a technique neither accidental nor unconscious nor copied. "I doubt if there is a chapter in my history," Adams said in 1910, "that I have written less than four or five times."[14] Writing history, as he saw it then, demanded sentences full of "either-or," "yes—but," "he did, except." Exaggeration and hyperbole, over- and under-statement, and sharp and astringent wit all emphasized larger truth. The pendulum of thought had to swing to extremes to show that truth is probably unknowable permanently.

When Adams declared in 1891 he cared more for one chapter or any dozen pages of his 1884 novel *Esther* than for the whole *History* (including maps and indexes) (Ford, I, 468), it is not sufficient to explain this statement on the basis of his tender feelings for a novel intimately though indirectly dealing with himself and his wife. A further explanation is that the novel form permitted an artistic expression of doubt, incertitude, confusion and inconclusiveness the rigorous demands of factual, documentary history did not allow. Not until he came to write *Mont-Saint-Michel and Chartres* did he find a sufficient skill to treat history openly as he found it must be treated—as incertitude. Esther was like the Virgin, human, a woman, and appealing. History like the dynamo, though just as mysterious in its genuine meaning, was repellent because inhuman and ignorant. In the last chapter of the *History* Adams wrote:

> No historian cared to hasten the coming of an epoch when man should study his own history in the same spirit and by the same methods with which he studied the formation of a crystal.

Knowing that man considers himself a separate factor in the scheme of things, he continued:

> Yet history had its scientific as well as its human side, and in American history the scientific interest was greater than the human. Elsewhere the student could study under better conditions the evolution of the individual, but nowhere could he study as well the evolution of a race. The interest of such a subject exceeded that of any other branch of science, for it brought mankind within sight of its own end (IX, X, 224–225).[15]

As always the "Yet" shows the double pull of contrary drives. The end is not described.

All nine volumes of the *History* add up to eight questions which in turn had grown from Adams' attempt to answer the seven questions he had asked as a prelude in Volume I, Chapter VI (184). As of 1800 he had asked if American society could "create and maintain in the mass of mankind those habits of mind which had hitherto belonged to men of science alone." As of 1817 he assumed habits of mind belonging to scientists had become common to all Americans: "They were scientific, and what control would their science exercise over their destiny?" (IX, X, 241–242) In 1800 he had asked if the American society could "transmute its social power into the higher forms of thought," and "Could it produce, or was it compatible with, the differentiation of a higher variety of the human race?" In 1817 the question shifted to a dead end: "They [the American people] were quick, but what solution of insoluble problems would quickness hurry?" The final question, also worded to imply a balance, presents a problem as current as our daily breath: "What object, besides physical content, must a democratic continent aspire to attain?" The last sentence in the work follows, a flat statement implying hollow laughter, "For the treatment of such questions, history required another century of experience."

Only a third position between oppositions remained—suspension. The end is open, indefinite, inconclusive, revealing Adams' position in the matter of history, a non-position most clearly revealed by his stylistic employment of balance in his phraseology.

II. *Mont-Saint-Michel and Chartres*

Mont-Saint-Michel and Chartres (1904) [16] differs in tone from the *History* and the *Education*, and from the "Rule" and the "Letter." It is joyous, warm and intimate, whereas the *History* is mostly flat and cold, the *Education* dismal and ominous, and the "Rule" and the "Letter" giddy. All the chapters but two or three (X, XII—and possibly the last one, XVI) end brightly in contrast to the regular downbeat of those in the *Education* or the open possibilities nearly always contrived in the *History* or the shattered and uncertain paragraphs that conclude the two final essays. It is chatty and familiar, full of you's and we's. It has a colorful air of youthful life quite at variance with everything else Adams wrote. Logic and reason, fact and detail, pomp and circumstance, all are toys here. Despite the concrete "facts" recorded, aphoristic distillations drawn from them are few. The book appeals strongly to the mist of "taste" and not to the crystallization of reason. The book is founded on learning that blends so smoothly with the story telling it is almost hidden. It is a chemical composition, not a mixture at all. Vernon Louis Parrington wrote:

Mont-Saint-Michel and Chartres is a beautiful book. . . . rich
and tender and wise, perhaps beyond anything else that his generation of Americans wrote, with a mellow scholarship that walks mod-
estly because it has learned how little it knows.[17]

It is a beautiful book, suggestive, fresh and memorable. And in addition to its loveliness it conveys a concentrated wisdom Parrington only
hinted at. The last three sentences read:

The delight of its [the Gothic Cathedral's] aspirations is flung up to
the sky. The pathos of its self-distrust and anguish of doubt is
buried in the earth as its last secret. You can read out of it whatever else pleases your youth and confidence; to me, this is all (377).

The first two sentences oppose each other but they do not balance, since
the second is the heavier weight carrying the major emphasis. Here the
pendulum swings not back and forth as in the *History* but up, then
down—and down. The antecedent of the "this" in the last sentence gives
a surface impression of applying to both ends of the pendulum's swing,
but it actually applies most strongly not to the single word "aspirations"
but to the double phrases "self-distrust" and "anguish of doubt" that
stay buried in the earth as a secret still.

Thus the wisdom of this volume is more of that with which the
History ended: Inconclusiveness unresolved because, as Adams wrote in
the *Education*, "complexity precedes evolution" (302) ". . . this is
all." The inconclusion is suspension. It must be this or it must be
despair. The incongruities Adams saw in the late middle ages he could
bear only with skepticism. Acceptance or denial was impossible since
either position rejects the possibility of knowing. Henry Adams was not
agnostic in the sense of thinking final explanations are unknowable,
though he did not think them known; nor was he the stoic he is usually
called for stoicism is acceptance too in that it is impassive and unresist-
ing. Silence alone is stoic; but in saying "Silence next to good temper"
is the mark of sense, a declaration Adams made in the beginning and
again at the end of the *Education,* good temper is more important than
quietude since it leaves the way open to further and perhaps endless
speculations, recognizings and additions.

To see the eleventh-century Mont-Saint-Michel against the thirteenth-century Amiens, the simple faith of William the Conqueror against the complex logic of Saint Thomas Aquinas; the plain Romanesque against the fanciful Gothic, God alone against the Holy Trinity—all this opposition produced full hyperbole of meaning. But for over half of this book we pause between these extremes at Chartres during the late twelfth century with the Virgin Mary; we hover there on a balance point and contemplate Unity. But Adams did not see twelfth-century unity as stability and position. It was a paradoxical absence of both for it was Transition. The harmony at Chartres cathedral is a mystery, one that combined the upright, square tower of the eleventh-century Norman with the sloping, many-sided spire of the Gothic, and the round, Romanesque arch of Mont-Saint-Michel with the pointed arch of the full thirteenth-century Gothic. More than this, Chartres is the mystery of Mary herself as she is opposed not only to the simple, single, masculine God of Mont-Saint-Michel but to the Holy Ghost of the Trinity that succeeded her in the thirteenth century.

In contrast to the rigorous statement of fact in the *History*, *Mont-Saint-Michel and Chartres* blurred fact when it did not ignore it. The goal was to capture "not a fact but a feeling" (14) because of course the force exerted by the Virgin can only be felt and not reasoned. Hence a literal translation of *Chanson de Roland* was of no consequence because "Poetry was not usually written to prove facts." (19) Mont-Saint-Michel itself is wholly masculine; Chartres is entirely feminine; both "feel" so. Saint Francis was the earthly representative of Mary's pure religion of love. Thomas Aquinas later, despite his virtue, was a shrewd and perhaps sly purveyor of orthodoxy. The three great queens of France, Eleanor, Blanche and Alice, completely dominated the actual world of their age as the Virgin absolutely dominated their church—this we feel: "Eleanor's real nature in no way concerns us," Adams declared. (210) "Tourists want as few dates as possible; what they want is poetry." (36) [18]

What tourists want, in short, is a living sense of a past 700 years dead when man did sense the Virgin as "the greatest force the Western world ever felt." Whether "symbol or energy," as Adams described her in the *Education* (388), she defied understanding. What if wars and pestilences and injustice and pain did exist as concrete fact? Are they more important than the exciting unity demonstrated by the life of Saint

Francis and seen with overwhelming validity in such gorgeous structures as the cathedral at Chartres? Can any tourist who studies this far-
gone time care for anything but the atmosphere and the attitude—and
the art? We are forced to agree with Henry Adams by asking with him
the rhetorical question, "What is the most sympathetic?"

No twentieth-century person can accept as literal the twelfth century
Adams described—its youth and exuberance and "purity of emotion,"
its naive Saint Francis with his sisters the birds and his Brother Fire,
and finally "our sister death." (341) These things contrast to their loss
with our modern sense of "the daily evidence of increasing and extending complexity." (375) They contrasted as well with the fearful list of
evils known in daily twelfth-century life. Despite this, the amazing *artistic* fact is that "Truth, indeed, may not exist; science avers it to be only
a relation; but what men took for truth stares one in the eye and begs
for sympathy" (376).

Underneath the joy of this great book runs the cold stream of Adams'
full appreciation of historical reality as painful, cruel, anti-human,
mean, and near (194, 364, etc.). Beneath this layer of recognition lies
another: the gamut of contradictions in the human mind was run 700
years ago; for a too-brief moment of splendor the point of the Gothic
arch hung in harmony over the half circle of the Roman, but it was an
excruciating harmony because it lasted so briefly. It is possible to see the
point of hesitation in reverse too, not as a zenith at all but as a nadir
since we do not know what is down or what is up.

Either way, the point of the Gothic arch and the harmony were
unmistakably inconclusive. They were both what Adams carefully and
constantly called them, "Transition." The late-twelfth-century pause did
not solve the problem of the universe. The multiple world seen in the
Education still posed the same questions. Substituting laboratory for
syllogistic science has provided no better answers since induction and
deduction still meet where we don't know. "I start from the universe,"
said William of Champeaux, the Platonic realist. "I start from the
atom," said Abélard, the nominalist. And "once having started, they
necessarily came into collision at some point between the two" (291).
The point of collision poses the real problem. "The attempt to bridge the
chasm between multiplicity and unity is the oldest problem of philosophy, religion and science," Adams wrote (299). Other terms can be

substituted: Fact and humanity, the creation and the creator, life and death.

> The schools argued, according to their tastes, from unity to multiplicity, or from multiplicity to unity, but what they wanted was to connect the two. They tried realism and found that it led to pantheism. They tried nominalism and found that it ended in materialism. They attempted a compromise in conceptualism which begged the whole question. Then they lay down exhausted (319).

The solution still eludes us all too, as Adams showed in his last essays; but men in the late twelfth century in France briefly "solved" their problems by suspending them in the Transition with the Virgin Mary as their representative.

> Men were, after all, not wholly inconsequent; their attachment to Mary rested on an instinct of self-preservation. They knew their own peril. If there was to be a future life, Mary was their only hope. She alone represented Love. The Trinity were, or was, One, and could, by the nature of its essence, administer justice alone. Only childlike illusion could expect a personal favour from Christ. Turn the dogma as one would, to this it must logically come. Call the three Godheads by what names one liked, still they must remain One; must administer one justice; must admit only one law. In that law, no human weakness or error could exist; by its essence it was infinite, eternal, immutable. There was no crack and no cranny in the system, through which human frailty could hope for escape. One was forced from corner to corner by a remorseless logic until one fell helpless at Mary's feet (250).

Such a unity was not really desirable at all because it was too confining. "If a Unity exists, in which and toward which all energies centre, it must explain and include Duality, Diversity, Infinity—Sex!" (259)

> God was Justice, Order, Unity, Perfection; He could not be human and imperfect, nor could the Son or the Holy Ghost be other than the Father. The Mother alone was human, imperfect, and could love; she alone was Favour, Duality, Diversity. . . . If the Trinity was in its essence Unity, the Mother alone could represent

47

whatever was not Unity; whatever was irregular, exceptional, out-lawed; and this was the whole human race (261).

To press on towards any firmer "solution" showed "the flimsiest bridge of all is the human concept, unless somewhere, within or beyond it, an energy not individual is hidden; and in that case the old question instantly reappears: What is that energy?" (299). The problem gets no easier. So Adams devoted his greatest attention in *Mont-Saint-Michel and Chartres* to an examination of the suspended moment of pause and of shift, of the Transition.

I conclude *Mont-Saint-Michel and Chartres* is a proper sequel to the *History*, "poetry" opposed to "fact," as within *Mont-Saint-Michel and Chartres* itself Adams opposed Chartres' poetic delicacy to the factual, the plain handsomeness and sturdy statement of the structure at Mont-Saint-Michel. And *Chartres* is an emotional stopping point on the way from the *History* to the *Education*. The latter is an appraisal of the human condition opposing the personal example of the world examined by one mind, a rational treatment, to the heart's desire of all mankind, the Virgin and Chartres. And *Mont-Saint-Michel and Chartres* also contrasts with Adams' final thinking expressed in the "Rule" and the "Letter." The last essays show the most suspended opposition of all: an intellectual appreciation of inconclusion that stands opposed to the "felt" emotional conclusion of the balanced Transition that so long ago represented a full and complete artistic understanding among men.

In commenting on the architecture of Mont-Saint-Michel, on its round arches, severe statement, military, useful, "masculine," terrestrial character, Adams said, "The Norman will be the practical scheme which states the facts, and stops." (Such a scheme was his architectonic intention in the *History*, but it was spoiled by a fact of another order: all the facts were not available for stating.) The point of importance was the stop. The eleventh-century Normans simply built at Mont-Saint-Michel clear, easy, definite arches in the midst of lines and rectangles. As Adams described it, the Norman builders were not bothered by any thought of insufficiency. But he was. The full Gothic that followed, the French scheme, was one that relieved the problem because it is "the graceful one, which states the beauties, and more or less fits the facts to suit them." Acceptable as this later structure might be to tourists who "want as few dates as possible," Adams found this alternative unacceptable too, despite its "sympathy." "Both styles are great," Adams says, but "both can sometimes be tiresome" (55). An astringent mind shrinks from either. It rests at last on the balance point between the Norman and the full Gothic—on the Transition, the old tower at Chartres, the late twelfth century, and the Virgin.

The notable emphasis in *Mont-Saint-Michel and Chartres* is on the old tower at Chartres. Adams sought to show its superior charm "lies in its unstable balance" (317). The most yearning, open desire of man is for a point of rest. It might be the accepted fact of Norman faith and Mont-Saint-Michel; it might be the logical assumption of the late Gothic as shown in the full Gothic of Amiens cathedral where "doubt ceases; emotion is trained in school; Thomas Aquinas reigns" (318). Adams' major books fit the same pattern. The *History* is Norman being fact as much as possible. The *Education* is late Gothic, being intricate, logical and reasonable but without end. Looked at in this way the *History* and the *Education* emphasize the Chartres book as the *balance* between two positions. Between all possible explanations lies lovely Chartres which is not fact, is not logic, but is emotion—it is art. And Chartres was the image of Transition. Adams could not be more clear about it than when he said:

> The Transition is the equilibrium between the love of God—which is faith—and the logic of God—which is reason; between the round arch and the pointed. One may not be sure which pleases most, but one need not be harsh toward people who think that the moment of balance is exquisite. The last and highest moment is seen at Chartres, where, in 1200, the charm depends on the constant doubt whether emotion or science is uppermost (317–318).

Man, a pendulum between feeling and thought, had for the moment paused.

III. The Transition

In developing his theory of the Transition in *Mont-Saint-Michel and Chartres,* Adams interpreted the Virgin herself as that very transition.

49

His discussion of the Trinity is a delicate yet convincing proof of his attitude. For thousands of years the natural family trio, father, mother and child, constituted any religious trinity. The Christian Church rejected this natural pattern and substituted the Holy Ghost for the mother because she seemed to be no mystery as a warm and human presence so real as to blend man with his creator—a figure who might be recognized as his creator alone, the "Mother of God." Adams explained that the Church of the twelfth and thirteenth centuries had to insist that one person in the Trinity be a mystery to create awe. Were it understood such knowledge would discredit the whole Trinity "under pretence of making it intelligible" (302): "The sin against the Holy Ghost was a haunting spectre, for no one knew what else it was" (301). But the eleventh- and twelfth-century builders of Chartres cathedral in creating this tribute to Mary alone in effect showed that the Mother absorbed the entire Trinity: Adams' description of the Virgin at Chartres shows that there she is the Church itself. As she was regent for her son and principal intercessor and mediator in heaven, a little more emphasis would have put her on the major throne—in the apsidal windows, in fact, ones seldom noticed, "She is there as Queen, not merely as intercessor" (194). Adams' explanation of her place, her character, her femininity, her maternity, makes her close to being the principal heavenly figure. She was much nearer to sinful man's heart's desire than any other figure the Church proposed:

> People who suffer beyond the formulas of expression—who are crushed into silence, and beyond pain—want no display of emotion —no bleeding heart—no weeping at the foot of the Cross—no hysterics—no phrases! They want to see God, and to know that He is watching over His own (194).

Whether she was God or not, people saw that Mary satisfied their desire for Him. She was pure love, interposed between the firm justice Mont-Saint-Michel demonstrated—to man's dismay—and the complex reason of Thomas Aquinas who in re-establishing the Trinity in the thirteenth century accentuated doubt and fret and discontent. The churches Thomas' architects built prove this. In the new tower at Chartres, for example, the juncture between the square base and the pointed spire grates and is painful; no amount of fussy architectural decoration could hide the fact that the thirteenth-century reconcilers of oppositions had trouble. They ended in presenting to the eye a result that reveals doubt about the juncture.

But the old tower at Chartres images successful balance and harmony where there is no real discord between the juncture of the square tower and the octagon spire. For the moment the atom and the universe joined. How? The problem a juncture presents was paradoxically solved by openly presenting it. It was

> the Gothic Transition. The quiet, restrained strength of the Romanesque married to the graceful curves and vaulting imagination of the Gothic makes a union nearer the ideal than is often allowed in marriage. . . . the strength and the grace join hands; the man and woman love each other still (33–34).

There was no forcing in the union. It does not jar because it is accepted, ignored, perhaps hidden; the "concealment of the transition is a beauty" (64).

As Adams more lushly described the Gothic Transition period of the late twelfth century it was a "passionate outbreak of religious devotion to the ideal of feminine grace, charity, and love" (50). That the passion lasted so short a time further demonstrates that only one law existed for Adams, the law of change, flux and instability that is forever working— and fully working for it can pause briefly itself to prove its own rule.

In explaining the Transition Adams considered another figure in addition to Mary: Saint Francis, who treated the human mind "half-serious, half-jesting" (333). A human embodiment of what Adams described as the meaning of the Virgin, Francis rejected reasonable theology and by implication the Holy Trinity:

> At Assisi, once, when a theologian attacked Fra Egidio by the usual formal arraignment in syllogisms, the brother waited until the conclusions were laid down, and then, taking out a flute from the folds of his robe, he played his answer in rustic melodies (333–334).[19]

Saint Francis displayed here the best of good tempers. By Adams' standards it amounted to a Marian disregard for rule either by law (Saint

Michael) or by logic (Saint Thomas). He concealed all difficulties with love. "The soul of Saint Francis was a rustic melody and the simplest that ever reached so high an expression. . . . he goes with Saint Bernard and Saint Victor through the religious idyll of Transition architecture" (334). Saint Francis was, perhaps, mankind's ultimate experience of object and goal (340).

Such conclusive equilibrium did not last. The Holy Ghost displaced the Virgin, the Mother. Thomas Aquinas succeeded Saint Francis. Thought began to operate again. Flow, momentarily interrupted, resumed. The wary eye looked again. The second tower at Chartres reveals doubt as shown in the worrisome juncture between its base and spire—it shows "signs of a certain tendency toward a dim and distant vulgarity" (66). Man again questioned the marriage of opposed principles. The unity of the old tower had exacted full indulgence in the emotion of absolute love and complete abandonment of a feeling for individual validity.[20] It cost, in fact, man's sense of humor in that it prevented personal suspension between clearly recognized horns of dilemmas by creating a suspension that was itself a thoroughly fixed position, with closed eyes. The silence here was unfortunately acceptance. And the temper here became so definite men failed for a time to know that Transition is no position at all—that Transition is movement of some kind, not stasis.

But while it lasted the devotion to Mary and to the Transition was intense beyond example. All the time of all the people of every class was spent in constructing churches in honor of Mary. The Archbishop of Rouen described the building of Chartres itself: "powerful princes of the world . . . nobles, men and women, have bent their proud and haughty necks to the harness of carts . . . like beasts of burden. . . . among such a multitude there was hardly a person present" (102). Architects and artists in stained glass or sculpture felt no need to put their names to their creations. If this does not prove enough, Adams said, "The measure of this devotion, which proves to any religious American mind, beyond possible cavil, its serious and practical reality, is the money it cost" (92). The capital of France invested cannot of course be fixed, "but in a spiritual and artistic sense, it was almost the whole . . . perhaps never even paralleled by any single economic effort [and here is the usual Adams barb] except in war" (92–93). This "intensity of conviction" invested in the Virgin was thus not founded on a spiritual base alone.

> Expenditure like this rests invariably on an economic idea. Just as the French of the nineteenth century invested their surplus capital in a railway system in the belief that they would make money by it in this life, in the thirteenth they trusted their money to the Queen of Heaven because of their belief in her power to repay it with interest in the life to come (93).

However invalid such an explanation is, however distorted such an interpretation of religious passion, the uncomfortable materialistic fact is that the Virgin was in large part a commercial enterprise.

> The [French] bourgeois had put an enormous share of his capital into what was in fact an economical speculation, not unlike the South Sea Scheme, or the railway system of our own time; except that in one case the energy was devoted to shortening the road to Heaven; in the other, to shortening the road to Paris.

It was an investment doomed. In the space of three generations (1200–1300) the French learned their mistake, that "Economically speaking" —always Adams' cautious check appears, one that does not disguise his meaning—the "enormous money-investment had proved to be an almost total loss" (96). To cap the proof: "The efforts of the bourgeoisie and the peasantry to recover their property, so far as it was recoverable, have lasted to the present day" (96–97). They were abetted by money-lenders and bankers because Mary's irresponsible views on their activities and values were "so feminine as to rouse in that powerful class a vindictive enmity which helped to overthrow her throne" (263).

The investors discovered simply that "prayer without money seemed to be quite as efficacious as prayer with money" (96). This is the Lutheran Revolution. (It was also a major thesis of Henry Adams' brother Brooks' *The Law of Civilization and Decay* in 1895.) More brutally: After the thirteenth century, French Mariolaters discovered they could keep their cash and possibly ride to heaven on faith alone; at least heaven was as reachable through simple faith as through good works.

But was it all money down the drain? Was this tremendous expenditure a mistake? It was if finality was what the investors thought they had bought. It was for those who had committed themselves to the Virgin and her proper housing. It was loss to minds that abandoned a middle position by—paradoxically—settling on it, wearied of swinging suspension. Otherwise it succeeded—as art, for example, which makes nothing happen and provides answers for nothing but its own problems, substituting activity for thought. It was beautiful illusion if not reality. Surely this is enough. The colors alone the Virgin insisted on in her house at Chartres, especially in the windows, "repaid to her worshippers a larger return for their money than the capitalist has ever been able to get, at least in this world, from any other illusion of wealth which he has tried to make a source of pleasure and profit" (97). "Illusion for illusion," this is true—just as "Illusion for illusion, courteous love . . . was as substantial as any other convention;—the balance of trade, the rights of man, or the Athanasian creed. In that sense the illusions alone were real." So history becomes (here at least) the story of illusions, or art perhaps: "if the Middle Ages had reflected only what was practical, nothing would have survived for us" (224).

A further buttress to Adams' cash explanation of this momentary period of fixed Transition is that churches like Chartres were firmly tied to the affairs of men in this world because they "created valuable industries" (104). "The mere masonry and structure made a vast market for labour" (105) in addition to the workshops for wood-carving, windows and sculpture. Saint Bernard may have been right when he objected that cathedrals became markets; we too may frown to see that the Chartres Adams so extravagantly described as expressing "an emotion, the deepest man ever felt," with the "thrust of the vaults, telling the unsatisfied, incomplete, overstrained effort of man to rival the energy, intelligence, and purpose of God"—that this splendid structure is "a cathedral or a world's fair" (104).

In dealing with this material Adams, as usual, practiced balance, but here it is of content rather than of phrases and clauses in sentences and paragraphs. The point of greatest importance is that it was a balance between oppositions.

God wanted contradictory things. . . . The schoolmen saw their duty in one direction; Francis saw his in another; and . . . after . . . five hundred years had been devoted to the effort, society declared both to be failures. Perhaps both may some day be revived, for the two paths seem to be the only roads that can exist, if man starts by taking for granted that there is an object to be reached at the end of his journey (339).

Where can the society Henry Adams describes be now if, though demanding unity, it has rejected the all-encompassing love of Saint Francis and the Virgin as well as the logic of Thomas Aquinas and the simple faith in God at Mont-Saint-Michel? We have no point to balance on. Mary, the Transition, failed, and so the pendulum swings again— "either God was harmony, or He was discord." Society insisted on both, on unity and its own free will; man

insisted that the universe was a unit, but that he was a universe; that energy was one, but that he was another energy; that God was omnipotent, but that man was free. The contradiction had always existed, exists still, and always must exist, unless man either admits that he is a machine, or agrees that anarchy and chaos are the habit of nature, and law and order its accident (366).

Thus the problem is a dilemma without solution, and to point it up Adams constantly employed his pen to accentuate opposed horns of it by writing a fairly constant series of hyperbolic statements somewhat obscured by what is usually the easy, soft flow of his language. So, for example, he wrote, "every French school-boy, if he knows no other poetry, knows . . . by heart" the verses describing the great death-scenes from *The Song of Roland*. "In the eleventh century they wrung the heart of every man-at-arms in Europe." "No modern singer ever employs such power over an audience as Taillefer exercised" (23). "History is only a catalogue of the forgotten" (34). Every, no one, all, none, only, instantly, always—these uncompromising words appear over and over again. But their extremity is counter-balanced constantly by the use of restrictive and cautious words—although, except, but, still— and the total effect leaves the reader alert but in doubt. More than this: the flashing quality of the writing is explained by Adams' use of various jokes founded on contrasts that sharply accentuate the points of transition by throwing bright looks on opposing items. These looks always discover incongruities that end finally in recognizing inconclusions to be regarded with good temper. Otherwise the thinking viewer himself can conclude only with complete stoicism or hopeless despair.

What permeates *Mont-Saint-Michel and Chartres* is Adams' refusal to accept a fixed position as certain, a truth as absolute—be it the faith represented by Mont-Saint-Michel and God, or the love that Chartres and St. Francis and the Virgin stand for, or the logic of Thomas Aquinas and the Holy Trinity, or flat doubt itself. He remains in a position of teetering inconclusion. In the book Adam always looked for other sides, noting what was not as well as what was. He checked any tendency to believe, always withheld himself from the certainly definite. He noted, for example, that the front facade of Chartres depicted the whole life of Christ from Nativity to Ascension except "the single scene that has been omitted is the Crucifixion." He concluded, "everything is there except misery" (70). Many sentences of this kind flow through his exposition: "Therefore, let us plod on, laboriously proving God, although, even to Saint Bernard and Pascal, God was incapable of proof" (129). A stricture like "although" corrects any tendency a reader might have to go too far in any direction. Joseph stood thus in regard to his wife: "Her husband, Saint Joseph, was notoriously uncomfortable in her Court, and always preferred to get as near to the door as he could" (175). "Always," Adams said; but this exaggeration stems from his habit of overstatement. He cannot be read literally because the "always" is cancelled by "except." So he explained the limitation of the "true scholar," who when he gets thoroughly to work, "his logic is remorseless, his art is implacable, and his sense of humour is blighted" (186).

Adams' sense of humor was seldom blighted. It has him object to a fixation of any kind.[21] ". . . monks and historians abhor emancipated women" he writes, then shakes the definite sense of such a statement by adding another view, "—with good reason since such women are apt to abhor them" (199). Other comments are more sly, containing cool strokes of warning: "Visionary as the courtesy was, the Holy Grail was as practical as any bric-à-brac that has survived of the time" (213). In speaking of King John of England, Adams defended him by saying, "Some redeeming quality he must have had," then spoiled the generosity with "but none is recorded" (222). Such examples are small ones that demonstrate one of the most remarkable qualities of *Mont-Saint-Michel and Chartres*, its genuine foundation on inconclusion, on the suspension of Henry Adams, on humor.

IV. Saint Thomas Aquinas

Another remark in *Mont-Saint-Michel and Chartres* cuts in several directions. Speaking of the mass of manuscript Thomas Aquinas left to the Church Adams said, "tourists will never know enough to estimate [it] except by weight" (343). Whether he meant to suggest only ignorance in the tourist or a ponderous Saint Thomas is uncertain; I think he meant the latter too, for this particular remark indicates Adams' whole treatment of this theologian. Saint Thomas weaves in and out of *Chartres*, and the final, climactic chapter of the book entitled "Saint Thomas Aquinas" indicates Adams meant him to represent the most important matter of his study.[22]

Who was this man treated with such prominence? Despite layers of sentences and paragraphs that established his importance he is perhaps a figure of fun at last, typical of all men who, in employing reason alone to solve universal puzzles, sinned through seriousness and were consequently doomed to failure in Adams' court. But a reader doubts what Thomas Aquinas was to Henry Adams. He was not a man Adams could fully admire because he wanted to fix the unfixable—the character of God, the riddle of the world, and man's place in the total scheme. Thomas Aquinas was too serious. "Outwardly Thomas was heavy and slow in manner, if it is true that his companions called him 'the big dumb ox of Sicily'; and in fashionable court circles he did not enjoy reputation for acute sense of humour" (343). The disclaimer "if it is true" does not eliminate the statement though it arouses doubt. To lack a "sense of humor," if I correctly interpret Henry Adams' mind, is to lack intellectual humility, the necessary constituent of wisdom. It is to lack uncertainty.

Adams took pains to show that Saint Thomas had difficulties:

Pope John XXII canonized him on the grounds that his decisions were miracles. . . . Innocent VI said that his doctrine alone was

57

sure. . . . Leo XIII very lately made a point [1879] of declaring
that, on the wings of Saint Thomas' genius, human reason has
reached the most sublime height it can probably ever attain (344).

This is all one side of the coin; Thomas was not automatically raised to
his eminence.

After fifty years of struggle [from 1274, the date of Thomas' death],
by use of every method known in Church politics, the Dominican
Order, in 1323, caused John XXII to canonize Thomas and in effect
affirm his doctrine (361).

To "affirm his doctrine" is a milder affair than to call it of "the most
sublime height."

Careful, detailed, thorough, even kindly, the total effect of Adams'
presentation shows that Saint Thomas erected a "completely studied
structure" (374) in his *Summa Theologiae*, an admirable product of a
blend in which "Science [logic] and art were one" (374). The converg-
ing lines of the spires of Chartres cathedral did point to a "unity beyond
space" (104) accepted on faith. But Thomas mistakenly used reason to
demonstrate this unity. So he failed. He built a structure like the cathedral at Beauvais. Both were "excessively modern, scientific, and technical, marking the extreme points reached by Europe on the lines of
scholastic science" (374). Like Thomas' thought, "Even the towering
fragment at Beauvais, poorly built from the first, which has broken
down oftener than most Gothic structures, and seems ready to crumble
again whenever the wind blows over its windy plains, has managed to
survive, after a fashion, six or seven hundred years" (108). Piece by
piece Adams shows us the mistake of Saint Thomas.

Dealing with the problems of creation, Thomas said every individual
who ever existed was created out of nothing. "The whole universe is, so
to speak, a simple emanation from God."

The famous junction, then, is made!—that celebrated fusion of
the universal with the individual, of unity with multiplicity, of God
and nature, which had broken the neck of every philosophy ever
invented.

Thomas erected his grand structure on the mere assertion, "It is so! it
cannot be otherwise!" (355). Adams had said earlier, "if ignorance is

allowed an opinion, even a lost soul may admire the grand simplicity of Thomas's scheme. . . . In Thomas's creation nothing intervened between God and his world; secondary causes became ornaments; only two forces, God and man, stood in the Church" (351). And even earlier Adams put a more subtle commentary in the mouth of a fictional "twentieth-century mechanic" (348). Thomas had begun by using the evidence of his senses, saying, "I see motion . . . I infer a motor! . . . I cannot infer an infinite series of motors: I can only infer, somewhere at the end of the series, an intelligent, fixed motor" (347). The mechanic replied, "Your inference may be sound logic, but is not proof. . . . In fact, if you are aiming to convince me, I will tell you flatly that I know only the multiple, and have no use for unity at all" (348). In sum, Adams implied Thomas' "grand simplicity" amounted to grand simple-mindedness—even though Adams admired Thomas' scheme and the late Gothic architecture, for in both the splendor of the arch fell "from the rosette on the keystone a hundred feet above down to the church floor," with nothing for the eye to see that would break "the sheer spring of the nervures" (351). (At Beauvais the vault was 160 feet high [108].)

But Thomas omitted the Adams essential, the point where the eye could glance both ways, the point of suspension, of transition, of jointure, existing between the unity of God at the rosette and inquiring man on the floor below. The marvelous Old Tower at Chartres did gloss over the junction but did admit its existence. Afterwards Thomas "simply" eliminated it. This caused his whole difficulty. As a result, the splendid simplicity of his arch from the atom up the nervure of thought to God the universe, with no bridge between, called for increasingly complex buttresses that arched over and over again. Adams viewed the late Gothic as a tendency to vulgarity. Balance and suspension were abandoned in favor of "the despotic central idea . . . organic unity both in the thought and the building" (374–375). Despotic ideas severely limit thought. Despots forbid suspension.

Thomas was clever, but probably in the shrewd rather than the noble sense of the word. Thomas assigned space in the Church to man, space "which he never can have in the galleries of Parliament or Congress" (372). He made man a creature of matter *and* mind, wholly apart from angels even (360). Adams admired this Thomas who "never wholly abandoned man in order to exalt God" (365) whereas he hinted that it is chilling to realize that Saint Francis in his total love of God did do this. Thomas even gave man more freedom to act than he gave to God: "Saint Thomas did not allow God even an undetermined will; He was pure Act, and as such He could not change" (372). Thomas boxed God in. "God could not think; He is." [23] Adams denied Thomas' God was a "divine maniac" (373) but suggesting the phrase plants the thought— and casts some suspicion on Thomas' thinking. The suspicion is enhanced when we see Thomas' philosophy does not account for final answers any more than any other broken-necked philosophy has ever done:

> Thomas conceded that God Himself, with the best of intentions, might be the source of evil, and pleaded only that his action might in the end work benefits. He could offer no proof of it, but he could assume as probable a plan of good which became the more perfect for the very reason that it allowed great liberty in detail (365).

The thought is as lovely as that of Adams' Virgin in her boudoir at Chartres dispensing mercy, loving-kindness and forgiveness to her erring children humbly kneeling before her. However, the details included among other things

> a picture of suffering, sorrow, and death; plague, pestilence, and famine; inundations, droughts, and frosts; catastrophes world-wide and accidents in corners; cruelty, perversity, stupidity, uncertainty, insanity; virtue begetting vice; vice working for good; happiness without sense, selfishness without gain, misery without cause, and horrors undefined (364).

". . . scoffers might add that he [Saint Thomas] invented . . . argument for proving the perfection of a machine by the number of its imperfections" (365). Indeed.

The whole presentation of Saint Thomas Aquinas is respectful, but it is finally derisive because, as time has unfolded during 700 years,

> Unity turned itself into complexity, multiplicity, variety, and even contradiction. . . . How was he [or any thirteenth-century man]

to know that these lines ran in every conceivable and inconceivable direction, and that at least half of them seemed to diverge from any imaginable centre of unity! (375)

Mont-Saint-Michel and Chartres ends at the real Transition, the suspension of all true men of humor. Saint Thomas Aquinas tried and even succeeded better than most:

Granted a Church, Saint Thomas's Church was the most expressive that man has made, and the great Gothic cathedrals were its most complete expression (377).

But Henry Adams could not grant a Church. He could not buy the closed faith of the Gothic arch. It opened wide again, and proved too cheap. It was not his idea of a thoroughly happy illusion. His faith failed because of his thought. His thought failed because of its weakness. Heaven was lost. Forced back from faith, repelled by the pointlessness of action, the only possible solution was "silence" and a try for good temper.

The Church, the Lord's house, is a unity. Unity is an artistic construction having reality only if not made to require final acceptance.

Considering the opposed positions represented by Mont-Saint-Michel, and by Thomas Aquinas' faith in reason, Adams dealt most fully with the latter because his set of mind was more similar to it. He objected to Saint Francis' "contempt and hatred for human intellectual processes" (340). So he objected to the mindless simplicity of Saint Michael's faith in obvious "facts." Conscious of the power of unreason, drawn to the comfort faith could provide, still logic appealed most to him. He early declared in *Chartres* that he sought to deal with taste and feeling, not with understanding; but the "feeling" that is conveyed to the "understanding" is a product of his inclination to respect the intellect more than the heart. He learned that neither is a trustworthy instrument for discovering answers. This hard realization led him to feel tender love for the Virgin and her maternal power; it led him to grave respect for Saint Michael and his masculine solidity; it led him to great sympathy for the pure mental processes Thomas Aquinas displayed. As a tentative third position, his inclination led him toward mind, Thomas Aquinas, but he could be nothing but tentative.[24] He had read Francis Bacon:

"Let men please themselves as they will in admiring and almost adoring the human mind, this is certain: that, as an uneven mirror distorts the rays of objects according to its own figure and section, so the mind . . . cannot be trusted . . ." (331).

He found Saint Bernard used the same figure in criticizing and condemning Abelard and his use of dialectics:

"he sees nothing as enigma, nothing as in a mirror, but looks on everything face to face" (311).[25]

Again he uses the figure to point up limitations:

the human mind was never better satisfied with itself than when thus absorbed in its mirror (333).

The only difference between man and vegetable "was the reflex action of the complicated mirror which was called mind" (370). It is clear Adams' doubt of mind itself explains his doubt of Thomas Aquinas and his "most expressive" construct, his Church. At the end of *Mont-Saint-Michel and Chartres* the same figure is used. In the beautiful final paragraph Adams equates "the irregularities of the mental mirror" to the other "haunting nightmares of the Church"—

The peril of the heavy tower, of the restless vault, of the vagrant buttress; the uncertainty of logic, the inequalities of the syllogism, the irregularities of the mental mirror (377).

Thomas Aquinas more bravely than any man had thrown to the sky the delight of man's aspirations. But he had been forced to bury pathetic distrust and anguished doubt deep into earth as the last secret. He taught Henry Adams that the juncture between oppositions called for a silent position of good temper, for humor.[26]

V. Mary

A different humor lies in Adams' treatment of the Virgin Mary, in part a lighter vein, but in part more deadly because Adams half destroyed the glorious cathedral of worship he had erected in her honor. A common view, supported by the poem he had written in 1901 entitled "Prayer to the Virgin of Chartres," is that Adams was a serious Mariolater. *Chartres* can be read as a tribute to the power of the Virgin who "was the highest energy ever known to man, the creator of four-fifths of his noblest art, exercising vastly more attraction over the human mind than all the steam-engines and dynamos ever dreamed of" (*Education*, 385).[27] She built Chartres; "her own hand is plainly shown" (*Chartres*, 115) "the church is Mary" (120). It was her own house, "the Virgin's wish" (107) "a child's fancy; a toy-house to please the Queen of Heaven."

> She was the greatest artist, as she was the greatest philosopher and musician and theologist, that ever lived on earth, except her Son, Who, at Chartres, is still an Infant under her guardianship (88).

> You may, if you have no imagination whatever, reject the idea that the Virgin herself made the plan; the feebleness of our fancy is now congenital, organic, beyond stimulant or strychnine, and we shrink like sensitive-plants from the touch of a vision or spirit (127).

The statements are so extravagant many readers conclude Adams went too far: the Virgin never held the dominant position Adams claimed for her.[28] But I think Adams was exercising hyperbole to create art, not history; he knew what fact was:

> For us the poetry is history, and the facts are false. French art starts not from facts, but from certain assumptions as conventional as a legendary window, and the commonest convention is the Woman. The fact, then as now, was Power, or its equivalent in exchange, but Frenchmen, while struggling for the Power, expressed it in terms of Art.

So the French in 1226 created a love affair between Thibaut-le-Grand and Queen Blanche which was probably not a fact, but as a drama to their contemporaries "Their loves were as real and as reasonable as the worship of the Virgin" (224).

Adams showed that the Virgin was no imaginative figure to late twelfth-century France, but a genuine reality, a living figure, a person, a divinity distinct from God, the Trinity and even the Church itself. Could this be true of an orthodox bishop of the Church?

> . . . since we are not members of the Church, we might be unnoticed and unrebuked if we start by suspecting that the worship of the Virgin never was strictly orthodox; but Chartres was hers before it ever belonged to the Church, and, like Lourdes in our own time, was a shrine peculiarly favoured by her presence. The mere fact that it was a bishopric had little share in its sanctity. The bishop was much more afraid of Mary than he was of any Church Council ever held (78).

Adams *seems* to say man's highest sense of his importance exactly paralleled his high faith in Mary who represented fulfillment and conclusion. Finally, however, she appears in a different light. She was a pause, a halt, an entr'acte because she was doubt as well as the reconciliation of all dualities. She was really diversity. She could mean only wonder in the long run of historical time for she became a suspension that crystallized. She was, in short, the Lotus for those who wanted to achieve complete forgetfulness—in the Greek sense of the word—or who as Asiatics wanted to cut themselves adrift from earthly reality to float in mystic being. I think Adams' most valuable contribution in *Chartres* is to point up the paradoxical position of Mary who as a unity existed by reconciling diversity through love alone.

To understand the Virgin Mary of Chartres we must remember the Romanesque arches at Mont-Saint-Michel. They are stout, masculine, warrior-like, definitive, terrestrial, down-to-earth, finite. We must then look beyond Chartres to the schoolmen of the thirteenth century, men of logic, men of words, whose architecture, the late Gothic, went far beyond the Romanesque. At Mont-Saint-Michel men believed simply but with certainty in the singleness of a just God. Two hundred years later God was the Trinity as reasonably explained by Thomas Aquinas and revealed by Beauvais and Amiens. The reliance on reason led to the rationalism and humanism of the Renaissance. In our day such a reliance on reason has for many eliminated the question of God altogether.[29]

But the brief period of Chartres and the Virgin in the late twelfth century was aside from God and justice and aside from reason, the

Trinity and the whole orthodox Church. It was a hesitation that throbbed and took breath, that laid law aside, and faith, and mind. It enthroned love as all although a love that "was certainly a passion . . . complicated beyond modern conception" (216). Mary was "the *only* court in equity capable of overruling strict law" (255). Law is God; but mercy is Mary; and Mary is the mother. In our contemporary terms such worship is easily interpreted as a retreat to the womb. Perhaps she was this to the twelfth century too. But what of the hard, the confused, the multiple world outside? Does it reconcile with that warm comfort? Does the warmth of Mary and the coldness of the world add up to unity? Adams said, "Children and saints can believe two contrary things at the same time" (337). Only they can accept at once both Mary and the world. Most men must choose. Only the few like Henry Adams, neither a child nor a saint, can remain apart in a third position between the two choices, in suspension.

The new artist at Chartres who broke the Romanesque arch to form the Gothic dropped "unwillingly the hand of his father or his grand-father" (106), that stout forebear who had built Mont-Saint-Michel. But drop it he did because the round arch could not do the work restless man demanded of an arch: "it could not rise; so he broke it, lifting the vaulting" and he "threw out flying buttresses." So the architect "satisfied the Virgin's wish."

But the broken arch did not work either because it resulted in two curved lines forced to converge at a point. And breaking the round arch to make it soar for better effect cost "two weak points," flying buttresses and wooden shelter-roofs. The first did not work, Adams says; besides the walls yielded anyhow. As for the roofs, they burned. No "permanent equilibrium" was achieved (107). If one translates this architecture into terms of philosophy and religion, he finds the great thing not achieved was the very unity that was the aim. To Adams then, as I have said earlier, the point was possibly not the peak but the nadir of man's achievement. And any weak points in religious art raise doubts about "the measure of human depth and sincerity," for "any triviality, any weakness cries aloud" (4). As much so as those two puzzles the *Pteraspis* and the *Terebratula* that spoiled Darwinism for Adams back in 1865. (*See* pages 132–135.)

Compare Chartres with the eleventh-century Norman:

Church and State, Soul and Body, God and Man, are all one at Mont-Saint-Michel, and the business of all is to fight, each in his own way, or to stand guard for each other. Neither Church nor State is intellectual, or learned, or even strict in dogma. Here we do not feel the Trinity at all; the Virgin but little; Christ hardly more; we feel only the Archangel and the Unity of God. We have little logic here, and simple faith, but we have energy (8).

Contrast this statement with one in the preceding paragraph:

Serious and simple to excess! is it not? Young people rarely enjoy it. They prefer the Gothic, even as you see it here, looking at us from the choir, through the great Norman arch. No doubt they are right, since they are young: but men and women who have lived long and are tired—who want rest—who have done with aspirations and ambition—whose life has been a broken arch—feel this respose and self-restraint as they feel nothing else. The quiet strength of these curved lines, the solid support of these heavy columns, the moderate proportions, even the modified lights, the absence of display, of effort, of self-consciousness, satisfy them as no other art does. They come back to it to rest, after a long circle of pilgrimage—the cradle of rest from which their ancestors started. Even here they find the repose none too deep (7).

The final sentence shows Adams' own suspension.

The Virgin Mary was a medieval woman. In *this* character Adams presents the subtlest matter of all, the most original, provocative and, more important, most humorous. A curious tone permeates Adams' whole treatment of her. Beautiful, she appealed to emotion alone. Diverse, she was anarchy. A creature of moods and fancies, she was quite outside logic and science. And for all her fascination she was imperious, careless of expense and an incitement to bankruptcy. She encouraged the spendthrift behavior called for by fairs like Chartres and all the other churches erected to "Notre Dame" in the twelfth and thirteenth centuries. In the end most cool-headed men found they could not afford her; like Adams himself, they were "in search of a father" (*Education*, 229)—of "God the father—Who never lied!" (*Chartres*, 48). I think Adams wanted the God of Truth, not a goddess of love. He preferred the God of fact, of Mont-Saint-Michel, one of justice hard as it might be; he admired the Trinity restored to the Church by the logic of Thomas Aquinas because it was God again, and so justice. He was the New England Puritan of George Santayana's Oliver Alden in *The Last Puritan* (1936), wistfully magnetized by the joyous Mediterranean world embodied in figures like Santayana's Mario and the twelfth-century Saint Francis, but Oliver Alden still.[30] Adams made it clear that Francis was not French but Mediterranean, "Greek in his joy of life" (334). "As an Italian or a Spaniard, Francis was in harmony with his world; as a Frenchman, he would have been out of place even at Clairvaux" (330), the abbey founded in 1115 by Saint Bernard, "a French precursor of Saint Francis" (90). More than this, Francis was "the nearest approach the Western world ever made to an Oriental incarnation of the divine essence" (12). Such a figure appealed tremendously to the heart of Henry Adams, but he did not let it capture his mind.

If it is true that "what man wanted most in the Middle Ages was not merely law or equity, but also and particularly favour" (260) why then did not the Virgin maintain her position as above, beyond, outside, over, aside from God and the Trinity? Why was she dethroned at all if she supplied an all-embracing love for mankind?

> Strict justice, either on earth or in heaven, was the last thing that society cared to face. All men were sinners, and had, at least, the merit of feeling that, if they got their deserts, not one would escape worse than whipping (260).

The answer is that love was not enough.

Part of the explanation is that she cost too much in hard cash, to put it quite plainly; and she did not pay off. Artists as well as other men who had "unwillingly" dropped the hand of father or grandfather in breaking the solid Roman arch to lift the vaulting at her command had for the time lost their senses. A clear fact of historical movement is that Thomas Aquinas for all his failure did reassert the power of independent reason at the great risk of being accused of pride, the worst sin of all. The thirteenth century followed his lead. Nobody remained content with Saint Francis or the Virgin even though

> The convulsive hold which Mary to this day maintains over human imagination—as you can see at Lourdes—was due much less to her

power of saving soul or body than to her sympathy with people who suffered under law—divine or human—justly or unjustly, by accident or design, by decree of God or by the guile of the Devil (274).

God and His justice triumphed again. Plain sense told men as it told Henry Adams that love and mercy however desirable are not the rule of the world. Some other force is at work, some other energy operates. To find and explain it cannot be done by abandoning thought for adoration. The Virgin wanted only love, gave only sympathy and mercy, comforted only as a mother can—*only* is the key. It is all contrary to the way of the hard and real world.

In no well-regulated community, under a proper system of police, could the Virgin feel at home, and the same thing may be said of most saints as well as sinners. Her conduct was at times undignified (257).

"Undignified" raises a shadow of low suspicion about her character: saints and sinners upset people, bother good conduct, worry orderly systems—like that system splendidly managed at Mont-Saint-Michel as well as the properly structured theology of the orthodox Church of the Trinity in the thirteenth century. No wonder the Trinity "could look on and see her dethroned with almost a breath of relief" (274).

Mary was simply too feminine in behavior for long toleration by—men. She was Woman in Command. ("Women have, commonly, a very positive moral sense; that which they will, is right; that which they reject, is wrong; and their will, in most cases, ends by settling the moral" [*Education*, 85]). Like Joan of Arc she could not be put up with indefinitely: "No one was surprised," Adams says, "when Jeanne did what she promised, or when the men burned her for doing it" (208). The rank and file of the French armies accepted Joan's leadership and followed her willingly, but the male leaders she challenged disposed of her. No major revolution followed her execution, for men cannot tolerate rule by woman since he knows she may at any time exercise not manly virtues but feminine caprice. Chartres, Mary's own house, was a haven for the hard-pressed and heavy laden—woman. Like Saint Joseph, the Thibauts, the Saint Louises and other men stood very near the doors.

It was woman's "kingdom." By implication it all declared that Eve was justified, Adam wrong. How long could this condition last? Must man abdicate?

Throughout *Mont-Saint-Michel and Chartres* woman appears with a surprisingly hard prominence despite the softness Adams constantly assures us she had.[31] Early he declared that the men of the eleventh century and the First Crusade "were astonishing, and its women were worth all the rest" (32). The rest of what? In Chapter XI, "The Three Queens," the funniest and liveliest chapter in the book, Adams' views on women show themselves a puzzle. This chapter and the following, "Nicolette and Marion," provide an elaborate background for the wonderfully subtle and misleading statement about himself in the *Education* that "no woman had ever driven him wrong; no man had ever driven him right" (85). The emphasis is on the word "driven." And Chapters XI and XII of *Chartres* demonstrate the woman of the late middle ages was a driver of the first order, usually; and unless she assumed them for purposes of wile was quite devoid of the pliability, gentleness, and docility male gallantry since the founding of the Courts of Love had chosen to endow her with; courts, be it realized, established by women.

Introducing the study of "The Three Queens," Eleanor of Guienne, her daughter Alice of France and then her granddaughter Blanche of Castile, Adams wrote:

The scientific mind is atrophied . . . when it comes in contact with the eternal woman—Astarte, Isis, Demeter, Aphrodite, and the last and greatest deity of all, the Virgin.

Clearly, the "scientific mind" is a male mind, for

The proper study of mankind is woman and, by common agreement since the time of Adam, it is the most complex and arduous.

He added immediately a scarcely worshipful statement:

The study of Our Lady, as shown by the art of Chartres, leads directly back to Eve, and lays bare the whole subject of sex (196).

He meant to remind us of the "woman problem." The most entrancing study in *Chartres* is of Our Lady Mary who leads us to Eve, who "stood in a Church of her own." She "cared not a straw for conventional morality" (274).[32] As for her tastes at the height of her power, "many ladies and gentlemen of the 'siècle' thought them disreputable" (273). Not only bankers and monks objected to her character:

> Mary's treatment of respectable and law-abiding people who had no favours to ask, and were reasonably confident of getting to heaven by the regular judgment, without expense, rankled so deeply that three hundred years later the Puritan reformers were not satisfied with abolishing her, but sought to abolish the woman altogether as the cause of all evil in heaven and on earth. The Puritans abandoned the New Testament and the Virgin in order to go back to the beginning, and renew the quarrel with Eve (274–275).

This explanation of the Protestant Revolution (which I have already suggested Adams showed was caused by the Virgin's failure as a money investment) added to another, rather unsettles men if they take it in slowly:

> Perhaps the best starting-point for study of the Virgin would be a practical acquaintance with bees, and especially with queen bees (196–197).

A more disturbing statement followed: "the French woman of the Middle Ages was a masculine character" (197).

Adams described the careers of the three great queens who dominated their age, its government, church—and men—by carefully showing they established the Courts of Love as instruments to soften men, restrict their more brutal excesses, and increase their own importance at man's expense:

> Side by side with the crude realities about them, they [Eleanor, Alice and Blanche] insisted on teaching and enforcing an ideal that contradicted the realities, and had no value for them or us except in the contradiction (211).

Adams illuminated what happened in describing the changes worked on the game of chess brought home from Syria by crusaders:

In the Oriental game, the King was followed step by step by a *Minister* whose functions were personal. The Crusaders freed the piece from control; gave it liberty to move up or down or diagonally, forwards and backwards; made it the most arbitrary and formidable champion on the board, while the King and the Knight were the most restricted in movement; and this piece they named the Queen, and called the Virgin (203).

That *men* did this clearly suggests medieval man's realization of woman's power; a more subtle commentary: "The ideals of Eleanor and her daughter Mary of Champagne were a form of religion." The result? It developed male evangels in Dante, Petrarch and Cervantes! (211). Cervantes ridiculed courteous love, Adams said (213), for his poor Don is shown a fool in practicing its "rules." Adams added item to item to prove woman's increasing "superiority." For any mistreatment of her by her man, any failure of his to recognize her superiority, she got even in the end. "As a matter of fact," said Adams, "probably she got more than even" as all "history, legend, poetry, romance, and especially the popular fabliaux . . . are all agreed" (198). Man's obedience to woman in the thirteenth century was "docile" Adams said; woman's devotion to man occurred "not because she loved him, for there was no question of love, but because he was *her* man, and she owned him as though he were her child" (207). Weak men may have desired such a position in relation to women, but it finally proved impossibly annoying for most.

> We do not, and never can, know the twelfth-century woman, or, for that matter, any other woman, but we do know the literature she created; we know the art she lived in, and. . . . We can collect from them some idea why the Virgin Mary ruled, and what she was taken to be, by the world which worshipped her (212).[33]

Christ's coming to man's estate did not alone retire Mary to the queen dowager's pavilion, though this happened. The revolt of the king against the queen's dominance does not explain it. The concerted power of an angry priesthood allied to disgruntled bankers in this world does not either. Nor is it the superior appeal of the logic of the schoolmen. More than likely the unconscious revolt by the majority of men against feminine control underlay the whole change. The development had Henry Adams' whole sympathy. It is to his point that in speaking of the "docile obedience of the man to the woman" in the thirteenth century, he reminded his readers of Lady Macbeth (207). And he reminded himself that the women of the twelfth century "seem always to have been more clean than the men, except when men painted them in colours which men liked best" (240).

Mont-Saint-Michel and Chartres is addressed to "nieces" who can read the account of Robin and Marion ("Le Gieus de Robin et de Marion" [241, ff.]) to preen themselves on woman's superiority if they wish. Like all women Marion "appears as the practical guide; the one who keeps her head, even in love." This is a touch undesirable. As for Robin, "He is tamed by his love of Marion, but he has just enough intelligence to think well of himself, and to get himself into trouble without knowing how to get out of it." Marion knows, though. She "loves him much as she would her child" (244). She teased, defended, scolded, flattered—and most of all used him.

> The man . . . was always getting himself into crusades, or feuds, or love, or debt, and depended on the woman to get him out. . . . The woman might be the good or the evil spirit, but she was always the stronger force. The twelfth and thirteenth centuries were a period when men were at their strongest; never before or since have they shown equal energy in such varied directions, or such intelligence in the direction of their energy; yet these marvels of history . . . all, without apparent exception, bowed down before the woman (244–245).

"Woman might be the good or the evil spirit, but she was always the stronger force." The suggestion is enough for anyone but nieces and other persons of their sex to see the joke that follows:

> Explain it who will! We are not particularly interested in the explanation; it is the art [etc.] (245).

People who are not nieces are most interested.

The explanation is double-edged as always, finally inconclusive. Woman's power was founded on her lack of morality. The Virgin substituted mercy for justice. So man could not accept her rule because she ended law, order, society, and increase of knowledge. Based on mind-lessness, woman's force was impossible to endure, to say nothing of having to worship it too.

Thus "the woman and the Rose became bankrupt" (248)—the Rose being "any feminine ideal of beauty, intelligence, purity, or grace—always culminating in the Virgin" (246). "The Frenchman had made what he called 'fausse route.' " The thirteenth-century man woke to "the dull memory of pain and sorrow and death that 'tout porrist,' " that all decays (248). The pendulum had swung again, proclaiming again that all—all is change, a realization that met anew can be felt only as one of two things: "Despair" (248)—or suspension and humor.

Mont-Saint-Michel and Chartres is a tribute to love. Lovingly written, compassionate, with a heavy undercurrent of sadness, it is regretful. The total matter for regret is that Transition cannot itself be a fixed point. Like the "idyll" Chartres represented, it could not stay (334). "Society could not remain forever balancing between thought and act" (342). The sentences could be rewritten to read, "Man cannot remain forever balancing on love between thought and act."

VI. Two Poems and a Novel

Three other, lesser pieces of Henry Adams all deal with this problem that constantly beset him, this relationship between love, thought and act in a world of constant change, the problem of faith and fact that all history seems to deal with. All three of these pieces conclude with an injunction to silence, but none provides in any forcible way grounds for the good temper that Adams later said is the basic mark of sense.

The first of these pieces is the poem Adams wrote in 1901 called "Prayer to the Virgin of Chartres." [34] He said to the Virgin, addressing her in the first part of the poem as "Gracious Lady,"

I brought you all my cares,
    And vexed you with the murmurs of a child;
You heard the tedious burden of my prayers;
    You could not grant them, but at least you smiled.

Here he expresses in a few lines the appeal the Virgin had for him as well as for late twelfth-century France as described in *Chartres*. But the smile was not enough. He was compelled to undertake a father's business:

> If then I left you, it was not my crime,
>> Or if a crime, it was not mine alone.
> All children wander with the truant Time.
>> Pardon me too! You pardoned once your Son!
>
> For he said to you:—"Wist ye not that I
>> Must be about my Father's business?" So,
> Seeking his Father he pursued his way
>> Straight to the Cross towards which we all must go.
>
> So I too wandered off among the host
>> That racked the earth to find the father's clue.
> I did not find the Father, but I lost
>> What now I value more, the Mother,—You!
>
> I thought the fault was yours that foiled my search;
>> I turned and broke your image on its throne,
> Cast down my idol, and resumed my march
>> To claim the father's empire for my own.

These lines express more than regret for losing the Mother. They explain in part that march soon to be recorded in the *Education* that was an outwardbound journey of the masculine mind pursuing truth. What Adams the traveler discovered was another force different from the Mother but as mysterious—the Dynamo. He addressed it in the second part of the poem as

> MYSTERIOUS POWER! Gentle Friend!
> Despotic Master! Tireless Force!

What he found was this:

> We know not whether you are kind,
>> Or cruel in your fiercer mood;

But be you Matter, be you Mind,
We think we know that you are blind,
    And we alone are good.

To ask this new idol questions,

What are we then? the lords of space?
The master-mind whose tasks you do?

got no answer but "Still Silence!" an answer that emphasized regret for
the abandoned Mother.
    The third part of the poem concluded with a return to the Virgin and
left the suppliant

Waiting I feel the energy of faith
Not in the future science, but in you!

It may seem that the poem ends with a return to religious faith, yet as I
see it, Adams is only too well aware that silence ends all search in
rushing time and stretching space. Man's "mimic sight" (the reflection
of the mirror), his "mocking art," "insect sense" and "baby load"
informed him finally of—the poem's last line—"The futile folly of the
Infinite!" Read too literally this intriguing poem of the early twentieth
century implies a retreat that is somber despair. Read for its "religion"
it recommends man should release hold on any rudders of thought to
float on without question, trusting mindlessly to love and to faith.
    In short compass "Prayer to the Virgin of Chartres" sets up the same
conflict he had dealt with in his 1884 novel *Esther*. Here Adams drew
portraits of two opposed characters, one of whom represented early
nineteenth-century man, who retained the faith of the middle ages, in
contrast to the other, a man of the twentieth century who without religious faith was committed to science—to logic. Tossed between these
two figures centuries apart is a third, the protagonist, Esther Dudley.
Adams presents here also the same horns of the dilemma he dealt with
later in *Chartres*, faith versus reason, with love in the balance. Here
Adams practiced in his own right the role of "Cornificci."
    Esther Dudley [35] was drawn to the solution of life's problems by the
orthodox religious faith of the Reverend Stephen Hazard, the pastor of a

fashionable Anglican church on Fifth Avenue in New York, a "medieval" man (28) who "had a sense of humor, except where his church was concerned" (100). She fell in love with Hazard after her father's death, hoping desperately that he and his religious conviction would supply solace, peace of mind, and satisfaction. "She had but to trust herself to him and all was sure to go well" (178). "Faith means submission. Submit!" her cousin George Strong advised her (202). He is the twentieth-century man of science. All would go well also if she could have done what her father advised just before his death: "Laugh, Esther, when you're in trouble! Say something droll! then you're safe" (150). But her mind interfered. She discovered it impossible to commit herself: "The trouble with you is that you start wrong," Strong told her. "You need what is called faith, and are trying to get it by reason. It can't be done. Faith is a state of mind, like love or jealousy. You can never reason yourself into it" (201). Esther knew this. "Some people are made with faith," she later declared; "I am made without it" (289). She loved Hazard and desired the comfort of his religion, but her thinking prevented her accepting him since she saw he and his religion were one.

Deeply disturbed she turned to Strong, a disciple of Darwin, a paleontologist, who declared no faith, not even in science: "Mystery for mystery," he said, "science beats religion hollow. I can't open my mouth in my lecture-room without repeating ten times as many unintelligible formulas as ever Hazard is forced to do in his church" (191). "I've not got one [thought] which I believe in myself," he said (272). His temper was so completely good though, he is doubtfully plausible:

> As for Strong he was always in good spirits. Within the memory of man, well or ill, on sea or shore, in peril or safety, Strong had never been seen unhappy or depressed (255).[36]

But he paid for this absolute good temper with an inability to love. Hazard could love though in his blind faith he was an extremist also. As a point between, only Esther appeals to one's sense of reality.

Quite simply Esther loved Hazard but could not resist Strong's appeal. She desired faith but mind attracted her more. She finally rejected her love to follow her thought, and in the end she could not marry

Hazard because he demanded too much. He was too decided. Hazard told her, "I am never afraid of pure atheism; it is the flabby kind of sentimental deism that annoys me, because it is as slippery as air" (224). He admitted a fear as great as hers—greater, really, in that he cravenly ran away:

> "As for myself, if I could have removed my doubts, by so simple a step as that of becoming an atheist, I should have done it. . . . I studied the subject thoroughly, and found that for one doubt removed, another was raised, only to reach at last a result more inconceivable than that reached by the church, and infinitely more hopeless besides. What do you gain by getting rid of one incomprehensible only to put a greater one in its place, and throw away your only hope besides? The atheists offer no sort of bargain for one's soul. Their scheme is all loss and no gain. At last both they and I come back to a confession of ignorance; the only difference between us is that my ignorance is joined with a faith and hope" (290–291).

Adams loaded the dice against Hazard; his real character is founded on faith, not hope. He said, "I accept tradition outright, because I think it wiser to receive a mystery than to weaken faith" (291). Such a creed was far too hazardous for Esther. "Why must the church always appeal to my weakness and never to my strength!" (299). Hazard lost the battle, and his temper too. Esther could not be bought. She could not understand how Hazard could "worship any person at all" (297). And "She knew that neither six months nor six years would make her a fit wife for Hazard, and that it would be dishonest to lure him on by any hope she could change her nature" (235).

"Hazard" names a character who represented certainty. "Strong" named one who represented uncertainty: Strong believed "N-N-No!" (270). Yet he exhibited a "hazardous" hope:

> "We may some day catch an abstract truth by the tail, and then we shall have our religion and immortality. We have got far more than half way. Infinity is infinitely more intelligible to you than you are to a sponge. If the soul of a sponge can grow to be the soul of a Darwin, why may we not all grow up to abstract truth? What more do you want?"

Esther asked, "Does your idea mean that the next world is a sort of great reservoir of truth, and that what is true in us just pours into it like raindrops?" Strong replied, "the figure is not perfectly correct, but the idea is a little of that kind" (273).

Such a view inspired Esther. Echoing Emerson, preceding Bergson, paralleling Huxley's and Spencer's cheery interpretations of evolution, its reasonableness countered but did not overcome the attraction of love (like that of Saint Francis and the Virgin Mother, the desires of the heart). Strong proposed marriage too. Esther answered, and the book ends, "But George, I don't love you, I love him."

Hazard was faith, love, conviction and unity. Strong was science, fact, thought and multiplicity. Esther shivered between the two, "infinitely dreary and absent" (302). She did not conclude. She ended without good temper, that vital essential for persons of sense.

A little-known Adams piece is his 1895 poem "Buddha and Brahma." Peculiar, involved, long and grim in matter, it penetrates deep into the conflicts and oppositions that increasingly occupied Adams. He wrote the poem aboard ship while he and John La Farge were returning through the Indian Ocean from their long South Seas trip in 1891, but it was not published until 1915, when it appeared in the October issue of *The Yale Review*.[37] In it Adams clarified his philosophy of silence more clearly than anywhere else,[38] but he did not exhibit in it much good temper.

A group of disciples are seated in the forest at the feet of Gautama Buddha after the Buddha had attained Nirvana through the "eight-fold way." The Buddha's earthly life is nearly over. One young disciple begs an answer to a question, one of the four "undetermined questions" the Buddha is supposed to have refused to answer during his lifetime: "Whether the World exists eternally." [39] Twice he asked the question and got no reply. The third time,

> Then gently, still in silence, lost in thought,
> The Buddha raised the Lotus in his hand,
> His eyes bent downward, fixed upon the flower.

The disciples pondered this response, and finally one left the group to seek out his father,

—an old man
Famous for human wisdom, subtle counsel,
Boldness in action, recklessness in war—
Gautama's friend, the Rajah of Mogadha.

Of him the young disciple asked the meaning of the Buddha's reply. Reluctant to answer, the Rajah warned the boy the Buddha meant this "deepest lesson" to be learned through "silent thought, abstraction, purity, / The living spirit of his Eight-fold Way." He advised his son to act, not to think.

But the boy insisted on an answer, claiming—what all conventionally thoughtful people believed—he could not act wisely without thought. Again the Rajah advised:

"Think not! Strike!
. . . I swear to you in truth
That all my wisdom lies in these three words."

Yet he finally consented to answer at last.

First he explained that he knew Gautama better than Gautama knew himself. In youth both the Rajah and the Buddha had been Kshatriya, members of the governing military caste, worldly men therefore, both of whom rebelled against the Brahman, the priestly caste ruling the Hindu world:

"We sought new paths, desperate to find escape
Out of the jungle that the priests had made.
Gautama found a path. . . .
I found none, and I stay here, in the jungle,
Content to tolerate what I cannot mend."

Their paths were separate, says the Rajah, but though they now seem worlds apart, "hold fast to this!—"

"The Starting-Point must be the End-point too!
You know the Veda, and need not be taught
The first and last idea of all true knowledge:
One single spirit from which all things spring:

One thought containing all thoughts possible;
Not merely these that we, in our thin reason,
Hold to be true, but all their opposites;
For Brahma is Beginning, Middle, End,
Matter and Mind, Time, Space, Form, Life and Death.
The Universal has no limit. Thought
Travelling in constant circles, round and round,
Must ever pass through endless contradictions,
Returning on itself at last, till lost
In silence."

All paths lead to silence. The silent raising of the Lotus supplied no answer to the disciples; but the Rajah sees the meaning: it points to "Brahma, the only Truth." And "Brahma," says the Rajah at the end, means this:

"Life, Time, Space, Thought, the World, the Universe
End where they first begin, in one sole Thought
Of Purity in Silence." [40]

But the Rajah too—the man of action, the defender of castes and the wielder of swords—"is an instrument of Brahma" as the Buddha is:

". . . in the life of Ruler, Warrior, Master,
The wise man knows his wisdom has no place,
And when most wise, we act by rule and law,
Talk to conceal our thought, and think
Only within the range of daily need,
Ruling our subjects while ourselves rebel,
Death always on our lips and in our act."

The *wise* man of action knows all the while knowledge and wisdom have no part in action. If a young man insists on understanding what the Buddha told "only by a mystic sign," he must desert the mystic way of Buddha. When he would insist to his warrior father

"You are wise;
I must have wisdom. Life for me is thought,
But, were it action, how, in youth or age,
Can man act wisely, leaving thought aside?"

he is told the harsh truth: action is necessity; wisdom is a thing apart. Man must fall back on silence, for thought is inadequate. A life of thoughtless action, a life of mystic contemplation, or the more difficult life that is full of action and silent contemplation, all are the same from the vantage point of Brahma. The last position, the Rajah's, is therefore like the second, the Buddha's; and both of these are no different from the first because they are all equally helpless.

A first reading of "Buddha and Brahma" shows it is identical with the *Education* (1907), with *Chartres* (1904) and with what Adams continually repeated in his letters: the answer was always silence. Action, faith, wisdom and thought taught nothing else. The major conflict in the poem, however, lies between but two of these choices, the Buddha's way of contemplation and the Rajah's way of action with thought in addition but hidden from it. The third way, the life of pure act, is not considered. Buddha was the most direct:

> "He breaks a path at once to what he seeks.
> By silence and absorption he unites
> His soul with the great Soul from which it started.
> . . . He has taught
> A certain pathway to attain the End;
> And best and simplest yet devised by man,
> Yet still so hard that every energy
> Must be devoted to its sacred law."

But, the Rajah says, other paths remain, and though "Gautama's way is best, but all are good," so the Rajah is also an instrument of Brahma; his way is as good as any other. It may even be superior:

> "This is the jungle in which we must stay. . . .
> We need no Noble Way to teach us Freedom
> Amid the clamor of a world of slaves.
> We need no Lotus to love purity
> Where life is else corruption."

Silence, the great fruit of wisdom, says the Rajah both proudly and scornfully, may be reached through act as well as through mystic trances. The Rajah speaks with force as well he might for his is the voice of Henry Adams. He wrote Elizabeth Cameron in 1891 of his journey to Anuradhpura in Ceylon:

> Of course we went at once to the sacred bo-tree, which is now only a sickly shoot or two from the original trunk, and under it I sat for half an hour, hoping to attain Nirvana. . . . I left the bo-tree without attaining Buddhaship (Ford, I, 526).

He never attained Buddhaship, nor could he, seek it as he would. Nor did he lose himself in worship of the Virgin. He could not. Thought always got in his way.

Nowhere else does Henry Adams more clearly explain himself than in "Buddha and Brahma." Like the Rajah of Mogadha, "No follower of Buddha, but a Brahman / Devoted first to Vishnu then to caste," he sought to preserve life as we have it, a genuine conservative like the God Vishnu the Preserver, the second of the Hindu trinity. This is the real character of what he later called a "conservative Christian anarchist" (*Education*, 405). Though a man of action during the most energetic years of his life (1867–1891) he was but partly this; he was capable of appreciating the Buddha's way of contemplation for he was also a man of thought. The Rajah told his questioning son:

> "Your Master, you, and I, and all wise men,
> Have one sole purpose which we never lose:
> Through different paths we each seek to attain,
> Sooner or later, as our paths allow,
> A perfect union with the single spirit."

He doggedly insists

> "Yet in this world of selfishness and striving
> The wise man lives as deeply sunk in silence,
> As conscious of the Perfect Life he covets,
> As any recluse in his forest shadows,
> As any Yogi in his mystic trances."

Man can live in the world and without Buddhistic means remain as conscious of Brahma as any Buddha. The result:

". . . we, who cannot fly the world, must seek
To live two separate lives, one, in the world
Which we must ever seem to treat as real;
The other in ourselves, behind a veil
Not to be raised without disturbing both."

Adams declared here more simply than in any other place that man can think and act at the same time if he realizes thought affects action in no effective way. His Rajah says,

"Thought
Travelling in constant circles, round and round,
Must ever pass through endless contradictions,
Returning on itself at last, till lost
In silence.

"This is the Veda, as you know,
The alphabet of all philosophy,
For he who cannot or who dares not grasp
And follow this necessity of Brahma,
Is but a fool and weakling; and must perish
Among the follies of his own reflection." [41]

It is only this realization, firmly held, that can provide the good temper beyond silence.

Chapter 3

The Educator

I. The Patterns of the *Education*

Adams wrote to William James in 1908 about his *Education* which he had published privately the previous year:

> As for the volume [*Education*], it interests me chiefly as a literary experiment, hitherto, as far as I know, never tried or never successful. Your brother Harry tries such experiments in literary art daily, and would know instantly what I mean; but I doubt whether a dozen people in America—except architects or decorators—would know or care.
>
> I care little myself, and have put too many such *tours-de-force* into the fire, to bother about explanation. This will probably follow the others, for I have got it so far into shape that I can see the impossibility of success. It is the old story of an American drama. You can't get your contrasts and backgrounds (Ford, II, 490).

The noteworthy referent is to "architects and decorators," and the noteworthy description is "literary experiment." Did Adams succeed in it or did he not? In the "Editor's Preface" (dated September 1918 and signed by Henry Cabot Lodge [1]) he wrote of the volume, "The point on which the author failed to please himself, and could get no light from readers or friends, was the usual one of literary form. . . . The scheme became unmanageable as he approached his end. . . . and he could not satisfy himself with his workmanship." He said the book was "avowedly incomplete" (vii–viii). What dissatisfied him? The book is clearly what he intended it to be, a sequel to *Chartres:* a study of twentieth-century multiplicity as opposed to the former's being a "Study of Thirteenth-Century Unity" (vii). The last three chapters, like the last three of *Chartres,* are the climax of all that preceded. He wrote Barrett Wendell in 1909 that he thought these six chapters comprised a single essay.[2] They do come to seem that—but one must read carefully everything else in the two volumes to see it.

It seems to me, therefore, that the whole matter of the *Education* must be dealt with in detail to see what its manner is—its architecture and its decoration. Adams said, as I quoted him at the beginning of this essay, "The pen works for itself, and acts like a hand, modelling the plastic material over and over again to the form that suits it best" (389). Like the painter, sculptor, architect, composer, photographer or choreographer, the writer as artist knows a satisfactory result comes only from finding a proper form for the matter of his thought. Each knows an idea in the depths and recesses of his mind communicates successfully only through proper form, and the final form is likely to be only an approximation of his fullest thought. All would-be artists are mutes until they learn speech, and none ever learns enough of that. Colors, lines, sounds, shapes and steps as well as words, unless they are ordered into intelligible *form*, remain gibberish, and the form that results, the "artistic product," must always seem to the artist insufficient. That Henry Adams was aware of this explains why he declared his *Education* "avowedly incomplete," why his workmanship dissatisfied him, why he failed to please himself. He did not realize his ideal. But to judge how far he did succeed in giving appreciable form to his material his readers must examine both, concentrating on the point where they meet, at the juncture.

A survey of the general impact of the *Education* shows that it provides surging waves of intricacies, of no certainties in the labyrinthine world. There is gnarliness, if waves could gnarl. Overall the book seems to be late Gothic architecturally speaking—or architectonically—in contrast to the Norman Romanesque of the *History,* a book that matches Mont-Saint-Michel with its presumed faith in flatly declared facts, in simplicity, in clarity, in weight and mass. In the *Education* a great wealth of facts clash against one another, startling facts, obscure facts, perhaps wrong ones. One reason they may even be excused when they are wrong is that, as Adams said in Chapter III, "Washington," describing a boyhood trip there in 1850, "the actual journey has no interest for education. The memory was all that mattered" (43). The actual history Adams reported in his study of education in the last two-thirds of the nineteenth century, meaning exactness in dates and other accuracies, is not significant to anyone but the student of fact. Facts are symbols in the *Education* as they are in *Chartres*; facts became images. When on that 1850 trip to Washington Henry visited the White House with his father, he wrote later he "half thought he owned it, and took for granted that he should some day live in it" (46). It is unimaginative to suppose that he meant to be literal. For the late Henry Adams facts helped little for, as he wrote in the *Education*, "all opinion founded on fact must be error, because the facts can never be complete, and their relations must be always infinite" (410).

Contortions of both sentences and matter produced peculiar distortions in the *Education*. Chapters end with downbeats that shatter the shore of a reader's perceptions. The entire tone is excessively lugubrious for a book about a presumably ebullient nineteenth century and not its *fin de siècle* decade alone. The sentences are so intricately and heavily weighted at the ends that they spoil any impression of flat statement. Their unbalance spoils that sense of rhythmic flux balanced sentences succeeded in conveying, I think, in the *History*. The clearcut order of the paragraphs themselves always counteract as sure as reefs the turgid flow of the sentences they contain. Jokes of all kinds curl atop powerful waves—sad, malicious, sharp, lightsome. They float above the somber tone, accentuating it. Sudden solemn aphorisms appear like islands or lifebuoys anchored in the ebb and flow of observations recording a movement called an education that beat about for nearly seventy years to end in the peculiar calm of "failure" at last, a word heavily charged with negation, loss, sorrow and hopelessness, the end to the storm of life. "Failure" is a cry from one drowning in a sub-aqueous world; it knells constant warnings about the uselessness of the human effort to learn about and finally to understand the content of the reefs, rocks and earthquakes, the whirlpools, cyclones, hurricanes and catastrophes that endanger all floating vessels seeking anchorage in peace and conclusion.

Most readers of Henry Adams agree with his brother Brooks who wrote of Henry in 1919, "he poses, more or less throughout his book, as having been a failure and a disappointed man." This is true enough, for one interpretation of the *Education* is that it is a treatise on failure. But Brooks added,

> He was neither the one nor the other, as he knew well. He was not a failure, for he succeeded, and succeeded brilliantly, in whatever he undertook, where success was possible; and he was not disappointed, for the world gave him everything he would take.[3]

Examined in the light Brooks used here the declaration is sound enough: the honorary degree Harvard offered Adams in 1892 proves his success as a professor of history there from 1871–1877 (Ford, II, 8, fn.). No one has found he failed as editor of the *North American Review* for the same period. And the current status his historical work enjoys demonstrates his triumph as an historian. Why then did Adams pose as a failure? The answer is that he sought success in places where, as his brother hinted, it was not possible. He arrived at manhood to find a society blasted and coarsened by a Gilded Age he found he could not understand. He studied a science that not only wrecked the foundations of accepted religion but could not explain itself—a science that uncovered the *Pteraspis* and the *Terebratula*, puzzling creations that jeered at pure evolutionary theory. This science in 1901 finally produced radium which threw into question all scientific law to that date. In general he failed constantly to be prepared or equipped for events and happenchance that occurred, nearly always experiences that surprised him.

But he meant failure in a worldly sense too, despite the surface evidence. He used a stronger light than his brother did. As a teacher, he said he did not know what to teach or for what purpose: "History is a tangled skein that one may take up at any point, and break when one has unravelled enough; but complexity precedes evolution." The *Pteraspis,* the first known vertebrate before whom there is no recognizable ancestor, "grins horribly from the closed entrance" (*Education,* 302). As an editor he chalked up another failure: he could only become "an authority on advertising" (308). And as an historian "He had no notion whether . . . [his histories] served a useful purpose" (315). He implied finally that they did not, and in the second of his last and most provocative studies, "A Letter to American Teachers of History" (1910) he showed that he saw the second law of thermodynamics to be the probable governing law of the progressive universe with Entropy— which is indeed silence—the likely goal. Thus he justified his claim of failure on broader grounds than his brother Brooks would admit to. One cannot therefore accept Brooks's assertion that it was merely a pose.

To Adams education fully thought of should contain training for aspects of life no school or educator had ever provided save Jean Jacques Rousseau, perhaps, whom he had praised in the first preface to the *Education,* but whose greatness as an educator was "in the manner of the eighteenth century" (ix). Beginning the chapter "Twenty Years After (1892)" he said, "education should try to lessen the obstacles, diminish the friction, invigorate the energy, and should train minds to react, not at haphazard, but by choice, on the lines of force that attract their world" (314). When, however, he discovered the lines of force were beyond knowing until too late, and that choice or no choice made no difference, then in training minds to act by choice education "may be shown to consist in following the intuitions of instinct" [4] while the conscious mind remained observant but silent—the most economical behavior. It is the position of the Rajah in the 1891 poem "Buddha and Brahma."

The great lesson Adams teaches in the *Education* is the old one of "Buddha and Brahma" with good temper added; he presented it concisely in the second preface to the book: "in the immediate future, silence next to good-temper was the mark of sense" (viii). The same statement occurs in the final chapter (501). In his letters he persistently said the same with slight variation, and with "good temper" implied in his wording. To Cecil Spring Rice, for example, he wrote in 1897, "All that remains is to hold one's tongue, and vomit gracefully, until the time comes when no man needs to be sea-sick more" (Ford, II, 122–123). In 1905 he wrote Margaret Chanler even more succinctly, "Silence alone is respectable and respected. I believe God to be Silence." [5] He did not arrive at this thought easily. It resulted from what he found was his incapacity to shape his own destiny, to influence the course of human affairs in society itself and, more important, to understand the meaning of human affairs and destiny itself. He wrestled perpetually, only to have this idea confirmed so often, thoroughly and finally that it is a considerable result.

The *Education* begins with a sophomoric question: "Where was he?—where was he going?" (21). The splendid irony is that wherever it has been asked the question is one unanswered by all philosophy and human thought.

Bernard DeVoto declared that after reading the book more than a dozen times he got

> an intense pleasure from perceiving how much of what Adams passes a magisterial judgment on he was altogether ignorant of, how superhumanly absurd much of his reasoning is, on the basis of what gigantic misconceptions he announced certainties where almighty God would have proceeded tentatively (*Op. cit.*, 516).

The comment typifies the resentful criticism Adams has received from many critics whose lack of perception I excuse because Adams did not succeed for them as an artist. Many take Adams' use of the word "ignorance" in too small a sense when he meant it to represent an ironic image of great inconclusion. Many so mistake Adams' pompous phraseology of exaggerated statements as "magisterial judgment" that they do not see the addition of circumlocutions, hesitations and elaborate protective phrases accentuate the ignorance he claimed by cancelling his boldest remarks. Many more than Mr. DeVoto see Adams' hyperbolic declarations as such "gigantic misconceptions" they are unable to see what appear to be "certainties" are only mock answers stated definitively to point up the fundamental fact of uncertainty, in nearly every case protected by some sort of "maybe."

Adams had said in *Chartres:*

> An artist, if good for anything, foresees what his public will see; and what his public will see is what he ought to have intended —the measure of his genius. If the public sees more than he himself did, this is his credit; if less, this is his fault (142).

Henry Adams' major failure has been, to date, as an artist. It is a failure I seek to correct. His "superhumanly absurd" reasoning was, I think, humor as I have explained it. So are his judgments—pretended—and his certainties—overly pronounced. His claim of ignorance was serious but not simple. The declaration, "He knew enough to be ignorant," is plain to the point of being annoyingly flat; and magisterial by itself it is even insulting if the reader emphasizes the "He." But its content as thought is hardly absurd if one reads on:

> His course had led him through oceans of ignorance; he had tumbled from one ocean into another till he had learned to swim; but even to him education was a serious thing.

Then follows a famous passage:

> A parent gives life, but as parent, gives no more. A murderer takes life, but his deed stops there. A teacher affects eternity; he can never tell where his influence stops.

Teacher-recruitment posters bear this quotation, a weighty inducement to the idealistic young to take up the task of affecting eternity through teaching. One hardly sees the caution implied in the final clause, but to consider the effect of ignorant tutoring sobers the view. The rest of the paragraph is just as decided, but it unmistakably corrects anyone whose ambition to shape eternity is overweening:

> A teacher is expected to teach truth, and may perhaps flatter himself that he does so, if he stops with the alphabet or the multiplication table, as a mother teaches truth by making her child eat with a spoon; but morals are quite another truth and philosophy is more complex still. A teacher must either treat history as a catalogue, a record, a romance, or as an evolution; and whether he affirms or denies evolution, he falls into all the burning faggots of the pit. He makes of his scholars either priests or atheists, plutocrats or socialists, judges or anarchists, almost in spite of himself. In essence incoherent and immoral, history had either to be taught as such— or falsified (300–301).

I think the *Education* adds up to humor in the largest sense: it is a treatise on inconclusion. The manner of its writing meets the chaos of its matter in a juncture that images suspension. "Gnarliness" is the word to characterize the complex description of movements in the lifetime of a man who ended nowhere, in the maze where he had begun, at no fixed point. Adams learned a powerful lesson. Not being positive but severely restrictive if not negative, it appears to many readers worth little. Simply stated it is this: failure described any education for the twentieth century that concludes understanding means something else than ignorance. Or: failure necessarily results from any education aiming at unified, orderly, patterned learning. Or: education properly considered results in silence.

But this was only part of Adams' education. Were it all, the *Education* should be consistently heavy and somber and gloomy. It is not. "Funniness" decorates the basic pattern, funniness of expression, of episodes, of thought; the whole elaborated hyperbole of the style encourages that essential beyond silence, "good temper," the only safe tower beyond tragedy. The *story* of the *Education,* as the writer himself defined it, deals with the adventures of Henry Adams "in search of an education, which, if not taken too seriously, tended to humor" (*Education,* 116).

One device that accentuates the humor is Adams' treatment of himself throughout the book as a littler man than he was in fact though that was little—five feet three inches high. He was a Lilliputian.[6] He was a tiny manikin, a "homunculus" (368) who crawled down gangplanks (112). He sat and stared helplessly into the future (280). He hid in rooms. He shook his "white beard in silent horror" (110). He flung up his little arms in helplessness, or he flung them around another figure, or he fell, nearly faint, into other arms outstretched.[7] But the "figure" that Henry Adams depicted finally emerges from his book as a reflection of one man's mental mirror, one finally very like that of Edward Gibbon, that "fat little historian" who when gazing at Gothic cathedrals "darted a contemptuous look on the stately monuments of superstition," but who must have felt respect for them as for any objects worthy of his "vast study and active mind" (386). Eighteenth-century Gibbon scorned the structures Adams succeeded in feeling in *Mont-Saint-Michel and Chartres,* but he would not have dismissed them. The picture of Gibbon Adams presents is only amusing until one realizes Adams gave strong respectability to the airs of this stout-minded little man. So Don Quixote also inspires respect if we think of him occasionally as Cervantes' ironic protest against woman-inspired "courtesy." A like air of respectability arises about short Henry Adams too whose cry of "Failure" sounds so specious. Like Gibbon, like the Noble Spanish Knight, Henry Adams stands up from his book so pitifully little and yet so greatly stout a man that the impression is miniature grotesque. He invites our laughter while he attracts our sympathy. By creating such a *persona* Adams went far in creating one of the effective paradoxes of his work.

The major result of my analysis of the *Education* shows it to be a careful work of art. Adams imposed artistic order on disorderly material, patterns on confusion; he gave a form to plasticity. Paradoxically, he fixed shapelessness on matter. He created art through successful technique. But he is far beyond artisanship. His technique is a success of mind, the final essential, I think, in the greatest art.[8] All the factors are linked—again I repeat it—to the point we must consider: at the juncture. In this case the principal factor of humor becomes by means of the writing the final matter of the work. Adams' pen finally traced out the main sequence of his thought. Realizing the necessity for striking out, what he left was purposeful. What may seem side-paths ultimately appear for what they are: necessary stops along the main lines of force. To avoid shapelessness he did employ his pen to model the plastic material of his education "over and over again to the form that suits it best" (389). The result was a very clear fundamental structure.

Chronology is the basic arrangement of the *Education* and each of the thirty-five chapters advanced Adams' story of education one or more years from 1838 to 1905. (Often Adams stepped into the future to look back on the experiences he related for a particular year, but when moving so he always showed he had not come to know later what he did not know at the time.) This arrangement provides the reader of the *Education* the common excitement of any narrative in ordinary time sequence; but it is somewhat deceptive since the material was always selected only from the experiences Adams claimed contributed to his education. In Chapter II, "Boston," he explained this in describing his education "at the moment when character is plastic" (29) from the years 1848 to 1854 when he was between the ages of ten and sixteen. He presented here a caution the reader should note carefully in reading all of the book:

This is the story of an education, and the person or persons who figure in it are supposed to have values only as educators or edu-

93

cated. The surroundings concern it only as far as they affect education (36).

Adams wanted his readers to consider him as an *image* of nineteenth-century education, an image that serves as a symbol;[9] in this way he could focus on the abstraction "education."[10]

In a letter to John Hay in 1883 Adams wrote:

> Trollope has amused me for two evenings. I am clear that you should write autobiography. I mean to do mine. After seeing how coolly and neatly a man like Trollope can destroy the last vestige of heroism in his own life, I object to allowing mine to be murdered by any one except myself (Ford, I, 347).

But to think of the *Education* as being what Adams meant by his autobiography so weakens its point that one can see then only a misleading account of a particular life that is unique and therefore limited. In the "Preface" dated 1907, Adams wrote at greater length on this issue:

> As educator, Jean Jacques was, in one respect, easily first; he erected a monument of warning against the Ego. Since his time, and largely thanks to him, the Ego has steadily tended to efface itself, and, for purposes of model, to become a manikin on which the toilet of education is to be draped in order to show the fit or misfit of the clothes. The object of study is the garment, not the figure. The tailor adapts the manikin as well as the clothes to his patron's wants. The tailor's object, in this volume, is to fit young men, in universities or elsewhere, to be men of the world, equipped for any emergency; and the garment offered to them is meant to show the faults of the patchwork fitted on their fathers (x).

If it is an autobiography, several sharp criticisms of the book are quite justified. One is that the use of the third person throughout would be a specious pretense of objectivity: Adams meant all along to insinuate himself into the reader's consciousness. Thus, goes this interpretation, Adams did in effect cheat. And Rousseau was more "honest" and so are all other autobiographers. Worse: if the book is autobiography, the gaps in Adams' account, explanations not given, sly hints not explained, references not followed out, all are further deception. The most spectacular omission is the story of the twenty years from 1871 to 1892. Only too briefly did he discuss his work as teacher, editor and historian then, in Chapter XX and XXI. An account of his marriage and his wife's suicide is missing entirely. Matched against the thoroughness with which he seemingly dealt with his life until 1871, the omission seems a fraud. But Adams included his own oblique defense, one not sufficiently noted. He began Chapter XXI, "Twenty Years After (1892)"

> Once more! this is a story of education, not of adventure! It is meant to help young men—or such as have intelligence enough to seek help—but it is not meant to amuse them. What one did—or did not do—with one's education, after getting it, need trouble the inquirer in no way; it is a personal matter only which would confuse him (314).

He was fully aware his book would call attention to himself, that the figure is of emphatic interest. He wrote in the last paragraph of his 1907 Preface:

> The mankin, therefore, has the same value as any other geometrical figure of three or more dimensions, which is used for the study of relation. For that purpose it cannot be spared; it is the only measure of motion, of proportion, of human condition; it must have the air of reality; must be taken for real; must be treated as though it had life. Who knows? Possibly it had! (x).

Thus the remark that what the manikin did with his education after getting it would only confuse the reader is true enough because personal matters would deflect the reader from the main sequence of his thought.

Such an interpretation explains more than the treatment of the prime manikin, Henry Adams. It explains the curious treatment of most of the other figures who appear in the book. The first one of importance is his father Charles Francis Adams, especially dominant because "His father's character was therefore the larger part of his education, as far as any single person affected it" (26). "Character" differs in direction of meaning from "man," the former being less whole than the latter; character is not necessarily the man. Adams presented a sensitive and subtle analysis of Charles Francis Adams but not a full portrait. He was, says his third son, the man of perfect poise who "stood alone" (28) [11] in his age in Boston and "set up a party of his own . . . [that] became a chief influence in the education of the boy Henry . . . and violently affected his character (29). The *character* of Mr. Adams that emerges from Henry Adams' presentation (some six to eight pages) is curiously cold and unloved. He did not, like the Presidents who were his father and grandfather (nor like at least two of his sons, Henry and Brooks) reveal restlessness. To his son Henry he "possessed the only perfectly balanced mind that ever existed in the name" (27). But his son rejected him finally as a useful educator because his balance was so fixed and settled, so fully an inheritance from Puritan ancestry (26). He was—I think the word must be—a grotesque. His "business in life was to get past the dangers of the slave-power, or to fix its bounds at least."

The task done, he might be content to let his sons pay for the pilotage; and it mattered little to his success whether they paid for it with their lives wasted on battle-fields or in misdirected energies and lost opportunity (26).

This may be a very personal complaint, but I think Adams meant not only his father's sons but all the following generation were forfeit to his father's fixed balance of mind. By strong implication though not by direct revelation Henry Adams exhibits strong objection to his father's character in the role of educator, though not to his father "personally" considered.

Yet if his perfection meant positively that his father was no snob, flatterer, or vilifier, nor envious, jealous, vain, conceited, arrogant or full of pride (28), why did Henry not profit from the education such character provided? Henry Adams was after all in "search of a father" (*Education*, 229; "Prayer," stanza eight). It is because Charles Francis Adams was a negative educational force. Henry Adams declared flatly:

The generation that lived from 1840 to 1870 could do very well with the old forms of education; that which had its work to do between 1870 and 1900 needed something quite new (26).

"Charles Francis Adams was singular for mental poise," yet his memory was hardly above the average; his mind was not bold like his grandfather's or restless like his father's, or imaginative or oratorical—still less mathematical; but it worked with singular perfection, admirable self-restraint, and instinctive mastery of form. Within its range it was a model (27).

The trouble was its narrowness of range, and in his son's analysis he appears to be what his critics found also, for "They called him cold" (28).

In contrast his father's intimates during the years 1848–1854 to whose talk young Henry listened constantly, John G. Palfrey, Richard H. Dana and Charles Sumner, seem warm and human. All of them together, however, provided no more education "fitting him for his own time" than anything else because they "were all types of the past" (32) convinced that their sort of world that "had always existed in Boston and Massachusetts Bay, was the world which he was to fit." They were part of the "same upper-class *bourgeoisie*" that comfortably felt the same way in France and in England and wanted to in Italy and Germany (33). In Boston it meant that "nothing exacted solution" because —the most succinct summation Adams provided in the chapter— "Boston had solved the universe" (34).

The education of Henry Adams in these years from all sources came to this:

All experience since the creation of man, all divine revelation or human science, conspired to deceive and betray a twelve-year-old boy who took for granted that his ideas, which were alone respectable, would be alone respected (33).

The list of specific items that began to make up his education is considerable, and all added up to nothing. His father belonged to the past. The church represented only the disappearance of religion (34). Emerson, who did protest in part, was *naïf* (35) if we consider him an element in education needed for the period 1870–1900. The reading he began caused him "In the want of positive instincts" to drift into "the mental indolence of history." The family "was rather an atmosphere than an influence" (36). Outside influences were negative. "He always reckoned his school days, from ten to sixteen years old, as time thrown away," because they failed to provide him with the four necessary tools he later needed—mathematics, French, German and Spanish (38). The amusements about him—skating, sleighing, billiards—taught him nothing "likely to be of use to him in the world" (39). He was, all told, educated as a standardized Boston type, and no one knew whether such a type was fitted to deal with life in the late nineteenth century (37). As it turned out it was not.

Amid this list of educational failures in his youth, one thing of value he did learn: "Only in one way his father rendered him a great service by trying to teach him French and giving him some idea of a French accent." Everything else of value is described grudgingly. "His father made no effort to force his mind, but left him free play, and this was perhaps best" (36). He had learned to read, and books remained the source of life, but "as in the eighteenth century," in the sense of the past. His happiest hours were devoted to Sir Walter Scott and raiding the garden for peaches and pears, he says finally. "On the whole he learned most then" (39). What *Ivanhoe* and peaches taught he does not say. Nor does he say they contributed to weaving any garment of education. At the age of sixteen Adams appeared to lack all but a thread of any patchwork of education and was about as naked of it as the day he was born. He had acquired only the stamp of education sealed in 1848 on the older Puritan generation, an inheritance he and other men whose lives were to "fall" in the generation between 1865 and 1900 had to get rid of if they were to "take the stamp that belonged to their time. This was their education" (26).

Despite the roughly chronological order of the material, then, the special selection and treatment of details all deal with education alone. This shows how far removed from usual autobiography the book is. Each chapter builds on the preceding one in a steady progression in simple narrative time but, more important, they all build into complexity. Adams never left his single, central subject, education, the clear, unifying element of the whole. He wrote of his friend Henry James that he "taught the world to read a volume for the pleasure of seeing the lights of his burning-glass turned on alternate sides of the same figure" (163). Adams did the same thing in reverse: He turned lights on the educative sides of various figures as they affected the same object, the garment of education.

Patterns of Education

In structure one sees the book in two parts. The first, Chapters I–XX, describes the material of a mid-nineteenth-century education (to 1870) to be used by the later nineteenth-century active man of the world. Passing by the twenty years of active life when Adams applied his first education, because that matter was personal as I have noted, the final half of the book rises above the specific details so fully mentioned in the first to a lofty plateau of observation and speculation. In it Adams largely disengaged himself from daily facts to deal with great ideas, using his chronology as a bare frame on which to build his thinking, a frame that gives movement to the whole. The chapter titles themselves show how he advanced in the treatment of his material. The first six chapters have simple place names. As the book progresses the chapter titles become increasingly more abstract until at the last (especially the very last one) they become obscure in meaning.

The simple chronology Adams employs disguises another arrangement of the material: The chapters fall into groups, and each revolves about a single object. There are six of these sections in all, each a fairly complete essay. The divisions are not notable as one reads the book since the author did not mark them off. But marked breaks occur in the subject matter. As I count the sections, they are as follows:

Section I —I–VI   : Education in Childhood and Youth
   "   II —VII–XV   : Education by Englishmen
   "   III—XVI–XX   : Education to Failure
   "   IV—XXI–XXIV   : Education in Indian Summer
   "   V —XXV–XXXII   : Education in Force
   "   VI—XXXIII–XXXV: Education as Inconclusion

A remarkable stylistic device Adams employed has to do with his paragraph structure. A glance shows the paragraphs run to a surprisingly uniform length, usually two to a page with few exceptions either very long or very short. And the chapters are uniform also in that they are roughly equal in the number of pages they contain, but more surprisingly in the number of paragraphs. One has forty-four, one but twelve, and the rest range from eighteen to thirty-three, the most common number being twenty-eight. Six chapters have that many. Only two contain more than thirty paragraphs, and five less than twenty. In blueprint form the book is steady and even, progressing, outwardly at least, step by even step, matching the steady progression of the chronology. Yet this even flow of paragraphs and years is not monotonous for it serves to create a counterpoise, counteracting the extravagant content *of* the paragraphs.

As I examined the paragraphs themselves one at a time I noted a general pattern of structure that has, again, a remarkable and almost monotonous consistency. Adams seldom varied the pattern. For the most part they are formal, textbook paragraphs similar to those of the *History*, each one a "free unit." More often than not the first sentence is the topic sentence, a declaration clamped by the final one that is a restatement of it and a half step beyond it, usually a step into generalization. In addition, a great many of the paragraphs are so constructed that the first sentence can be read with the last to make considerable sense. One gets the firm impression that Adams set up his paragraphs with his final sentence well in mind as he proceeded to develop his initial topic sentence. A few paragraphs chosen at random will demonstrate this framework:

1. Pp. 44–45: (First sentence:) "The boy could not have told her [his aunt]; he was nowhere near an understanding of himself." (Last sentence:) "Even at twelve years old he could see his own nature no more clearly than he would at twelve hundred, if by accident he should happen to live so long."
Paragraph content: The confused impression of Washington on the Boston boy of twelve, who had a taint of Maryland blood.

2. P. 201: (First sentence:) "Least of all did Motley mean that the taste or the manners were perfect." (Last sentence:) "He meant something scholarly, worldly, and modern; he was thinking of his own tastes."
Paragraph content: The extreme contrast between the badness and the best qualities of English society.

3. Pp. 264–265: (First sentence:) "Badeau took Adams to the White House one evening and introduced him to the President and Mrs. Grant." (Last sentence:) "Adam, according to legend, was such a man."

100

Paragraph content: To compare Grant to Garibaldi to show that each was archaic.

4. P. 429: (First sentence:) "Rid of man and his mind, the universe of Thomas Aquinas seemed rather more scientific than that of Haeckel or Ernst Mach." (Last sentence:) "Mind and Unity flourished or perished together."
Paragraph content: The ironic fact that Aquinas really demonstrated more unity by far than modern science, though unscientific.

But what lies between these sturdy first and last sentences of such conventional paragraphs is an elaboration of details and arguments into sentences that particularly distinguish Adams' style. In a sense he drove these two sentences apart with those that lay between, those remarkable, rich sentences so very full of lively thought, so involved and so various. These sentences forming the contents of the paragraphs are, in fact, so convoluted, containing so rich a vocabulary and wealth of allusions, the underlying structure is hardly evident at all since the sentences within them compel such attention from the reader the signs of their framework are almost entirely obscured. Furthermore, the paragraphs are not free units at all in the sense that they can usually be extracted from the larger whole for their fullest meaning. Time and again the reader cannot discover this until well into a following paragraph, sometimes well beyond the next two or three. So, stylistically, Adams created a paradox. The ordered unity of the paragraphs is countered by the gnarly content within them to result in a series of struggling sentences that dispel the very artistic order the paragraph form appears to give them.

One other fact is evident as one studies the structure of the book. It clearly shows Adams' conscious artistry. Key words such as chaos, multiplicity, failure and force are all used sparingly at first. Their use gradually and unobtrusively picks up until the frequency of their appearance is, though not overbearing, particularly heavy and noticeable. So, for example, the word "force" appears in Chapter I nine times. But in Chapter XXV it occurs forty-two times. And in Chapter XXXIII, seventy-four times, nine times in the first two paragraphs alone.

II. Education in Childhood and Youth

I wish now to examine in detail "Quincy," the first chapter of the *Education*, attending especially to that profusion of captivating passages that strike the reader's awareness. Once this chapter is understood, the rest of the book becomes much clearer.

I have earlier quoted Elizabeth Stevenson who said Henry Adams' most pervasive manner was that of "wit" (*Henry Adams: A Biography*, 242). This is true in large part, especially in the modern sense of the word. Once meaning only "reasoning in general" or "activity of mind," wit now means a lively activity of mind, lively fancy, clever statement, indicating "that quality of speech or writing which consists in the apt association of thought and expression, calculated to surprise and delight by its unexpectedness"; and indicating also "the power to evoke laughter by remarks showing swift perception, especially of the incongruous, and verbal felicity." [12] So defined, wit is the word that aptly describes innumerable quick phrases, sharp sentences, unusual metaphors and bright words in Henry Adams' works. In addition, a further quality appears in the *Education*, a special variety of wit: mock sententiousness.

In Chapter I, Adams defined politics wickedly as "the systematic organization of hatreds" (7). Of a schoolmaster he said, "that is, a man employed to tell lies to little boys" (9). Or of Quincy in the 1840's, "a simpler manner of life and thought could hardly exist, short of cave-dwelling" (10). He said his grandfather President John Quincy Adams in the role of an adult was a boy's "natural enemy" (12), a man who as a disciplinarian was "a tool of tyranny" (13). He mentioned in passing that certain fine old trees still remained "unless they have been improved off the ground" (14). He spoke of the New Englander's "long struggle with a stingy or hostile universe" as resulting in his learning "to love the pleasure of hating; his joys were few" (7). He played on his own name: "a system of society which had lasted since Adam would outlast one Adams more" (16). He spoke of his grandmother's "silver teapot and sugar-bowl and cream-jug, which still exist somewhere as an heirloom of the modern safety-vault" (18). And he referred, in his discussion of the difference between his Adams tradition and the wealthy material inheritance of his maternal background, to "the fatted calf of his grandfather Brooks" (22). The great profusion of these witticisms, like those in the *History* (where they are fewer), are short, quick, succinct, easy—even automatic, indicating a mind always alert to the possible incongruities and other rich possibilities words and their use can present. Astringency is their special quality.

A more extended passage that is also "wit" covers two pages (12–14). It exemplifies the lively fancy and verbal felicity of *Chartres* with some of the same lightness of tone and yet it has the formal words and phraseology of the *History*. The combination of these qualities enhance the witty perception of the story told. It is a step forward in style. One summer morning when he was seven, Henry had refused to go to school, "a passionate outburst of rebellion against going to school . . . . he met all efforts at compulsion by successful, though too vehement protest." Finally "without a word" his elderly President grandfather had appeared, taken his hand and walked him nearly a mile to his seat in the schoolroom. Looking back at the scene in his own old age, Adams found that he had even then admired the fact that this "natural enemy," this "tool of tyranny," "Above all . . . had held his tongue."

> Probably his mind at that moment was actually troubling itself little about his grandson's iniquities, and much about the iniquities of President Polk, but the boy could scarcely at that age feel the whole satisfaction of thinking that President Polk was to be a vicarious victim of his own sins, and he gave his grandfather credit for intelligent silence (13–14).

The intelligent silence his grandfather exhibited, whatever its true cause, got Adams' "instinctive respect."

> He admitted force as a form of right; he admitted even temper, under protest; but the seeds of a moral education would at that moment have fallen on the stoniest soil in Quincy, which is, as every one knows, the stoniest glacial and tidal drift known in any Puritan land (14).

Again we see in a trivial example exaggeration that extends to hyperbole —a characteristic quality of all of the *Education*. Again we see balanced sentences with the heaviest weight of meaning, force and tone on the final swing. The pattern is common, exhibited time and again, in even what appear to be the plainest sentences of exposition: Adams described Louisa Johnson, John Quincy Adams' wife-to-be, as she was in 1794.

> Louisa was charming, like a Romney portrait, but among her many charms that of being a New England woman was not one. The defect was serious. Her future mother-in-law, Abigail, a famous New England woman whose authority over her turbulent husband, the second President, was hardly so great as that which she exercised over her son, the sixth to be, was troubled by the fear that Louisa might not be made of stuff stern enough, or brought up in conditions severe enough, to suit a New England climate, or to make an efficient wife for her paragon son, and Abigail was right on that point, as on most others where sound judgment was involved; but sound judgment is sometimes a source of weakness rather than of force, and John Quincy already had reason to think that his mother held sound judgments on the subject of daughters-in-law which human nature, since the fall of Eve, made Adams helpless to realize (17).

The third sentence is overblown. Its final clause is not easily understood. In what way is "sound judgment sometimes a source of weakness rather than of force"? Why would John Quincy have "already had reason to think that"? Especially since his human nature made him "helpless to realize" it? The next sentence explains: he was 3000 miles away from his reasonable mother and "far in love." So the reason is that force is equated to human nature which in turn stems from the fall of Eve. Eve, we can recall from *Mont-Saint-Michel and Chartres,* represents a force clearly superior to human judgment and reason—sex.

But because human judgment is weak does not make it wrong. Two pages later we see Abigail had been right about Louisa after all. Adams suspected later that Louisa's lack of efficiency had passed down to her descendents, appearing as "those doubts and self-questionings, those hesitations, those rebellions against law and discipline, which marked more than one" of them (19). Adams came to see Louisa had bequeathed qualities that made him no pure scion of New England stock, but one "half exotic"; it reveals the irony of an Adams being anything but New England in ancestry, as well as the correctness of Abigail's suspicions.

Much more important than this: in these first few pages appears the word that is fundamental to the book. It is as striking as any leit motif of Richard Wagner's: it is the word *force*. But in this first chapter no more than anywhere else does Adams reveal any true understanding of it. It remains the "mysterious power" he called it in "Prayer to the Virgin of Chartres." "Tireless" in its pressure on man, it is irresistible.

Thus early Henry Adams introduced the major theme of his book, the conflict between the limited human mind and all the mighty other elements that confront it, counter it, confuse it, and finally tend to cancel it—elements that are all *force* of one kind or another, taking such turns, appearing in such a variety of forms, pushing the mind into such extreme, detailed, intimate or minute crossways, as to make the reader along with Henry Adams finally dizzy with inconclusiveness. The conflict is operative paradox contrasting that unity man claims to be with the multiverse surrounding him. To present an attitude towards this contrariety calls for either hopelessness and despair or, if one continues with "a tendency to regard every question as open," for suspension—for humor.

Adams' use of the term "force" is interesting in every instance in Chapter I. In each case it implies mysterious, irresistible pressures on man that call for humor. In addition to force cited as adult power over children and as sex, he used the word in other contexts, each of which implies mystery. In the second paragraph of his book it appears in this sentence:

> Whether life was an honest game of chance, or whether the cards were marked and forced, he could not refuse to play his excellent hand (4).

The "whethers" do not allow free choice—the two possibilities are chance or force alone. In another paragraph Adams wrote:

> for numberless generations his predecessors had viewed the world chiefly as a thing to be reformed, filled with evil forces to be abolished. . . . Boys naturally look on all force as an enemy, and generally find it so (7).

A bit later, in setting up pairs of conflicting elements in his childhood education, he spoke of one as "force and freedom"; force he linked to winter, cold and town, all limitations of freedom. Finally the word occurs in a very emphatic sense:

> The bearing of the two seasons on the education of Henry Adams was no fancy; it was the most decisive force he ever knew (9).

So Adams introduced the reader to his increasing use of the word throughout the book. To confront the various mysteries of force calls for blind groping. Could the writer's pen work as a blind man's staff in such perplexities? It was the problem Adams set himself to solve in preparing his book, in seeking to find the form that would contain the contradictions of his experience that complicated the queries he put to the mystery. Thus he writes of the puzzle of the two seasons mentioned above, extending their meanings so that they serve as images for several other things:

> The double exterior nature [the freezing cold and boiling heat of New England] gave life its relative values. Winter and summer, cold and heat, town and country, force and freedom, marked two modes of life and thought, balanced like lobes of the brain (7).
>
> Life was a double thing (9).

If life was a double thing, both aspects had to be held somehow in concurrent consciousness. Only balance, a third position that is suspension, could provide any position between fluctuations if the balance was tentative.

The passages I have already labelled as wit also demonstrate a quality in Adams' thinking I have only named—mockery. It is present in the very first sentence:

> Under the shadow of Boston State House, turning its back on the house of John Hancock, the little passage called Hancock Avenue runs, or ran, from Beacon Street, skirting the State House grounds, to Mount Vernon Street, on the summit of Beacon Hill; and there, in the third house below Mount Vernon Place, February 16, 1838, a child was born, and christened later by his uncle, the minister of

the First Church after the tenets of Boston Unitarianism, as Henry Brooks Adams (3).

The sentence is full, flowing, detailed, solid, informative. However, the buried phrase "a child was born" echoes later. Its biblical reference is unmistakable, and unless we suspect an ego that will shortly alienate us entirely, we must see such a phrase as a deliberate intent to set a certain tone. Anyone who writes at all knows a first sentence is carefully wrought no matter how speedily much else of any given piece is written. Had Adams stopped the sentence with the phrase and begun anew with "He" his effect would be too obvious. It was Adams' constant manner to plant a phrase amid a thick surrounding of words that served as a cloak against too definite assertion. So in Chapter II in a statement of larger importance Adams wrote, "That the most powerful emotion of man, next to the sexual, should disappear, might be a personal defect of his own" (34). In the context of the extended paragraph in which this occurs, one dealing entirely with religion, a hasty reader will miss the "next to the sexual" phrase; yet in the sentence as in the paragraph the trip phrase declares sex to be the basic human instinct.[13] The wit here is part mockery, I think, and another of those constant assertions demonstrating the inconclusion Adams came to because he insisted on seeing all sides of possible questions.

The second paragraph of the first chapter contains three words that point up this kind of half mockery—mock mockery. After explaining his similarity to a fully established Israel Cohen of orthodox Jerusalem Jewry, he spoke of the weight of his own ancestral associations as a "nest," as "troglodytic." A short pause to think reveals that lumping the First Church, the Boston State House, Beacon Hill, John Hancock and John Adams into a *troglodytic nest* implies a ridiculous prehistoric situation. The final jibe is the last word of the long sentence, "solution." A solution to what? Adams must mean one that concludes the career of such a baby born as he had been. But his career ended in the twentieth century when that certainly marked baby was nearly seventy years of age. His career ended unresolved, misunderstood, and solved only because it ended. Surely he mocks. Several pages later, talking still of the special weight of national history that was so personal a pressure on his boyhood—Revolutionary patriots, Presidents, Queen

Anne Mahogany, and Stuart portraits for which one "had to pay"—he said, "Americans commonly believed that they ruined" a young life, and he declared that "perhaps the practical common-sense of the American mind judged right." "The practical common-sense of the American mind" is not the whole American mind (20).

Aphorisms depend on witty word play for effectiveness. To be memorable or pithy they must exaggerate; they must flatly assert. The aphorist is therefore to be suspected of mockery. Henry Adams says:

> Politics, as a practice, whatever its professions, had always been the systematic organization of hatreds, and Massachusetts politics had been as harsh as the climate (7).

The reader gets an impression of aphorism—he may quote Adams by stripping away the verbiage of modifications to reveal the bald statement that "politics is the systematic organization of hatreds." He may even forget and omit the word "systematic" as I have done on occasion. Adams did not write this, though the phrase "whatever its professions" encourages one to over-emphasize the kernel of the sentence. The result reveals subtle intent. Such subtlety is a form of mockery. And when a schoolmaster is defined as "a man employed to tell lies to little boys," the reader forgets the lies are not garden variety falsehoods but a much more serious kind—assertions by men who pretend "Winter and summer, town and country, law and liberty" are not hostile forces (9). The mockery here has become somewhat grim.

Let me examine another paragraph in this first chapter.

> The attachment to Quincy was not altogether sentimental or wholly sympathetic. Quincy was not a bed of thornless roses. Even there the curse of Cain set its mark. There as elsewhere a cruel universe combined to crush a child. As though three or four vigorous brothers and sisters, with the best will, were not enough to crush any child, every one else conspired towards an education which he hated. From cradle to grave this problem of running order through chaos, direction through space, discipline through freedom, unity through multiplicity, has always been, and must always be, the task of education, as it is the moral of religion, philosophy, science, art, politics, and economy; but a boy's will is his life, and he dies when

it is broken, as the colt dies in harness, taking a new nature in becoming tame. Rarely has the boy felt kindly towards his tamers. Between him and his master has always been war. Henry Adams never knew a boy of his generation to like a master, and the task of remaining on friendly terms with one's family, in such a relation, was never easy (11–12).

The kernel here is the presentation of Henry Adams' definition of education's task—not, it must be noted, of education itself—in the middle of the paragraph, suddenly gotten past by the quick tripping phrase, "as it is the moral of. . . ." Careful readers underline "running order through chaos, direction through space, discipline through freedom, unity through multiplicity, has always been . . . the task of education." Surrounded by a thick verbal hedge it is the main line of the passage, not a bog or a side-path. The rest of the phrases are in effect that.

In such writing Henry Adams' particular artistry appears. His wit created aphoristic declarations that are half mockery produced by circling assertions, contradictions, and a feigned weariness of language that finally remind one of an Oscar Wilde or of H. L. Mencken's tired pose of sophistication later. "He was to see many great functions—funerals and festivals—in after-life, till his only thought was to see no more" (21). The assertion is an insertion here, as it is so often, a phrase that exaggerates opposed extremities enough to create weariness in the reader too. Exaggeration permeates this initial chapter, usually with sanguinolent touches that seldom appeared in *Chartres*, but which remind the reader of the *History* and its frequent flashes of cutting comment. In the second sentence in the *Education,* Adams used the word "circumcised" and he added "branded." The atmosphere of his childhood education made it seem "as though he were steeped . . . in the odor of political crime" (7). The Adams family's quarrels in the historic past had broken into "riot, bloodshed, personal feuds, foreign and civil war, wholesale banishments and confiscations" (21). Such exaggerations in wording occur constantly. They create sharp pictures of absolute thoughts that in the very act of overstatement demonstrate their tentative truth.

For him, alone, the old universe was thrown into the ashheap and a new one created. He and his eighteenth-century, troglodytic Boston

were suddenly cut apart—separated forever—in act if not in senti-
ment, by the opening of the Boston and Albany Railroad (5).

Heavy words abound: extremes, violence, boiled (7), drunken, scorch-
ing, glare, harshness, blaze, intense, strong (8), violent, intense, hostile
(9), crush, rage (12). But such words are countered by understatement
and words of reservation: he was "moderately interested"; (5) he was
"enjoying much of it" but not all (7). His President greatgrandfather
had " 'pledged his life, his fortune, and his sacred honor' to secure the
independence of his country and so forth" (15–16).

The extreme words are countered more frequently by concrete details,
specific descriptions and brief scenes that give the reader a trustworthy
sense of solidity—but a solidity spoiled in the long run by the undercurrent theme of uncertainty that when finally seen shows all the story adds
up to inconclusion. It is satisfying to read of actual experiences young
Henry Adams had in his President grandfather's library at Quincy, "He
hung about the library; handled the books . . . the caterpillars . . .
cut-glass . . . caterpillars" (14). It is good to see the list of activities
boys engaged in when they "swam in the *salt* ocean," or took to "the
pine-woods and the *granite* quarries," or "hunted *snapping*-turtles in the
swamps" (9). One feels sure of the facts when Adams describes his
name as written on the fly-leaf of his volume of Nursery Rhymes "in the
President's *trembling* hand" (15); or reads of his grandmother's
writing-desk, "with *little glass* doors above and little eighteenth-century
volumes in old binding, labeled 'Peregrine Pickle' or 'Tom Jones' or
'Hannah More' " (16) or of her "*heavy* silver teapot and sugar-bowl
and cream-jug" (18). Short, personalized similes provide for the reader
a sense of truth and stability the involved sentences point up:

To the boy she seemed singularly peaceful . . . an exotic, like her
Sèvres china (18).

Such a figure was even less fitted. . . . She was Louis Seize,
like the furniture (19).

Sanguinolence, mockery, weariness of tone and statement, circum-
locution, concrete words; lengthy, delayed statements, reversals, negative declarations, over-positive assertions: The total effect of such
gnarly, baroque, even rococo sentences is beguiling, bewildering, puzzling and finally uncertain. They offer a startling contrast to the clear,

hard sub-structure—the organization of the even-flowing paragraphs, the formality of the great bulk of the paragraphs themselves, the smooth progression of the chapters, the clear divisions of these chapters into sections, and the sharply significant break half way through the book. Here Henry Adams achieved a major success in prose composition. He made his manner fit his matter to produce the uncertainty that is humor.

It seems, however, that he only created confusion, as Yvor Winters has contended. In Chapter V, "Berlin," Adams concluded a paragraph: "In November, 1858, London was still vast, but it was the London of the eighteenth century that an American felt and hated." He did not say why. We must assume he meant the enemy London of the eighteenth century the Adams clan had fought then. In the next paragraph, picking up the last word, he wrote, "He liked it best when he hated it." He must have meant that London had dwindled away from the lively presence it had been to eighteenth-century Adamses; that as it flowered otherwise in the nineteenth century it came to represent to an Adams of his ancestry an alien clime. But what did he mean when he followed this sentence with the aphoristic one, completely confusing at first glance: "Education began at the end, or perhaps would end at the beginning" (73)? It takes a stretch of the reading mind to follow through here. The next sentence says simply that from London, going to Antwerp, he was carried back to the sixteenth century. This was the source period of the Adams mind and conscience, in Puritanism. Antwerp took him even farther back in time to medievalism and beyond that to Christ himself and His descent from the Cross. He ended the paragraph:

> He never dreamed of trying to educate himself to the Descent from the Cross. He was only too happy to feel himself kneeling at the foot of the Cross; he learned only to loathe the sordid necessity of getting up again, and going about his stupid business (74).

Now where are we? Are we really in confusion? In part, yes, but weaving throughout all this mass and mixture, constantly shimmering, regularly shuddering (if anyone prefers the final word of the *Education*) is the solid thread of meaning which is a matter of contradictions, oppositions, balance and paradox.

Adams recognized his matter (his plastic material) was essentially formless, and it seems to me he made his recognition clear just by this means of filling in his blueprint, his structural base, with sentences that in themselves create confusion at first glance and inconclusiveness finally. In writing of winter and summer early in the first chapter he said, "The violence of the contrast was real and made the strongest motive of education" (7). That is: the stimulation of opposing elements. In this first chapter alone the list of doubled terms that exist together and are in opposition is long and staggering. The entire tone is established by the phrase beginning the second half of the second sentence of the book: "but, on the other hand" (3). Following this occur:

Whether life was an honest game of chance, or whether the cards were marked and forced (4)

whether it had fitted or unfitted them for success (6)

the passion for companionship and the antipathy to society (6)

good or bad (6)

stingy or hostile (7)

Winter and summer, cold and heat, town and country, force and freedom (7)

Town was restraint, law, unity. Country . . . was liberty, diversity, outlawry (8)

summer was drunken. . . . The opposites or antipathies, were the cold grays of November evenings (8)

Life was a double thing (9)

Winter and summer, then, were two hostile lives (9)

Summer was the multiplicity of nature; winter was school (9)

life was double (9)

Winter and summer, town and country, law and liberty, were hostile (9)

double nature (9)

He liked the Adams [Quincy] side best. . . . Yet he felt also that Quincy was in a way inferior to Boston [the Brookses], and that socially Boston looked down on Quincy (10)

this problem of running order through chaos, direction through space, discipline through freedom, unity through multiplicity (12)

Abigail was right . . . where sound judgment was involved; but sound judgment is sometimes a source of weakness rather than of force (17)

Add to this list of doubles and oppositions one of words and phrases of uncertainty:

[He was engaged in a game—of life] of which neither he nor anyone else back to the beginning of time knew the rules or the risks or the stakes (4)

the practical value remains to the end in doubt (4)

The habit of doubt; of distrusting his own judgment and of totally rejecting the judgment of the world; the tendency to regard every question as open; the hesitation to act except as a choice of evils; the shirking of responsibility (6)

perplexing, warring, irreconcilable problems, irreducible opposites (9)

the boy found himself standing face to face with a dilemma that might have puzzled an early Christian. What was he? Where was he going? (21)

and could never decide (22)

Beginning then with a statement of his fortunate birth, he advanced through twenty-two pages of remarks in Chapter I to demonstrate that his seventy years of education following his auspicious birth (a heavy burden, that noble birth) left him still wondering whether the wealth of his eighteenth-century Adams inheritance should have been abandoned for the material advantages of State Street in Boston. He concluded: "Sixty years afterwards he was still unable to make up his mind" (22).

The uncertainty Adams expressed in this first chapter forewarns the reader of the subjects he was to develop in the rest of his book. He introduced the ominous word "force" which appeared thereafter as commonly as "Virgin Mary" had in *Mont-Saint-Michel and Chartres*. That men lie when they pretend law and liberty are not hostile forces (schoolmasters) is the only statement in this chapter jeering at unitarian thinking, but it is the first of many similar remarks that followed. By implication every doubled term denied unity too. Finally, the respect young Henry had for his grandfather despite the latter's use of force grew because his grandfather had not only kept silent while doing his disreputable work but had "shown no temper." Such a performance came to seem the acme of human achievement to Henry Adams for his creed became "Silence next to good-temper was the mark of sense."

The rest of the first section of *The Education of Henry Adams* and the rest of the book elaborated these manners and this matter to produce finally so reiterated a series as to amount to an inconclusiveness and a suspension that at last demands good temper, that demands humor, to appreciate it. Chapter II, "Boston," finds Henry Adams in the eighteenth-century past reading the romances of Scott. Chapter III, "Washington," concludes that by 1854 he "had as yet no education at all" (53). Chapter IV, "Harvard College," finds him a Harvard graduate, but "Education had not begun" (69). Harvard provided "a mind on which only a water-mark had been stamped" (55) a reinforcement of a particular social type good enough for any previous age, but insufficient "for success in the next generation" (65).[14] Chapter V, "Berlin," condemns the city as useless—what Adams liked in Germany was the old Germany of the eighteenth century, not what was emerging in 1858. And Chapter VI, "Rome," concludes with the statement that after two years in Europe he started home for Boston in the autumn of 1860, twenty-two years old, with "mixed emotions but no education" (97).

He had learned nothing to fit him to be a young man of the world "equipped for any emergency"; nor did he as a "subject of education," a "certain form of energy," gain "economy of his force" (x). His training only increased his awareness of obstacles. Direct application of effort, especially during his two years at Berlin, Dresden, Rome and Paris, left him "floundering between worlds passed and worlds coming, which had a habit of crushing men who stayed too long at the points of contact" (83). In brief, at twenty-two he was quite unprepared to do what was necessary to get rid of the stamp of 1848, 1776, and the eighteenth century, and to take the stamp that belonged to his own age, the period from 1865 to 1900 (25–26). At "any other moment in human history" except 1854 (or 1860) his education would have been quite the best a young man could have because it provided a "political and literary bias." All past moments had shown "invariable sequence" in man's experience (52). Fifty years later he looked back to see a dismaying fact:

in essentials like religion, ethics, philosophy; in history, literature, art; in the concepts of all science, except perhaps mathematics, the American boy of 1854 stood nearer the year 1 than to the year 1900 (53).

He needed training as an *economist* to live successfully in the late nineteenth century. This does not mean a "scientific education" because the world wasn't scientific (88). Henry's older brother Charles Francis Adams, Jr., became such an economist in railroading, but the latter's *Autobiography* shows such a career was no more successful ultimately than that his younger brother followed into failure.

In a thorough way Henry Adams was thus crushed between the worlds of the eighteenth and the late nineteenth centuries by forever after having to stay "at the points of contact," at the *junctures*. The task of education from cradle to grave, he said, was the problem of "running order through chaos, direction through space, discipline through freedom, unity through multiplicity" (12). He came to realize the points where the two parts of these conflicting doublets met was the only goal to be realized as he came to learn in studying Chartres that the moment of transition was what marked the success of the medieval church.

Throughout this first section of the *Education* Adams implied education should be intellectual training. Southerners like his college classmate "Roony" Lee had temperament but no mind and were thus doomed to defeat in their attempts to acquire education (57). But neither did Adams get concrete and helpful lessons to provide a solution to the problem of running order through chaos. Seeing Antwerp in 1858 and realizing the medieval smell of it, he "got drunk on his emotions, and had then to get sober as best as he could." Sobriety is clear-headed appraisal, but Antwerp was "education only sensual." The meaning of the Descent from the Cross did not bother him at twenty; he was happy only to feel himself kneeling at its foot. Later in life "he learned only to loathe the sordid necessity of getting up again, and going about his stupid business" (74) which was his inner compulsion to continue to reason. He buttressed this implied view of education as intellectual understanding when he explained in Chapter III the impression the Southern slave power made on him as a New England boy in 1851: it forced him back on Puritanism, back to "Stuart kings and Roman popes.

Education could go no further in that course, and ran off into emotion"
(48).

A succinct statement of Adams' realization of irony is "Better take
sides first, and reason about it for the rest of life" (84). It is the *"Think
not! Strike!"* advice of 1891 in "Buddha and Brahma." [15] This practical advice permits decision, then action. Reason emphasized contradictions, impeded solutions. The earliest "motive" to education he received
was the contrast between the "extremes of sensibility" (7) in which his
life was lived as a child, the "bearing of the two seasons":

> . . . it ran through life, and made the division between its perplex-
> ing, warring, irreconcilable problems, irreducible opposites, with
> growing emphasis to the last year of study (9).

When in later life he speculated about George Washington who had his
sources in the "sum of all wickedness" (48) the slave power, and still
remained to the end of Adams' life the one steady Pole Star (47), he did
not solve the problem except by "concluding" with yet another puzzle,
that

> In practice, such trifles as contradictions in principle are easily set
> aside; the faculty of ignoring them makes the practical man; but
> any attempt to deal with them seriously as education is fatal (48).

A page later this remark begins to look cynical when Adams explains
that his boyhood hero Charles Sumner though too noble to sell his vote
openly to proslavery Democrats in Massachusetts in 1850 still accepted a
senatorship as the result of a bargain, "too good to take part, but not too
good to take profit" (49). Sumner solved a life problem by taking sides
first.[16] But he solved no problem of Henry Adams' education because to
run order through chaos is not only the task of education, "it is the
moral of religion, philosophy, science, art, politics, and economy" (12).
But how does one solve the problem of morality? In 1859 when Napoleon III declared war on Austria and set out to rob it, Adams wondered:
where is the moral justification? To rob and kill the wicked is permitted
"without a qualm; but it might happen that the good were robbed.
Education insisted on finding a moral foundation for robbery. . . .
Education founded on mere self-interest was. . . . Machiavelli translated into American" (84–85). In Section II, "Education by English-

men," Chapters VII through XV, a good deal of Adams' discussion is devoted to further speculation about this essential problem of education, morality.

Let me count up the positive gains in education Henry Adams made through his twenty-second year.

1. He learned the color yellow, the taste of baked apples and the feel of discomfort as he was once half-stifled under a blanket (5–6).

2. He learned the increasingly emphatic lesson that "irreducible opposites" occur again and again (9).

3. His father gave him "some idea of a French accent." His father made no effort to force his mind (36).

4. He learned a dislike of school "so strong as to be a positive gain" (37).

5. He learned as an adolescent to read books—as of the eighteenth century (39).

6. He learned that women possessed domestic virtues but not that they "had more to give" (40).

7. He learned blackguardism in Boston which was "only too educational" (41) and he learned violence—if that "were a part of complete education" (42).

8. He went to Washington as a boy of twelve and learned only that it fixed in memory the stages of a boy's thought in 1850 (43).

9. He learned a "vague sense of feeling an unknown living obstacle in the [political] dark" of 1851—a reference to the political machine that the later nineteenth century would produce (49).

10. At Harvard he learned Southerners were as fitted for nineteenth-century life as Sioux Indians (56, 58).

11. He learned that he should perhaps go to Europe for amusement —only perhaps Harvard had not even taught him that (63).

12. At Harvard somehow he was encouraged to write—but to write what (66)?

13. Setting off for Europe on his first ocean voyage he learned the seriousness of sea-sickness (71). ("he could never see the humor of sea-sickness.")

14. He learned that impressions gathered in travel teach if one is able to sort them out so that some lead to wisdom (71).

15. In Berlin he learned the purpose of state education is to mold young minds to its ends (78).

All these learnings as a part of education were forthright but clearly no help out of chaos. What really "taught" was accident:

1. He learned Beethoven in a German beer hall (80).

2. He learned Italy by going there. In both cases music and Italy became "not a means of pursuing life, but one of the ends attained" (85).

3. He learned the limits of landscape education at an Alpine pass in 1860 (86–87).

4. He learned to be a tourist after two years in Europe—to look, to see, but not to understand (88).

Adams showed himself a devotee of reason and reasonable plans, but finally he demonstrated the helplessness of reason in finding order in chaos—or, here, direction through the space of his future: "He could have done no better had he foreseen every stage of his coming life, and he would probably have done worse," he said (62). Looking back in 1905 he saw, "For success in the life imposed on him he needed, as afterwards appeared, the facile use of only four tools: Mathematics, French, German, and Spanish" (38). He gained only a partial use of one tool, French, and enough German only to enable him to read it as though it were English "which proved that he knew little about it" (77). "Negative results in plenty he could trace" (63), he said in telling about these first twenty-two years of education, and he produced an overpowering quantity of them, all too obvious to require listing.

One wonders how seriously to take Adams at this point; but I think it should be very. A final note confirms the negative-ness he meant to convey: near the end of Section I he wrote, "All experience is an arch, to build upon." He added immediately, "Yet Adams admitted himself unable to guess what use his second winter in Germany was to him, or what he expected it to be" (87). And the section ends with a discussion of Rome as increasingly raising the question, the more experience he had of it, of "Why! Why!! Why!!!" (92) and with the exotic experience of interviewing Garibaldi in Palermo in 1860, a man who said of himself later that he had not understood his own acts and who taught Adams "the extreme complexity of extreme simplicity" (95). In concrete terms this expressed what he had earlier said: "Education began at the end, or perhaps would end at the beginning" (73) [17] and even earlier why "The more he was educated, the less he understood" (44). I therefore interpret this arch of experience as another image of suspension; the confusion hardly permitted Adams a firm reach to solid firmament, and once again we are back at the juncture where the style that likens experience to an arch becomes the matter and both become suspension, the only unity Adams ever achieved.

III. Education by Englishmen

The second section of the *Education* is the longest of all six, made up of Chapters VII, "Treason," through XV, "Darwinism" (140 pages). It deals with the effect on Henry Adams' education of the years of his early maturity from age twenty-two to thirty in England during the Civil War while he served as "assistant son" to his father during the latter's term of service as Minister to England from 1861–1868. Adams concentrates on the effect of a number of people, mostly Englishmen of various kinds, and what they taught, or rather did not teach.[18] In describing this time in his book, he continued to employ the stylistic devices he began with.

Extravagance was the keynote of his expression still, and he continued with overstatements, understatements, negative declarations, acidity, sanguinolence, mockery, and keen quick phrases embedded in or quickly following what were generally fairly heavy and even ponderous sentences. The heaviness of wording underscores the flow of witticisms: a thick skull, for example, is a "thick cortex of fixed ideas" (170). This somewhat pompous, Jamesian manner helps flashing wit to gleam through. Often it is slashing wit: an English duke he met as a boy playing leap-frog, met off and on in the course of the next thirty years "singularly enough, was always playing leap-frog." He scored off a dowager duchess who forced him to perform a highland fling in public with the daughter of the Turkish ambassador as "a terrible vision in castanets" (118). The wit is very often acid. He spoke of the Southern secessionists as "fit for medical treatment." He derided the notion that intelligent people could treat Southern statesmen *as* statesmen because "the Sioux Indians would have taught less mischief" (100). And the wit is occasionally an unexpected contradiction provided by an insertion as when he says "the habit of reticence—of talking without meaning—is never effaced" (114). As before, sanguinolence is common:

> the vultures descended on it [Washington] in swarms that darkened the ground, and tore the carrion of political patronage into fragments and gobbets of fat and lean, on the very steps of the White House (108–109).

And:

> he could plainly discern in history, that man from the beginning had found his chief amusement in bloodshed (128).

Sanguinolence led into overdone lugubriousness:

> the month of December, 1861, in Mansfield Street, Portland Place, would have gorged a glutton of gloom (119).

Such overstatements occur constantly; so he said flatly, "Not one man in America wanted the Civil War, or expected or intended it." But his dogmatism was never absolute, and such a statement is always protected by one following which disperses the too-firm declaration:

> Possibly a few Southern loyalists in despair might dream it as an impossible chance; but none planned it (98).

For the sake of his image occasionally an overstatement of itself showed it is not to be taken literally, as when he said that in July of 1863 when England began to hear of Yankee successes on the battlefield, "Londoners were stupid with unbelief" (169).

The negative is always present. Speaking of Quincy in November he said,

Nowhere else does the uncharitable autumn wreak its spite so harshly on the frail wreck of the grasshopper summer (98–99).

Overdone, the remark is followed by one even more so:

yet even a Quincy November seemed temperate before the chill of a Boston January (99).

And when he described his reaction to Thomas Carlyle's sympathy with the Southern cause he produced a fine and negative figure:

Doubts cast on his stature spread far into general darkness like shadows of a setting sun (131–132).

This whole section of nine chapters is the funniest in the entire book, for Adams treats himself as a figure of fun, an obscure, ignored, humiliated young man of no position and no appeal in the diplomatic world, exaggerating a picture of insignificance and half-comic bewilderment, but at the same time revealing stoutness and validity even so, as when he speaks of himself as one of the small fry of the London legations who were admitted to Lady Palmerston's receptions in 1862 where, though hardly recognized, they could "at least stand in a corner and look at a bishop or even a duke" (134). Adams seldom failed to mock. The impression the reader gets is of a young Henry Adams who was a naive young porpoise (he called himself "a young mosquito" [103] which is a more dangerous specimen than a playful porpoise, smaller though he may be) swimming about in the "surf of a wild ocean" (111) of war and international diplomacy and giant whales, trying his innocent best to learn from his elders and his betters what made the world go round. The experience was

one of the most perfect educational courses in politics and diplomacy that a young man ever had a chance to pursue. The most costly tutors in the world were provided for him at public expense —Lord Palmerston, Lord Russell, Lord Westbury, Lord Selborne, Mr. Gladstone, Lord Granville, and their associates, paid for by the British Government; William H. Seward, Charles Francis Adams, William Maxwell Evarts, Thurlow Weed, and other considerable professors employed by the American Government.

Still "there was only one student to profit by this immense staff of teachers. The private secretary alone sought education" (149). But what he learned was all wrong.

Forty years after these teachers had completed his diplomatic education, forty years after he had shuffled all these expensive tutors of the 1860's into their proper niches of importance and validity, he came to see he had been mistaken in particularly crushing ways. He discovered "a picture different from anything he had conceived" and this "rendered worthless his whole painful diplomatic experience" (178).

He had entirely misjudged the principal English figures he knew as they affected England's American diplomacy. He had thought Prime Minister Palmerston was an active and decided friend of the Confederacy, an enemy to the North. Chancellor of the Exchequer Gladstone he thought was the most thoughtful and thorough in his plan to recognize the Confederacy in 1862. Foreign Minister Russell he thought was privately at least the best friend of the North in the British Government. In all cases the reverse was true. After forty years Adams discovered Palmerston was "so simple as to mislead the student altogether" : "The world thought him positive, decided, reckless; the record proved him to be cautious, careful, vacillating" (164). The record revealed he was a man who had lost his nerve. He found Glastone was "the sum of contradictions. The highest education could reach, in this analysis, only a reduction to the absurd" (164–165). Gladstone himself revealed in his memoirs that he was to be charged not with "conspiracy—of policy—of logic and connection in the affairs of man" (165) but with *no* set plan to break the Union, with *no* conspiracy, with *no* sense to see the results of his own acts: he was in fact "not quite sane."

As for Lord Russell, he seemed to have been verging on senility (166). (But: "Russell's generation were mostly senile from youth. They had never got beyond 1815" [168].) He turned out to be the enemy, not the friend, of the American Minister and the Union cause. Worse: he ended up appearing so unaware of his own acts as to conclude himself that despite the damage he caused he was honest (164). Adams had wanted to believe Russell "had foresight and persistence of which he was unaware" (175). Forty years later Adams found in no revealed documents that such was the case—"Russell proved that he had been feeble, timid, mistaken, senile, but not dishonest" (176). He cost his government twenty million dollars in reparations paid for the Alabama Claims by his "senility," and the effect on Adams as a student of diplomacy rendered worthless all the diplomatic education he thought he had gained (178). Gladstone wrote in after years that he *"always"* held "that politicians are the men whom, as a rule it is the most difficult to comprehend." He claimed for his part to "never have thus understood, or thought I understood, *above one or two."* Henry Adams, as he drew up his later years' conclusion, declared he "thought" he had also "understood one or two." They were certainly not Palmerston, Russell and Gladstone: "The American type was more familiar" (179).

In this section Adams expanded the *"I* don't know" of Section I to "They don't know either." Speaking of Lincoln, Seward and Sumner, for example, in Washington in the spring of 1861, he said, "they knew less than he" (109). That spring, "all were as ignorant as himself; none knew what should be done, or how to do it" 106). He said flatly, "in all great [political] emergencies he commonly found that every one was more or less wrong" (108). He began Chapter VIII on "Diplomacy" by saying of the outbreak of war in April of 1861:

a million young men [were] planted in the mud of a lawless world. . . . They asked few questions, but if they had asked millions they would have got no answers. No one could help (110).

The whole of this section demonstrates the ignorance Adams found all about him as a young man, revealed as images in the figures of Palmerston, Gladstone and Russell, whose activities never appeared later to be founded on their own knowledge of what they were about: Lord Russell, in after years "affirmed . . . that he had meant nothing at all; that he meant to do right; that he did not know what he meant" (174–175). Adams had earlier reminded his readers

This is not a story of the diplomatic adventures of Charles Francis Adams, but of his son Henry's adventures in search of an education, which, if not taken too seriously tended to humor (116).

Commenting later on a critical diplomatic problem faced by his father in June of 1862, Adams provided only the bare facts of the case, explaining that "the story belongs to history, not to education." As educational value it was another puzzle of reconciling contradictions—in this case that the weak American Minister could succeed in "muzzling" the powerful British Prime Minister (136).

Adams found no order, direction, discipline or unity in his experiences in diplomacy. The moral eluded him too.

Education in diplomacy should be education in diplomatic morality. The educational values of Thurlow Weed, the astute politician from New York who came to London to help Minister Adams in 1863, provided what Adams called "a complete American education in himself" (146). He was an education in humor. Weed was successful, wanted no offices for himself, displayed apparent unselfishness. "He grasped power, but not office. . . . he gave, but he did not receive," unlike the earlier hero, Charles Sumner. He was interested in playing the game, not interested in rules; what young Adams thought he should conclude from Mr. Weed's stories he put in the form of a question, asking,

"Then, Mr. Weed, do you think that no politician can be trusted?"
Mr. Weed hesitated for a moment; then said in his mild manner:
"I never advise a young man to begin by thinking so" (147).

Mild the statement is, but it was one Adams learned as a lesson forty years later when he discovered *no* law operated, for Lord Russell, though ignorant, had proved that he was neither honest, dishonest, nor anything else (175). Conclusion of any sort was mistaken. Only open possibility remained.

The successful American lawyer William M. Evarts was "an economist of morals, but with him the question was rather how much morality one could afford. 'The world can absorb only doses of truth,' he said; 'too much would kill it.' " Adams commented, "One sought education in order to adjust the dose" (148). I doubt Adams was very serious here. Earlier he had declared "the chief obstacle to the youth's [his] education . . . was his honesty; his simple-minded faith in his intentions" (83). Mr. Evarts' talk unsettled him because "he liked lofty moral principles and cared little for political tactics" (108). Finding that an actual politician like Evarts and the entirely different variety Thurlow Weed both taught relativity in values, he had difficulty:

Principles had better be left aside; values were enough. Adams knew that he could never learn to play politics in so masterly a fashion as this: his education and his nervous system equally forbade it, although he admired all the more the impersonal faculty of the political master who could thus efface himself and his temper in the game (148).

Adams sought an operative moral—principles, motives and firm explanations. He did not find them.[19] So when he read Lord Russell's admission in his *Recollections* that he had been at fault in important affairs (150) Adams said it was not a question of fault. What was his intent? "To a young man, getting an education in politics, there could be no sense in history unless a constant course of faults implied a constant motive." There seems to have been no constant motive. This increased the importance of what he thought he had learned as law, "that in politics no man should be trusted" (151) because, worst of all possibilities, men were not necessarily wicked but not even sure of their own interests:

> Here, then, appeared in its fullest force, the practical difficulty in education which a mere student would never overcome; a difficulty, not in theory, or knowledge, or even in want of experience, but in the sheer chaos of human nature (153).

Forty years later new information about this busy time in history (1862) showed,

> All the world had been at cross-purposes, had misunderstood themselves and the situation, had followed wrong paths, drawn wrong conclusions, had known none of the facts. One would have done better to draw no conclusions at all. One's diplomatic education was a long mistake (161–162).

Thus Adams ended where he began, but his search for an education "if not taken too seriously, tended to humor" (116). Again humor was inconclusion, and education was suspension. Reexamine as he would the diplomatic struggle in London from 1861–1863, he never found a mistake in the American campaign or in the American assumption that the major figures of the British government had persistently worked to establish the Confederacy (173–175). Yet "to the total derision and despair of the lifelong effort for education" (175) he found Lord Russell, at least, proved that such was not his intention. And regardless of any individual's intentions or lack of them the *determining* force was beyond any individual, for the force lay with the mass. So "The problem would have been the same; the answer equally obscure" (166).

Section II dealt with more figures of prime value than Section I did, where Charles Francis Adams appeared as the principal human factor in Henry Adams' education. Two other men appeared before Adams on this English stage who did not teach diplomacy or morality, but who did add experience. They did teach inconclusion, too, and this was the important issue. One was Richard Monckton Milnes, Lord Houghton. He appeared as a counterpart to the other figures. A "man of the world" representing the ideal for whom Adams wrote his book, he seemed to have been a living image of suspension. A social power in London, he affected social eccentricity, was indifferent to ridicule, was the first wit in London, and had great intelligence behind "his almost Falstaffian mask and laugh of Silenus." He went everywhere and knew everybody.

> He was a voracious reader, a strong critic, an art connoisseur in certain directions, a collector of books, but above all he was a man of the world by profession, and loved the contacts—perhaps the collisions—of society.

He was the "good-nature of London" (124).

Adams portrayed Milnes as a successful man of the nineteenth-century world. Adams admired him greatly. He was of that rare company in Adams' book who showed no serious blind spots. "Monckton Milnes himself was regarded as an eccentric, chiefly by those who did not know him, but his fancies and hobbies were only ideas a little in advance of the time; his manner was eccentric, but not his mind" (184). His intelligence protected him from the charge of frivolity. In Parliament he later "made speeches, chiefly criticized as too good for the place and too high for the audience" (124). What particularly endeared him to Adams, I think, is that his intelligence in rejecting reverence allowed him non-commitment. This is shown by the experience he reported of a call on the great Victor Hugo some years after this period, an episode I have earlier mentioned:

"I was shown into a large room," he said, "with women and men seated in chairs against the walls, and Hugo, at one end throned. No one spoke. At last Hugo raised his voice solemnly, and uttered the words, 'Quant à moi, je crois en dieu!' Silence followed. Then a woman responded as if in deep meditation: 'Chose sublime! un Dieu qui croit en Dieu!' " (143).

Adams loved this story and admired Milnes for seeing the foolishness of such great commitment.

A fairly lengthy passage deals with the second figure, Charles Algernon Swinburne, who struck Adams when he first met him in 1862 at Milnes' country house as a genius. He was the first such person Adams had ever been conscious of meeting. But the portrait of Swinburne ends so qualified that he appears in a distinctly hard light that exposes him. Swinburne was a year older than Adams (twenty-three) "a tropical bird, high-crested, long-beaked, quick-moving, with rapid utterance and screams of humor, quite unlike any English lark or nightingale" (139). Listening to the torrent of his talk and the evidence of his "incredible memory and knowledge of literature" and his recitations of his as yet unpublished work, Adams was stunned. "Then, at last, if never before, Adams acquired education. What he had sought so long, he found; but he was none the wiser; only the more astonished" (140). This seems perverse.

I think Adams meant Swinburne's astonishing brilliance indicated a completely finished man who contained in abundance all those qualities the late nineteenth-century world demanded of a successful man, including perhaps flexibility. I think he meant Swinburne had found a direction in space. He appeared to have in rich profusion the makings of a garment of education. He had managed "economy of his force." He had cleared away obstacles. His superiority impressed Adams strongly enough to elicit the remark that "no number of centuries could ever educate him to Swinburne's level, even in technical appreciation" (142–143). Swinburne tested him by his two measuring sticks, Victor Hugo and Walter Savage Landor, and Adams failed the test for he "had to admit that both Hugo and Landor bored him." That was enough for

Swinburne, since "One who could feel neither Hugo nor Landor was lost."

At this point one begins to suspect a trick, for Adams' display of humility is too extravagant. Adams said "he knew he was no companion for Swinburne; probably he could be only an annoyance" (142). It might work the other way around: after admitting that he could never reach Swinburne's level, Adams said quietly, "yet he often wondered whether there was nothing he had to offer that was worth the poet's acceptance" (143). Homage was not enough. *Then* follows the story Monckton Milnes told of Victor Hugo as a god. It reveals, I think, that Adams seriously doubted the validity of Swinburne altogether; the education he provided left Adams none the wiser and "only the more astonished" (140) because "so enabled a man" (to use Emily Dickinson's phrase) was too complete, no different from any dogmatist, a man like Charles Sumner, for example, who was also fixed in a certain attitude "forever" (102). Adams concluded the account of Swinburne by saying he later read his poetry, and "If he had sinned and doubted at all, he wholly repented and did penance before 'Atalanta in Calydon,' and would have offered Swinburne a solemn worship as Milne's female offered Hugo, if it would have pleased the poet. Unfortunately it was worthless" (143).

It is too much. Adams doubted and continued to. After all—a very subtle thrust—Adams had declared Swinburne, in comparison with his companions at this country house party of Milnes', was "millions of ages far from them" all. This is not to say *above* them all. Adams added that the distinguishing phrase to describe Swinburne, according to Stirling, one of the house guests, was that he was "a cross between the devil and the Duke of Argyll!" Carefully, Adams explained that he didn't know the devil "at least in person" but to a Scotsman like Stirling, Argyll meant (to skip past Adams' sly smoke screen of words here) "what the French call *moyenâgeux*, or mediaeval with grotesque turn" (141). So much for Charles Algernon Swinburne. Witnessing Swinburne's virtuoso performance all one long evening in this English country house in December of 1862 left Adams unable to judge what contribution to real wisdom he provided. It is well to note here that Adams came to think both Swinburne and his touchstone Victor Hugo were men who, unlike himself, could bring into "common relation with an ordered social system tending to orderly development" such perplexing spectacles as the sight of Garibaldi at one great London house being lionized by duchesses, and the famous beauty of the Second Empire, Mme. de Castiglione, at another being rudely stared at by "the most refined and aristocratic society in the world." Swinburne (and Hugo) could have reconciled these two sights, but Adams would have rejected any reconciliation as superficial or supernatural (198–199).[20]

Each of the last four chapters of this section of the *Education* which I have labelled "Education by Englishmen" is a side-path if considered separately. As individual essays they make great sense, for each is informative. Chapter XII, "Eccentricity," discusses the peculiar character of the individual Englishman. Chapter XIII, "The Perfection of Human Society," deals with individuals added into social systems. Chapter XIV, "Dilettantism," relates Adams' fruitless struggle to learn from artists and critics uniform standards in art. And Chapter XV, "Darwinism," the most important of the four, penetrates into fundamental questions raised by the spectacular advances made by the scientific theories of Charles Darwin.

In "Eccentricity" Adams showed that peculiarity in behavior may be all right in the English surroundings which allowed individual freedom, but it was of no value to his education. "The English mind was one-sided, eccentric, systematically unsystematic, and logically illogical. The less one knew of it, the better" (180). It is stupidity essentially because it is conviction—witness John Arthur Roebuck's headlong confident support of the Confederate cause. He was opposed by John Bright; but he underestimated Bright's courage to fight back (188). What is the value of an extreme confidence if it blinds the possessor to functioning realities outside his bliss?

Henry Reeve, the editor of the *Edinburgh Review*, exhibited a contradictory variety of this English eccentricity—Adams called it "oscillating reserve"—an attitude that forbade publishing any article dealing with a matter on which sides were not already fixed. Such caution was more troublesome than outright conviction like Roebuck's, or the "reckless hostility" to the Northern cause of Carlyle: one "never could be sure what preposterous commonplace it might encourage." Where is education in repetition of the commonplace? Adams' concluded eccentricity was weakness because by implication it was contradiction. It did not provide unified thought. It only displayed multiplicity (193).

Many chapters later, in Chapter XXIV, "Indian Summer," Adams introduced the subject of eccentricity once again. This time he dealt with the contrast between the American artists John La Farge and James Whistler in their art and their behavior in public. "To La Farge, eccentricity meant convention; a mind really eccentric never betrayed it. True eccentricity was a tone—a shade—a *nuance*—and the finer the tone, the truer the eccentricity" (370). This was in conversation, not in artistic work, for there his mind "asserted his personal force with depth and vehemence of tone never before seen" (371–372). Whistler, on the other hand, "in his art carried the sense of *nuance* and tone far beyond any point reached by La Farge, or even attempted," but exhibited a vehemence in company that gave all the appearance of demonstrating extreme eccentricity when it was not. At a dinner in Paris during the Boer War, Adams watched the behavior of both artists. La Farge was silent, but Whistler declaimed against England for two hours, "witty, declamatory, extravagant, bitter, amusing, and noisy; but in substance what he said was not merely commonplace—it was true!" Thus he showed "a willingness to seem eccentric where no real eccentricity, unless perhaps of temper, existed" (371). La Farge was the eccentric in the quietude of his daily life then, but Whistler was the more eccentric in his art. What this meant as education was that the more refined an art may be the more it adds to the evidence of multiplicity.

Chapter XIII, "The Perfection of Human Society," reveals that "society" in England was perfect in the social life of London dinner parties and in English country houses on weekends, which one friend told Adams such perfection meant. Meaning perhaps "something scholarly, worldy, and modern" (201) it was the taste of only a few. And the taste was antiquated: Adams

> conceived that the perfection of human society required that a man should enter a drawing-room where he was a total stranger, and place himself on the hearth-rug, his back to the fire, with an air of expected benevolence, without curiosity, much as though he had dropped in at a charity concert, kindly disposed to applaud the performers and to overlook mistakes.

Like the watermark gained at Harvard, such learning helped education not at all. The knowledge was still "ignorance to the next generation" (202). What was "society" anyway? In a funny but biting figure Adams said, "Society had no unity; one wandered about in it like a maggot in cheese." (197).

One hopeful note closed this chapter, one parallel to that ending the far grimmer chapter "Failure" later. Adams made a friend, Milnes Gaskell. I think Adams himself interpreted the "perfection of human society" to mean discovering friendship; but then, "Intimates are predestined" (205), not to be found through education.

Chapter XIV, "Dilettantism," deals with education in art. The figures named, described and quoted all come to life as persons of dogma and conviction—Francis Turner Palgrave, an art critic, Thomas Woolner, another, and Stopford Brooke, the sculptor. They taught Adams that art was another world of chaos. Taste in England was a "garden of innate disorder" (214) yet taste in art "was the most alluring and treacherous" of all things.

> Once drawn into it, one had small chance of escape, for it had no centre or circumference, no beginning, middle, or end, no origin, no object, and no conceivable result as education (213).

It proved another dead end. As an end in itself art was as valuable as Beethoven, Italy, Alpine scenery, the charm of women over thirty or forty, even the poems and ballads of Swinburne. But for Education the pursuit of art was fruitless because it was "fragmentary by essence."

Where else could Adams look for education? His inclination was to history; but to follow the British was to fall into "the sink of history— antiquarianism." All British historians were guilty of "antiquarianism or anecdotage." Henry Thomas Buckle alone attempted to link history to ideas and he was thought to have failed. Macaulay and Carlyle were dramatists, painters and poets—story tellers (221). Where was a method to study history as a way out of chaos? There was none. Nevertheless Adams took to his pen, aiming to fit himself for the press, not with much faith in its value as a career, however:

> Yet the press was still the last resource of the educated poor who could not be artists and would not be tutors. Any man who was fit for nothing else could write an editorial or a criticism (211).

131

But he had to have a career. He began by doing a three-month study of the John Smith and Pocahontas story and succeeded in placing it with the *North American Review*. At last he had undertaken an action that succeeded. But what was the result for education? It had no relationship to it, for it was "American antiquarianism, which of all antiquarianism he held the most foolish." The chapter concluded: "He had wholly lost his way" and must begin education anew (223).

Chapter XV, "Darwinism," began with a summary of Adams' education up to 1867: "Politics, diplomacy, law, art, and history had opened no outlet for future energy or effort" (224). So far he had found no "means of pursuing life," which is the most forthright definition of education Adams produced in the whole of the *Education* (85). He decided to pin his hopes for education on the new science of Charles Darwin. (He could not stomach Marxism, he said [225], though by 1867 he could not have known about it.) Darwin promised a prospect that "seemed to lead somewhere—to some great generalization which would finish one's clamor to be educated" (224). But the science of evolution fell to pieces before his eyes and, far from learning progress, pattern, order, "All he could prove was change" (230). What is change? It is catastrophe, or rather "castastrophe was the law of change" (313).

More so than any previous attempt at education, that in Darwinism proved the greatest disappointment to Adams because he had hoped for so much from it; he had been "a Darwinist before the letter; a predestined follower of the tide" (224). Natural Selection; Natural Evolution; Natural Uniformity: these gave at least a pattern, an order, almost a religion (225). They promised unity at last and, furthermore, the process of reaching it had the logical appeal of being the more certain *a posteriori* method of the new science of the nineteenth century, not the doubtful *a priori* method of a Spinoza (226). But if it did not comfortably assume unity to begin with, the new science did set about to prove it as the end of the process. Its difficulty was to make the proof stick:

> If one were at liberty to be as lax in science as in theology, and to assume unity from the start, one might better say so, as the Church did, and not invite attack by appearing weak in evidence (227).

Thus four objections to Darwin arose as Adams dug into the case in 1867 while preparing an essay that was a review of a new edition of Sir Charles Lyell's *Principles of Geology*. They were so unanswerable they completely ruined the beautiful unity:

1. Sir Charles Lyell, the geologist and supporter of Darwin—he had published in 1863 his *Antiquity of Man* "in order to support Darwin by wrecking the Garden of Eden" (225)—advanced his theories concerning the uniformity of the glacial period by only *assuming* uniformity. He could not prove it. Where was the evidence (227)?

2. The *Terebratula* (a kind of invertebrate mollusc) was admittedly uniform, "identical from the beginning to the end of geological time" (228). So much uniformity cancelled the corollary law of Natural Selection.

3. The *Pteraspis* was the first vertebrate on record. But there was no known predecessor. Before him was an "eternal void." Where did he get his backbone? So where is Natural Evolution? He would seem to be "older than evolution itself." (230)

4. And all these scientific defeats emphasized a more basic question: What explains the evolution of mind? Darwin or Lyell provided no explanation, whether of Selection, of Uniformity, or Whatever.

The major conclusion is one of pure suspension. Wishing nothing better than to believe in Darwinism, still

when he came to ask himself what he truly thought, he felt that he had no Faith; that whenever the next new hobby should be brought out, he should surely drop off from Darwinism like a monkey from a perch; that the idea of one Form, Law, Order, or Sequence had no more value for him than the idea of none; that what he valued most was Motion, and that what attracted his mind was Change (231).

In suspension Adams struggled for good temper also for, unlike his ancestors who struggled for truth alone, he came to admit, exaggerating as usual, "he really did not care whether truth was, or was not, true. He did not even care that it should be proved true, unless the process were new and amusing. He was a Darwinian for fun" (231–232). But to develop a program of action forced him to lay aside doubt regarding Darwinism. Evolution must be assumed, the goal of unity believed in. He had to act on Will. Otherwise he'd end up no more practically useful than Bluebeard's curious wives (232).

Such mental resolution was immediately successful: he wrote and had accepted and printed two articles on another subject, on money problems. He gained "the freedom of the press" (234). Activity paid off even though he discovered in his research that financiers did not approve the exercise of Will in managing money matters (233).

Adams ended his education by Englishmen with the equivalent of an Oxford degree not unlike the empty Harvard degree he already had. Seven years in England had taught only disillusion. He possessed less certainty of Unity, more conviction of Multiplicity, and nearly absolute belief in Change. At the age of thirty, no longer a truly young man, no longer able to be a student in any original sense, he "could see only one great change, and this was wholly in years" (236). He was compelled to go on with his life "submissive" (313). The following three years of "education" in American politics and the American press led him to the same conclusion. Good temper was lacking.

IV. Education to Failure

A chapter of defeat, "Darwinism" ends the second section of the *Education*. The following section containing Chapters XVI through XX concludes with an even more spectacular chapter of defeat entitled "Failure"—the title I give to the whole section. Back in America following the Civil War, Adams described his career in Washington (1868–1870) as a writer on politics for some New York periodicals and the *North American Review*, and he offered some generalized remarks on the next twelve years, the seven at Harvard as an assistant professor of history and editor of the *North American Review*, and the following five years back in Washington as a writer on American history. As before, the actual events Adams described of his participation in real life are not designed to present the manikin but to explain why he did not get an education. In all of his undertakings during these fourteen years he succeeded in ways that many would envy. But constantly, constantly, he queried, "What was the effect of these activities for education?" He found none still except enlarged chaos and increased failure.

Observing and commenting on federal politics in Washington should have produced success. After all:

> [no one] had a keener instinct, an intenser energy, and a freer hand than he—American of Americans, with Heaven knew how many Puritans and Patriots behind him, and an education that had cost a civil war (238).

What then went wrong? He was a stranger after nearly ten years away (237), one among all the new Americans, aware that this new world "was one of energies quite new," of the railroad, for example, with whose advent "life took on extravagance" (239). Another energy with increased force was money, for "The world, after 1865, became a banker's world." For Henry Adams such a world was appalling. An eighteenth-century child could hardly comprehend railroads; and Adams could hardly join bankers. As an Adams he could not feel anything toward them except "the narrow prejudice which the serf feels to his overseer" (247). The new Boston of 1865 and after only "meant business" (241). He had no education for it even though he'd have liked to help build railroads.[21] And he concluded that in undertaking an active career in the press he found "nine-tenths of his acquired education was useless, and the other tenth harmful" (253). He aimed at becoming a political authority, at getting a share of power himself (258–259). Waiting for General Grant to assume office in March of 1869 he was hopeful and enthusiastic, for Grant, a great soldier, promised reform, good government, order and progress. A general who had successfully organized an army of a million or so men "must know how to administer." And he was needed, even though Adams thought

> The task of bringing the Government back to regular practices, and of restoring moral and mechanical order to administration, was not very difficult; it was ready to do it itself, with a little encouragement (260).

135

But in Congress a different situation existed. Adams wickedly quoted one cabinet officer on the subject of representatives: "A Congressman is a hog! You must take a stick and hit him on the snout!" When Adams asked, "If a Congressman is a hog, what is a Senator?" the question only petrified his interlocutor as it did "any executive officer that ever sat a week in his office." So:

> Senators passed belief. The comic side of their egotism partly dis-
> guised its extravagance, but faction had gone so far under Andrew
> Johnson that at times the whole Senate seemed to catch hysterics of
> nervous bucking without apparent reason. Great leaders, like
> Sumner and Conkling, could not be burlesqued; they were more
> grotesque than ridicule could make them; even Grant, who rarely
> sparkled in epigram, became witty on their account; but their ego-
> tism and factiousness were no laughing matter. They did permanent
> and terrible mischief, as Garfield and Blaine, and even McKinley
> and John Hay, were to feel. The most troublesome task of a reform
> President was that of bringing the Senate back to decency (261).

But when Grant announced his cabinet appointments the weakness and futility of the list "within five minutes, changed his [Adams'] intended future into an absurdity so laughable as to make him ashamed of it." Grant proved simply that "A great soldier might be a baby politician." Adams discovered that "no thought of effectual reform could revive for at least one generation" (262). Wanting something to support, he found nothing in Grant's administration to give his energy to. Not wanting to "go into opposition" he was thus left with nothing to do in Washington (267).

In the following chapter, "Free Fight (1869–1870)," Adams explained that the most disturbing learning of all was that apparently moral law was dead. He had come to Washington "fresh from the cynicism of European diplomacy." Within a few months (September of 1868 to March of 1869) he discovered to his thorough dismay that he had returned "fresh from the rustic simplicity of London" (272). The American political system had been the hope of the world, one that society needed if it was to succeed at all. But he found the system had broken down because of a moral collapse. American democracy had shaken his nerves to pieces as it was to shatter those of his heroine Madeleine Lee in his 1880 novel *Democracy*. Corruption was so ram-

pant (was Grant at fault? Was the Secretary of the Treasury? Was it
Jay Gould?) the Grant Administration so "outraged every rule of ordinary decency" (280) Adams could only conclude flatly that "The moral
law had expired—like the Constitution."

> Society hesitated, wavered, oscillated between harshness and laxity,
> pitilessly sacrificing the weak, and deferentially following the
> strong. In spite of all such criticism, the public nominated Grant,
> Garfield, and Blaine for the Presidency, and voted for them after-
> wards, not seeming to care for the question.

As far as Adams could see, "The system of 1789 had broken down, and
with it the eighteenth-century fabric of *a priori,* or moral, principles."
What such recognition was worth as education he "could not guess"
(280–281).

This whole section, as well as the one following, like those preceding
it, is speculative sociology and "political science" about the American
scene.[22] Not until the final two sections on "Force" and "Inconclusion"
does Adams really get beyond this. Like nearly all the great thinkers of
the pre-Darwinian West, like Spinoza and Thomas Aquinas, who had
asserted unity *a priori,* Adams too began his various studies with
assumptions. To begin with he assumed righteousness, honor and intelligence in the American political world. All proved to be false for the
late nineteenth century, because men were interested then only in
workaday successes that had no connection with large principles. This
new society was only amused at the dishonesty of its elected governmen-
tal representatives: it "laughed a vacant and meaningless derision over
its own failure" (272). But it was a failure Americans did not admit, so
intent were they on railroads and foundries. Still "immoral and immor-
tal" (273) society would go on, regardless.

Is such learning education? It is in the sense that Adams increasingly
recognized chaos was reality. Only one attitude could demonstrate good
sense and Adams had not yet acquired it—good temper. Adams was
badly stung by the iniquity of United States politics in Washington in
1868–1870, solaced only by the splendid "vast maternity" of nature
displayed by the beautiful District of Columbia countryside (282) from
which views of the Capitol dome gave to it a purified charm it did not
possess under its shelter. Not yet had he found serious reason to doubt

nature as a source of abiding comfort despite his childhood experience of her doubleness in Quincy and Boston. The extended summers of Maryland and Virginia were like the splendid summers of Quincy; the one had healed the frostbite of harsh Boston winters, the other moderated the cold knowledge of American political corruption. Adams was alert to what V. L. Parrington calls "the Great Barbecue," that period when overlords of financial banditry used the whole American people as an ox which they roasted on a spit to satisfy their gross appetites, to the admiration of the victims themselves, the majority of their fellow citizens. Adams retreated to the stony towers of Harvard and after that to the sink of history, antiquarianism. He had come to see with a bleeding, pulsing realization that the world he had to make his way in was unpredictable, out of kilter, and unmanageable.

The chapter called "Chaos" tells finally what in 1870 fixed forever Adams' view that the future could not be predicted or controlled. In this year he suffered three blows that ended forever his hope of finding unity in his world and integrity in that "education" he demanded. In the spring of 1870 he went to London to place with Reeve at the *Edinburgh Review* what he thought was his best piece of writing: an essay on the New York Gold Conspiracy. He was pleased with himself. He deemed himself "already a man of action, and rather far up towards the front" (285). "Never had the sun of progress shone so fair. Evolution from lower to higher raged like an epidemic" (284). But "In this year of all years, Adams lost sight of education" only to be so sharply drawn back to a consideration of it as to shatter his complacency.

> The first shock came lightly, as though Nature were playing tricks on her spoiled child, though she had thus far not exerted herself to spoil him. Reeve refused the Gold Conspiracy (286).

So was it refused by the *Quarterly*. What had happened? Adams did not know and could explain these refusals by the English press only on the basis of that English eccentricity he had already largely experienced.

This blow, however, was slight. The confusion it caused in Adams' thinking was minor compared to what followed when he was called to Italy to the bedside of his sick sister. When he got there, "Tetanus had already set in."

The last lesson—the sum and term of education—began then. He had passed through thirty years of rather varied experience without having once felt the shell of custom broken. He had never seen Nature—only her surface—the sugar-coating that she shows to youth. Flung suddenly in his face, with the harsh brutality of chance, the terror of the blow stayed by him thenceforth for life, until repetition made it more than the will could struggle with; more than he could call on himself to bear. He found his sister, a woman of forty, as gay and brilliant in the terrors of lockjaw as she had been in the careless fun of 1859, lying in bed in consequence of a miserable cab-accident that had bruised her foot. Hour by hour the muscles grew rigid, while the mind remained bright, until after ten days of fiendish torture she died in convulsions (287).

The incisive writing of this paragraph, mounting to the last sentence of short, abrupt phrases like hiccups, is, I think, among the most successful passages in all of Adams' writings. It is likewise typical in that it contains reversals, long delayed sentences, an aphorism, concrete words, sanguinolence, exaggeration, and hyperbole.

The three paragraphs that follow make up with it a complete essay. Each paragraph enlarges on the subject of his sister's death. Each through contrast presents the effect on his thinking. In the first Adams contrasts the beautiful Italian summer with the dying human being, concluding: "For many thousands of years, on these hills and plains, Nature had gone on sabring men and women with the same air of sensual pleasure" (288). "Hills," "Nature," "sabring," and "sensual" had already appeared in other sentences in the paragraph. The final statement draws all the threads of thought together. The next paragraph contrasts nature's "insanity of force" with the religious anodynes of society. The paragraph concludes: "God might be, as the Church said, a Substance, but He could not be a Person." The last of the four paragraphs contrasts the "chaos of anarchic and purposeless forces" that is Mount Blanc, with the "illusions of his senses" which clothed it with beauty: that sugar coating nature shows to youth. This paragraph ended with a concluding sentence that is also a transition to the discussion of the third shock Adams received in 1870—the news of the outbreak of the Franco-Prussian War:

Nature was kind; Lake Geneva was beautiful beyond itself, and the Alps put on charms real as terrors; but man became chaotic, and before the illusions of Nature were wholly restored, the illusions of Europe suddenly vanished, leaving a new world to learn (289).

Of all the shocks, that of his sister's death was the most striking; it was personal. In such a sentence as this Adams shows the intellectually realized impact of it:

Society became fantastic, a vision of pantomime with a mechanical motion; and its so-called thought merged in the mere sense of life, and pleasure in the sense (288).

More: The shock broke his heretofore comfortable "shell of custom" (287) and educated him to a profound indignation:

Stoicism was perhaps the best [attitude]; religion was the most human; but the idea that any personal deity could find pleasure or profit in torturing a poor woman, by accident, with a fiendish cruelty known to man only in perverted and insane temperaments, could not be held for a moment. For pure blasphemy, it made pure atheism a comfort.

The third shock, although not personal, was one that fixed the total lessons of Adams' political education, demonstrating conclusively his failure to learn how to predict political developments. In 1870, against all expectation and in the face of all he thought he knew of international diplomacy, suddenly France and Germany engaged in battle and all Europe was "in full chaos of war" (289). What it meant was lost on him.

Thus in three ways in 1870 Adams was tossed back once again to beginnings. He did not know where he was. Returning to America he found a kind of success: Two of his essays were pirated by the Democratic Party as campaign documents; his reward was to be called a begonia—a name he clearly resented since "the honors of piracy resemble the colors of the begonia; they are showy but not useful" (292). He accepted an assistant professorship in medieval history from Harvard's new president, Charles W. Eliot, though he felt that "the appointment of any professor at all seemed to him unnecessary." Eliot flattered him curiously by saying, "If you will point out to me any one who knows more, Mr. Adams, I will appoint him" (294). Along with the appointment went the editorship of the *North American Review*, which "would lead to the daily press." But Adams did not depart from his major position that he was ignorant:

> He could see no relation whatever between himself and a professorship. He sought education; he did not sell it. He knew no history; he only knew a few historians; his ignorance was mischievous because it was literary, accidental, indifferent.

Pious though the apology reads, and false though it is to the testimony of his students during the seven years of his professorship, fundamentally the statement does not contradict Adams' final position regarding all learning: the bits and pieces he learned were insufficient to construct a unified view of the universe. In accepting the appointment he had the grim wit to realize that "it could not much affect the sum of solar energies whether one went on dancing with girls in Washington, or began talking to boys at Cambridge" (293).

He did not go to Harvard willingly, he said. He was "to begin a new education, on lines he had not chosen, in subjects for which he cared less than nothing; in a place he did not love, and before a future which repelled." Should he have stayed in Washington? Later he looked back to see that from 1870–1895, search as he would, he could find among men who had remained in Washington "little but damaged reputation" (294). But there he had been engaged in a career he liked. To leave Washington was to retreat though "all America" advised him to do so because Washington was "barren and dangerous" (297). Was this the fault of the American character? If so, "what accounted for American character?" (296). It "showed singular limitations which sometimes drove the student of civilized man to despair" (297).

The chapter ends with a pitiless analysis of what the American character consisted of, at least that of the American businessman. He seemed "ignorant that there is a thing called ignorance." He may have thought himself "a restless, pushing, energetic, ingenious person, always awake and trying to get ahead of his neighbors," but such an idea "was not correct for Washington." "Work, whiskey, and cards were life." Work was a form of vice. The American was "ashamed to be amused . . . he could not face a new thought." He was oriented in one direction—the acquisition of money and power which he never cared about after winning. Populated then with such men, Washington was fatal to thirty-two-year-old Henry Adams "who never played cards, and who loathed whiskey" (297–298).

By the end of this chapter it is clear that Henry Adams was a disappointed, not-so-young man.

In the final chapter of this section, "Failure," Adams drew together the results of his education from all the various sources on which he had fed from childhood. He produced no real "sum" though his exaggerated manner and mock dogmatism give an impression of finality. He found no order or direction or discipline or unity up to this his thirty-third year. So he "stopped his own education in 1871, and began to apply it for practical uses, like his neighbors" (314). He went to Harvard where for seven years he "could never satisfy himself what to do" (300). What was he to do? History was a scandal, "less instructive than Walter Scott and Alexandre Dumas." All the great historians had only "stirred the scandal" (301). As for the students, only one in ten "sensibly reacts" to instruction (302). (But this was just as well since any method employed "led nowhere" [303] since "one has but the loosest relative truths to follow up" [302].)

What then could he teach his students that would be "not wholly useless" (302)? Perhaps the way might be to learn along with the students, since he had no knowledge to profess, and to encourage them to investigate ideas to their sources. But source preceded source, and real explanations were lost in that dim period preceding evolution.[23] It was thus wasteful, and "What was the use of training an active mind to waste its energy?" (303). If he could have created "conflicts of thought among his students" by setting a rival assistant professor opposite him, he might have produced some education of value (as the thirteenth century had done in its conflicting schools), but "no irregularity shocked the intellectual atmosphere so much as contradiction or competition among teachers" (304).[24] He discovered one concrete fact. One student when asked what he thought he could do with an education if he got it answered, "The degree of Harvard College is worth money to me in Chicago" (305–306). Adams concluded, "In his own opinion the greatest good he could do them [the students] was to hold his tongue. They

needed faith then; they were likely to need more if they lived long"
(306).

His education as an editor was thinner still (307). A "helpless
drudge," he had little time to edit and none to write; "an editor became
an authority on advertising." One thing, however, his editorship brought
him: he became acquainted "at a distance with almost every one in the
country who could write or who could be the cause of writing" (308).
Among them all, "one stood out in extraordinary prominence as the
type and model of what Adams would have liked to be, and of what
the American, as he conceived, should have been and was not" (309).
This was Clarence King.

Adams met King for the first time in the summer of 1871 in the Far
West of Wyoming where King was working for the Fortieth Parallel
Survey as a geologist. Adams devoted several paragraphs of extravagant praise to this talented man who joined John Hay, John La Farge
and Augustus St. Gaudens as Adams' most intimate American friends.
No other figure of whom Adams wrote received such thorough admiration. "He had in him something of the Greek—a touch of Alcibiades or
Alexander" (311). What especially attracted Adams was King's powerful strength of certainty about the future, firmly founded on the best
possible base—science:

> King had moulded and directed his life logically, scientifically, as
> Adams thought American life should be directed. He had given
> himself education all of a piece, yet broad. Standing in the middle
> of his career, where their [Adams' and King's] paths at last came
> together, he could look back and look forward on a straight line,
> with scientific knowledge for its base. . . . Whatever prize he
> wanted lay ready for him—scientific, social, literary, political—and
> he knew how to take them in turn. With ordinary luck he would die
> at eighty the richest and most many-sided genius of his day
> (312–313).

When King did die in 1901 he was almost sixty years old. He died of
tuberculosis and other ailments, nearly penniless, leaving practically
nothing of the several fortunes he had made. He did leave a record of
wrong guesses, unsuccessful endeavors, several mulatto children born to
his much-loved Negro mistress-wife. (Adams only hints at King's vari-

ance from the more usual American pattern in this regard: "King had no faith in the American woman; he loved types more robust" [313].) And as King's biographer shows,[25] he left a history full of such confusion that one of the bitterest failures of Henry Adams' education was that in expecting so much of King he had guessed so wrongly about what was needed for success in the later nineteenth-century world.

> In 1871 he had thought King's education ideal, and his personal fitness unrivalled. No other young American approached him for the combination of chances—physical energy, social standing, mental scope and training, wit, geniality, and science, that seemed superlatively American and irresistibly strong.

King's ruin "taught whatever the bystander chose to read in it; but to Adams it seemed singularly full of moral, if he could but understand it" (346). Not only Adams saw in King a splendid model: other men King knew "worshipped not so much their friend, as the ideal American they all wanted to be" (313). Several chapters later Adams quoted John Hay's summation of King's career, and I think he means to present it as his own view:

> "There you have it in the face!" he said—"the best and brightest man of his generation, with talents immeasurably beyond any of his contemporaries; with industry that has often sickened me to witness it; with everything in his favor but blind luck; hounded by disaster from his cradle, with none of the joy of life to which he was entitled, dying at last, with nameless suffering, alone and uncared-for, in a California tavern. *Ça vous amuse, la vie?*" (416) [Actually, King died in a new brick cottage in Phoenix, Arizona, in the presence of a servant and the local doctor.]

But this was thirty years later. In 1871 "the West was still fresh" (309) and King and Adams were both fresh too. Meeting for the first time, the two men instantly found themselves friends, in nearly complete agreement. Adams sounded here the note he was to develop so thoroughly and so extensively in the last two sections of this book and in the final essays: he found that he and King "felt no leanings towards the simple uniformities of Lyell and Darwin; they saw little proof of slight and imperceptible changes; to them, catastrophe was the law of change." Like Adams, "King loved paradox." What especially delighted Adams was to encounter a scientist who was his contemporary and who did not insist that unity governed the universe. King, in short, merrily granted a multiverse.

A further result of Adams' contact with this brilliant man is only slightly stated, but one of considerable importance as it shaped Adams' choice of a career, I think. Adams said the paradoxes King advanced "delighted Adams, for they helped, among other things, to persuade him that history was more amusing than science" (313). Though King had "moulded and directed his life logically, scientifically, as Adams thought American life should be directed" (312) Adams quietly chose history for his career as an active man and steadily pursued it for twenty years until he completed a monumental historical work. He sought to be "scientific" in his rigorous statement of what facts seemed to be in sequence, but his activity was not in science. I think Adams wished us to know King's example somehow taught him the limitations of science itself. Not that he was deeply convinced of the superiority of history. I think his encounter with King is an accurate *image* of what his thought had led him to even this early, the paradoxical contradiction between history and science, a contradiction that he came to deal with at great length in the final essays. The exorbitant eulogy of King he balanced by the brief but telling phrase, "history was more amusing than science."

Here appears another example of the difficulty of reading Adams. He went beyond balance into a still more elaborate use of hyperbole. He overstated King's superiority and understated the appeal of history by using only the word "amusing." Very often paragraphs repeat this same pattern of large, sweeping, heavy sentences that are negated by such a short phrase or even a single word at the end. (See the last sentence in the book.) In this example the progressive matter covers four pages, and the negation is proportionately reduced in size. The result is intellectual grotesquerie of thought that either misses or puzzles too quick a reader. This trick of writing makes it hard to scale Adams' remarks to ordinary common sense. Why such over-complication? It is because of Adams' artistry. He knew that all representational artists necessarily distort in making compositions by rearranging facts to convey a sense of reality. He was trying to convey a kind of reality that defies a reader's almost instinctive desire for order and unity. He meant to convey the reverse—his conviction of chaos and multiplicity and thus the implied necessity for suspension.

The concluding paragraph of this chapter on "Failure" drags the reader back to the grim conclusions of all the other chapters of the *Education*. It is in tone with the whole chapter, one that piles defeat on defeat; however, when read as a finish to the bright discussion of Clarence King that immediately preceded it, it is a startling contrast:

> No more education was possible for either man. Such as they were, they had got to stand the chances of the world they lived in; and when Adams started back to Cambridge, to take up again the humble tasks of schoolmaster and editor he was harnessed to his cart. Education, systematic or accidental, had done its worst. Henceforth, he went on, submissive (313).

So ends one half of the book.

V. Education in Indian Summer

The section of four chapters, XXI through XXIV, I have called "Education in Indian Summer." It is a transition between the quite full account of "active education" in Henry Adams' childhood, youth and young manhood and the final and most powerful two sections of the book, one dealing with "Education in Force" and the other, "Education as Inconclusion." In this section Adams raised his tone. His pendulums of thought ranged far wider over the world; he was less concrete, less specific, more speculative, more ruminative. A more immediate sense of current time is evident. The educational garment is far more prominent than the manikin. Little sense of growth existed any more in age and maturity.[26] As the section began Henry Adams said of 1892 he

> would rather, as choice, have gone back to the east [to the South Seas where he had been in 1890–1891 with John La Farge], if it were only to sleep forever in the trade-winds under the southern stars, wandering over the dark purple ocean, with its purple sense of solitude and void. Not that he liked the sensation, but that it was

the most unearthly he had felt. He had not yet happened on Rudyard Kipling's "Mandalay," but he knew the poetry before he knew the poem, like millions of wanderers, who have perhaps alone felt the world exactly as it is. Nothing attracted him less than the idea of beginning a new education (316–317).

But an even greater effort was required of him, for he had to try to realize the most difficult half of his motto, "silence next to good-temper was the mark of sense." He had "submitted" without too noisy protests to the unmanageable aspects of his world. But could he in the time remaining to him during the Indian Summer of his life beginning at age fifty-four also manage to acquire good temper? Near the beginning of Chapter XXI he said

He had enjoyed his life amazingly, and would not have exchanged it for any other that came in his way; he was, or thought he was, perfectly satisfied with it; but for reasons that had nothing to do with education, he was tired; his nervous energy ran low; and, like a horse that wears out, he quitted the race-course, left the stable, and sought pastures as far as possible from the old. Education had ended in 1871; life was complete in 1890; the rest mattered so little! (316)

Yet he had begun this chapter:

Once more! this is a story of education, not of adventure! It is meant to help young men—or such as have intelligence enough to seek help—but it is not meant to amuse them (314).

We are thus warned to look forward to the remaining 200 pages of this book as the most serious matter of all. If we can read it intelligently we can perhaps be "helped" to education.

The section begins quietly. Adams spoke of this time from 1892–1900 as an interlude. All his family and friends were settled and busy (318) ; only he was adrift. Not only was he at low ebb. So were the times. "Everywhere was slack-water" (325). With his active career at an end he attempted to sum up the results.

He came to no conclusions except that he discovered more questions.

Was he a success? What was success? Neither Hay nor King nor Adams knew. It should have to do with money, but in America "The American mind had less respect for money than the European or Asiatic mind, and bore its loss more easily; but it had been deflected by its pursuit till it could turn in no other direction" (328). Even so in the American world, "The forgotten statesman had no value at all; the general and admiral not much; the historian but little; [and] on the whole, the artist stood best . . . of course, wealth rested outside the question, since it was acting as judge" (326). He talked of value in terms of "consideration" awarded by one's contemporaries. But how was one to measure it? He estimated his ten or twelve years of labor on his *History* cost him at least $100,000 for expenses, on a salary of $5,000 a year, and "he had but three serious readers." But he said he was "amply satisfied with their consideration," and was willing to let all others go (327). In these terms, was he a success? Had his career been successful? He could not tell. If he had satisfied himself perhaps that would have been enough, but clearly he had not.

The chapter concludes with a contrast of images foreshadowing what was yet to follow—the Augustus St. Gaudens statue erected over the grave of Marian Adams at Rock Creek Cemetery in Washington as matched against the railway system, that "one active interest, to which all others were subservient, and which absorbed the energies of some sixty million people to the exclusion of every other force, real or imaginary" (330). This is another form of the contrast between the Virgin and the Dynamo, those two symbols of contradictory force that bemused Adams for so much of his later career in thought and whose stimulating contrast constitutes in large measure the great contribution he made to twentieth-century thinking in general.

St. Gaudens was commissioned to do the bronze sculpture while Adams was in the South Seas in 1891. Adams found on his return that the artist had done well. A grave and serious figure, seated, the statue is sexless, hooded, bleak with "steadfast, deep, inexorable eyes" (as Cecil Spring Rice described it) brooding with gaunt solemnity and "Set look inscrutable, nor smile nor frown." [27] The shallow-minded (the clergy especially), Adams wrote, found in it a "figure of despair, of atheism, of denial." But "Like the others, the priest saw only what he brought. Like all great artists, St. Gaudens held up the mirror and no more."

It is generally named "Grief." But I doubt it is supposed to be this any more than what most tourists thought it to be, a "portrait-statue" (329).

Adams' intimates reflected a fuller understanding of Adams' idea even though they too saw what they brought. John Hay wrote Adams to give his impression of the figure before Adams himself had seen it:

> It is full of poetry and suggestion. Infinite widom; a past without beginning and a future without end; a repose, after limitless experience; a peace, to which nothing matters—all embodied in this austere and beautiful face and form.[28]

And Spring Rice saw it much the same, saying it shows that "after all, the end is peace" (*Op. cit.*). Adams himself once implied it meant "thought," [29] and it is that of course, a figure that gropes within itself, eyes hooded, the hand raised along the face, gently caressing the mind in a gesture of concentration common to all humanity. But it is more than thought, for it is itself the lotus—the peace of God, because like God it is silence.[30] Above all else I see it as brooding suspension. As such it is a sculptured embodiment of Henry Adams' most "conclusive" thought.[31]

Adams declared that American viewers could make nothing of it because they "had lost sight of ideals" (329). "The American mind . . . . shunned, distrusted, disliked, the dangerous attraction of ideals, and stood alone in history for its ignorance of the past" (328). What would have been felt as a "nursery-instinct to a Hindu baby or a Japanese jinricksha-runner" was a closed book to the American eye. Americans were concentrated on railways, not on ideals; on practical production, on coal, telephones, bicycles, and electric trams (329–330). They could apparently see nothing but the present, not caring for a future life or even the future thirty years hence (352). But where was education in seeing this contrast between the railway system and "the oldest idea known to human thought," which art "From the Egyptian Sphinx . . . had wrought on this eternal figure almost as though it had nothing else to say" (329)? The answer is only a giddy note at the chapter's end: "At past fifty, Adams solemnly and painfully learned to ride the bicycle" (330). Did he ride to Rock Creek Cemetery?

Chapter XXII on "Chicago" is further transition. Adams began the chapter with a variation of a common figure in speaking of himself as

"Drifting in the dead-water of the *fin de siècle*" (331). But the reader begins to see a growing crystallization of his thought that is a firm contrast to the uncertain, hopeless floundering of the first half of the book. In 1893 Adams began to see more clearly; for one thing he saw that a shift in values had occurred in America. He recognized a new element in American politics, revealed by the silver question:

> He knew well enough all that was to be said for the gold standard as economy, but he had never in his life taken politics for a pursuit of economy. One might have a political or an economical policy; one could not have both at the same time. This was heresy in the English school, but it had always been law in the American.

As an heir to the Adams tradition he himself saw politics as morality. The new age saw it as a matter of money. Was the eighteenth century then so dead? Apparently so, for morality was "a private and costly luxury" in 1893 (335). The symbol of this change was Senator James Donald Cameron of Pennsylvania, his personal friend. Senator Cameron was a type from the same mold as President Grant (that caveman) (333). But he was also from Pennsylvania, the home state of Albert Gallatin, the American statesman Adams respected most, and the state Adams was inclined to think had "set up the Government in 1789; saved it in 1861; created the American system; developed its iron and coal power; and invented its great railways." Cameron's "qualities and defects united in equal share to make him the most useful member of the Senate," which was a paradox to Adams. True, Adamses and Camerons had always distrusted one another—Adamses thought Camerons lacked moral principle—but they had always worked together (334). This particular Cameron only helped create confusion: In 1893 the silver question was at its height. Cameron's legitimate interest was in gold and the corporations. Yet he supported silver for unknown and suspicious reasons. Adams was likewise inclined to gold out of personal interest, yet he supported silver on "moral principles." A third man, E. L. Godkin, editor of the New York *Evening Post,* also was a gold man and came out for gold stoutly. Clearly, "one of the three was a moral idiot." Which one of them was it (336)? The popular vote declared in favor of Godkin. Does a majority vote then determine morality?

A new statement follows. The mysterious Panic of 1893 that nearly bankrupted Adams brought him to a point where "at last he had got hold of his world and could finish his education, interrupted for twenty years." He seemed to feel "something new and curious was about to happen to the world" (338). New forces were at work, among them one of impressive significance: acceleration, the speed of which "passed bounds" (339). He had earlier become aware of it on returning from Europe aboard the "Teutonic" in 1892 where he found the ship so vast an "improvement" he could not take it in:

> Wonder may double—even treble. Adams's wonder ran off into figures. As the Niagara [the ship on which he had gone back to Europe in May of 1861] was to the Teutonic—as 1860 was to 1890—so the Teutonic and 1890 must be to the next term—and then? (319)

He attended the Columbian Exposition at Chicago in 1893. The Cunard exhibit confirmed his earlier thought:

> still a student hungry for results found himself obliged to waste a pencil and several sheets of paper trying to calculate exactly when, according to the given increase of power, tonnage, and speed, the growth of the ocean steamer would reach its limits. His figures brought him, he thought, to the year 1927; another generation to spare before force, space, and time should meet (341).

Acceleration he discussed at length in the final section of the *Education* and in the final two essays.

Another new force was the dynamo. What was it? "did it pull or did it push? Was it a screw or thrust? Did it flow or vibrate? Was it a wire or a mathematical line?" (342). No one could tell him, and it produced futility, for it was a mechanical sequence that was unknown. Heretofore though historians could only feel helpless before metaphysical, theological or political sequences, they had been able to trust to one certainty: the unity of natural forces. Is the dynamo a unity? Adams found he did not know enough even to state the problem. If he could have his education would have been complete at once. One thing was observable: Chicago of the Exposition showed that Americans "might still be driving or drifting unconsciously to some point in thought" and "Chicago was the first expression of American thought as a unity" (343).[32]

Back in Washington was the second such expression. Congress in voting for the single gold standard demonstrated that another unity had developed. Gold meant the triumph of capitalism, of concentrated economic power into trusts and of course trades unions, a mechanical consolidation of forces that would end in monopolies and crush forever simple industrial forces and the kind of eighteenth-century political thought Adamses had always cherished, meaning non-centralization and economic control not by bankers but by producers and manufacturers (344).

Little so far at the beginning of his new education provided Adams with much basis for good temper. In the next chapter, "Silence," he brooded on the matter of the earlier two in this section. Money had triumphed as a result of 1893. What was the relation of money to education? Many envied the wealthy their money but hardly respected them for it (347). Yet society paid uneducated administrators and managers ten times what it paid educated linguists and mathematicians (348). To use money as the measuring stick did not solve the problem after all. Clarence King was the most fit of any American of Adams' generation, because he had a scientific education, but his fortunes perished, apparently because without money to back it a scientific education was a failure (347). On the other hand, William C. Whitney "who was not better educated than Adams, had achieved phenomenal success" (348). In 1894 Adams found he needed still what he needed forty years before, the "facile use of the four old tools: Mathematics, French, German and Spanish," for with these he could "make his way to any object within his vision" and "would fear none" (38, 348). This is not to say these things would provide education however much they might lead to power. The question of "what an American education ought to be in order to count as success" remained (348).

The object of Adams' education took a new direction—to discover "what the mass of mankind did care for, and why" (353). This led him finally back to Chartres, beyond it, then forward again. He had added to his studies examinations of statistics and of the religious press—aware of his own "aching consciousness of religious void" (352)—additional travel in Cuba, the Far West, Mexico and the Caribbean. They all led to nothing.

> Accidental education could go no further, for one's mind was already littered and stuffed beyond hope with the millions of chance images stored away without order in the memory. One might as well try to educate a gravel pit. The task was futile (353).

The lesson of this new study therefore seemed to be this: keep silent. The chapter end once again echoes the thought that recognition of ignorance is great wisdom:

> all philosophy . . . affirmed that no man, even at sixty, had ever been known to attain knowledge; but that a very few were believed to have attained ignorance, which was in result the same. More than this, in every society worth the name, the man of sixty had been encouraged to ride his hobby—the Pursuit of Ignorance in Silence . . . . but perhaps elsewhere the world might still hide some haunt of *futilitarian* silence where content reigned . . . and so the pilgrimage began anew! (359)

The final sentence two paragraphs later picks up a note in this passage and a reference to Brook Adams' theory of the relationship between civilization and centers of trade. It deftly concludes:

> His hobby [horse?] had turned into a camel, and he hoped, if he rode long enough in silence, that at last he might come on a city of thought along the great highways of exchange (361).

It is one of the few hopeful notes to conclude any chapter of the *Education*.

The conclusion to this section of transition and interlude is the chapter "Indian Summer (1898–1899)." More than ever in these years Adams, now sixty years old, said he felt solitude. But cut off, "Adams could go back to his own pursuits which were slowly taking a direction" (366).

> . . . the solitude did what the society did not—it forced and drove him into the study of his ignorance in silence. Here at last he entered the practice of his final profession.

This began with a "methodical survey—a triangulation—of the twelfth century" (369). (It finally resulted in *Mont-Saint-Michel and Chartres*.) He was visited by John La Farge who repeated the telling charge Adams only too ruefully admitted: "Adams, you reason too much!" (370). Adams' cross and burden, of course, as well as his virtue, was that this was true—what he had called in the previous chapter "a certain intense cerebral restlessness" that, at sixty, survived when, he says (with what proved to be exactly the contrary, considering the work that followed), "the artist began to die" in him (351). His approach to the twelfth century in 1900 was quite different from that of his Harvard teaching days, an astonishing contrast between "the twelfth century of his thirtieth and that of his sixtieth years" (368). As I have shown, and as any one can read it, *Mont-Saint-Michel and Chartres* is basically the result of intense cerebral restlessness. In seeking to learn more than cold reason had taught him, he turned to artists for instruction, and contact with one, La Farge, brought his education "a step backwards towards Chartres" (372).

The conclusion to the chapter and to the section became irony, for in retreating to an examination of the unity of the twelfth century Adams undertook what he repeatedly scorned as antiquarian study. And had he remained there; had he not come back again after *Mont-Saint-Michel and Chartres* to produce the *Education;* had he not gone even further in his most extreme endeavor, seeking to relate science to the uses of history in the final two essays, then I think we would be justified in calling Adams a minor figure in American literary and intellectual history. Since he did not retreat but only backed up to try again, and since he persisted to the very end to grapple with the problems of thought of 1900 and of the future, we are forced, I believe, to award him high distinction and must conclude that his work is of major importance to us.

VI. Education in Force

A study of Chapter XXV, "The Dynamo and the Virgin," begins a direct study of force, what Adams dealt with in this and the following seven chapters. The best known of all those in the *Education* (it is often

anthologized) this chapter is the most important in the book. It has a
strength that is accounted for, I think, by the fact that it contains so
much in so few pages—eleven pages, eighteen paragraphs. Adams here
set up in opposition his two best-known and most successful images: the
Virgin, representing the unifying force of religious faith to late medieval
western Europe, and the Dynamo, representing the multiple forces of
power in the twentieth century. The prose discussion of these two forces
is more cerebral than it is in the 1901 poem "Prayer to the Virgin of
Chartres." The latter was a personal reaction to the two forces: love of
and desire for faith in the Holy Virgin Mother as opposed to fear of that
force the Dynamo represented.

> You come in silence, Primal Force,
>   We know not whence, or when, or why;
> You stay a moment in your course
> To play; and, lo! you leap across
>   To Alpha Centauri!

In prose he said it differently later: "the dynamo became a symbol of
infinity" (380). And as he brooded about it at the Paris Exhibition in
1900, "he began to feel the forty-foot dynamo as a moral force, much as
the early Christians felt the Cross":

> this huge wheel, revolving within arm's-length at some vertiginous
> speed, and barely murmuring—scarcely humming an audible warn-
> ing to stand a hair's-breadth further for respect of power—while it
> would not wake the baby lying close against its frame. Before the
> end, one began to pray to it; inherited instinct taught the natural
> expression of man before silent and infinite force. Among the thou-
> sand symbols of ultimate energy, the dynamo was not so human as
> some, but it was the most expressive (380).

In the poem he had said more expressively:

> We know not whether you are kind,
>   Or cruel in your fiercer mood;
> But be you Matter, be you Mind,
> We think we know that you are blind,
>   And we alone are good.

Considering the twelfth-century Virgin as equal to the twentieth-century dynamo is no paradox in one sense. Both are forces. Both are silent. Both deny explanation. Thus they are alike. The contrast is simple too. The Virgin is the appealing and human unifying force as Adams had fully shown in *Mont-Saint-Michel and Chartres*. The dynamo, though a symbol of "ultimate energy" and "not so human" (380) is force of multiple power. But a further mystery appears:

> No more relation could he discover between the steam and the electric current [coal to steam to wheels to electricity] than between the Cross [the Virgin] and the cathedral.

His scientist friend Samuel Pierpont Langley was no help since he didn't understand the dynamo either. Its forces were "anarchical." Worse, the wholly new force of radium was completely baffling; it was "little short of parricidal" in its wicked spirit towards science for "Radium denied its god." It denied the truths of science. In short, radium ruined the theory of fixed elements.[33] It, the X-ray, the actual discovery of the atom which had been only a fiction of thought before, all products of the past seven years (before 1900), meant that "man had translated himself into a new universe which had no common scale of measurement with the old" (381). Langley, to Adams' wonderment, seemed prepared for anything, even for an indeterminable number of universes interfused— "physics stark mad in metaphysics."

And with this phrase Adams indirectly resolved the real paradox of the Virgin and the dynamo and even presented an ironic unity after all. It was the unity of chaos and multiplicity: physics, science, was no closer to solutions than Thomas Aquinas was, no closer to the discovery of infinity or of ultimate energy or of God himself. Thomas Aquinas had simply asserted unity and God; he could not prove it. Still Adams was dogged in continuing. He "insisted on a relation of sequence" (382). But how to find it? He had ended his "Prayer to the Virgin of Chartres" with the final stanzas each in turn beginning:

> Help me to see!
> Help me to know!
> Help me to feel! [and finally]
> Help me to bear!

Force

He did not quit.

Satisfied that the sequence of men led to nothing and that the sequence of their society could lead no further, while the mere sequence of time was artificial, and the sequence of thought was chaos, he turned at last to the sequence of force; and thus it happened that, after ten years' pursuit, he found himself lying in the Gallery of Machines at the Great Exposition of 1900, his historical neck broken by the sudden irruption of forces totally new (382).

Is it possible to convert all these forces to a "common value"? What should be its measure? The only one is "that of their attraction on his own mind" (383). So he set out to translate rays into faith, reversing the historical process.

The faith he now talked of was that in the Virgin. Here he presented one of his most penetrating speculations, one far in advance of the proprieties of Victorian thought. To Americans the Virgin was idolatry. Her pagan predecessor Venus was a scandal. No American had ever felt the force of either. Both were women. Both were really sex. But to Americans sex was sin whereas to all other ages woman had been force, "the animated dynamo; she was reproduction—the greatest and most mysterious of all energies" (384). Thus the Virgin and the dynamo have this relationship: they are forces and they are mysteries. Is there a more direct relationship between them? This was true: the Virgin was "the highest energy ever known to man, the creator of four-fifths of his noblest art, exercising vastly more attraction over the human mind than all the steam-engines and dynamos ever dreamed of" (385). This is a succinct epitome of the lengthy treatment of the Virgin in *Mont-Saint-Michel and Chartres*. But in the *Education* the impressive fact is the attention brought to the *two* attractions, the Virgin and the dynamo, the latter somehow the twentieth-century descendant of the former who was the easily documented force that absorbed the twelfth century.

What followed was a further subtilization of much of this speculation. Adams talked of Augustus St. Gaudens, an artist even more inarticulate than John La Farge. At Paris in 1900 St. Gaudens was showing his equestrian statue of General Sherman. "For a symbol of power, St. Gaudens instinctively preferred the horse" (388)—that is, like most Americans, he did not realize the power in woman, in sex. One can note that the Rock Creek statue is sexless. Why is this so? Why was sex so peculiarly hidden in America? One paragraph in this chapter, which can stand as representative for many, contains so much it must be considered in detail:

> The question, which to any plain American of the nineteenth century seemed as remote as it did to Adams, drew him almost violently to study, once it was posed; and on this point Langleys were as useless as though they were Herbert Spencers or dynamos. The idea survived only as art. There one turned as naturally as though the artist were himself a woman. Adams began to ponder, asking himself whether he knew of any American artist who had ever insisted on the power of sex, as every classic had always done; but he could think only of Walt Whitman; Bret Harte, as far as the magazines would let him venture; and one or two painters, for the flesh-tones. All the rest had used sex for sentiment, never for force; to them, Eve was a tender flower, and Herodias an unfeminine horror. American art, like the American language and American education, was as far as possible sexless. Society regarded this victory over sex as its greatest triumph, and the historian readily admitted it, since the moral issue, for the moment, did not concern one who was studying the relations of unmoral force. He cared nothing for the sex of the dynamo until he could measure its energy (385).

Very few nineteenth-century Americans even seemed to wonder about the power of sex. Physicists like Langley were helpless before it—as useless for help as that blind popularizer of Darwinian theory, Herbert Spencer. "The idea survived only in art." "Art" meant the intermediary between the absoluteness of religious faith and the convictions of science. It seems to me that Adams here revealed a great deal. Either faith or science decided issues; only art reflected them. Thus for Adams art was a position of suspension; it represented humor therefor. His flat declaration, "American art, like the American language and American education, was as far as possible sexless," is dogmatic, incisive, definitive. But it is hyperbolic to the point of mockery. The suggestive quality of such a statement ramifies in the reader's mind.

The whole paragraph is scattered, giving an impression of giddiness. But it moved to a point in the last sentence. The Virgin was sexual energy; the dynamo is energy without sex. Perhaps one must measure energy in its effect on art: "the power embodied in a railway train could never be embodied in art. All the steam in the world could not, like the Virgin, build Chartres." And Chartres is an "action on man": "by action on man all known force may be measured" (388). At this point (1900) Adams saw that one definite force of history was at least clear, that although "The secret of education still hid itself somewhere behind ignorance,"

> Symbol or energy, the Virgin had acted as the greatest force the Western world ever felt, and had drawn man's activities to herself more strongly than any other power, natural or supernatural, had ever done (388–389).

To study the Virgin, then,

> to follow the track of the energy; to find where it came from and where it went to; its complex source and shifting channels; its values, equivalents, conversions

—all this was his historian's business. The Virgin looked the "easiest to handle" of all the powerful forces available for study, easier than the dynamo.

The chapter ends with that fine and rich explanation of his method I have chosen as the key quotation for this study, the explanation of Henry Adams' literary art:

> In such labyrinths, the staff is a force almost more necessary than the legs; the pen becomes a sort of blind-man's dog, to keep him from falling into the gutters. The pen works for itself, and acts like a hand, modelling the plastic material over and over again to the form that suits it best. The form is never arbitrary, but is a sort of growth like crystallization, as any artist knows too well; for often the pencil or pen runs into side-paths and shapelessness, loses its relations, stops or is bogged. Then it has to return on its trail, and recover, if it can, its line of force. The result of a year's work depends more on what is struck out than on what is left in; on the sequence of the main lines of thought, than on their play or variety (389).

"Twilight," Chapter XXVI, continued the more lofty, distant speculation of the final half of Adams' book. Disillusioned comment on the
politics and diplomacy of 1901, accentuated by the sad announcement of
King's death and then Hay's increased weariness, reflected Adams' own
mood. The added years produced increased complexities and multiplici-
ties. Adams found himself walking a path more solitary than ever,
leading him "further and further into a wilderness where twilight is
short and the shadows are dense" (395). Here occurs one of the most
moving paragraphs in the book:

> The sunshine of life had not been so dazzling of late but that a
> share of it flickered out for Adams and Hay when King disap-
> peared from their lives; but Hay had still his family and ambition,
> while Adams could only blunder back alone, helplessly, wearily, his
> eyes rather dim with tears, to his vague trail across the darkening
> prairie of education, without motive, big or small, except curiosity to
> reach, before he too should drop, some point that would give him a
> far look ahead. He was morbidly curious to see some light at the
> end of the passage, as though thirty years were a shadow, and he
> were again to fall into King's arms at the door of the last and only
> log cabin left in life. Time had become terribly short, and the sense
> of knowing so little when others knew so much, crushed out hope
> (396).

Yet the paragraph is not so much personal as it is symbolic. A reader
not knowing *Mont-Saint-Michel and Chartres* and the two final essays is
tempted to assume here a weariness and despair that is even mawkish.
But I think Adams meant to declare his renewed effort to seek, still, an
education that might provide some means of "triangulating" the course
of human events toward the future, "beyond the curvature of the horizon" (395).

He retreated to his desk to brood over an age-old contradiction of
forces, the magnet and gravity. The mysterious magnet was well known
to have always done what the new force radium did in that it radiated
an energy not understood at all. Another force also radiated mysteri-
ously—the human mind. Add this to radium, to the magnet, to gravity
—the dynamo, the Virgin, capitalism and all other operative forces—
and indeed one gets futility. Everyone struggled for unity and even

found it in "God who was unity," opposed to "Satan who was complexity," but what was the truth (397)? It must be the "multiplicity of unity." Each of the forces Adams had examined was in itself a unity, and the world contained many, the number increasing as an aging man continued to look farther and farther ahead. Unity, after all, is "vision," a faculty of the young alone (398). In any case its measure like that of all energies was in the mind of man, in his thought.

Once again reexamining his old friend the *Pteraspis* whose backbone had no known source, he found that no more than ever before could he find actual proof of uniformity or that natural selection operated:

> He wished to be shown that changes in form caused evolution in force; that chemical or mechanical energy had by natural selection and minute changes, under uniform conditions, converted itself into thought (399).

The source of thought was as lost as ever. If one can measure only by the effect on man's mind, then the mystery deepened. For unity one must then borrow from the Church and impose a "larger synthesis" (401) but "For human purposes a point must always be soon reached where larger synthesis is suicide," because such a synthesis only assumes a unity that is not proved and only ends speculation. At this point Adams found himself in the "corridors of chaos" which would be all right since it would permit him to float with the stream if only he "knew which way the current ran" (402). The year 1901 was twilight.

And 1901 was "Teufelsdröckh" also (Chapter XXVII) which means, variously, to students of Carlyle's *Sartor Resartus,* a "diabolic garment," or "devil's dung." Teufelsdröckh was a man who lived in a town called "Weissnichtwo—who knows where?" He was Adams. Back in Paris, sixty-three years old, Adams saw more chaos. He went to Baireuth for the first time to the Wagner festival, but he was decades too late. The world had moved far beyond the staid rococo of Baireuth.

Adams' comments on Wagner are a transition to the mention of his new party, the Conservative Christian Anarchists, designed to "restore true poetry under the inspiration of the 'Götterdämmerung'" (405). This device served Adams as a means for commenting again on the "larger synthesis." He pointed out that his new party was founded on the "great principle of contradiction" and would thus permit but two members. What held it together was an agreement of a sort—to accept the "law of contradiction" (406).

> He could not affirm with confidence, even to himself, that his "largest synthesis" would certainly turn out to be chaos, since he would be equally obliged to deny the chaos.

So the "Conservative Christian Anarchist" turns out to be a truly suspended figure who settled nowhere and who denied to demonstrate that he took no stand whatever. A following commentary on the American character goes far to explain the appeal this book has for me and, by extension, I think, the appeal Henry Adams' mind should have for most Americans.

> In America all were conservative Christian anarchists; the faith was national, racial, geographic. The true American had never seen such supreme virtue in any of the innumerable shades between social anarchy and social order as to mark it for exclusively human and his own. He never had known a complete union either in Church or State or thought, and had never seen any need for it. The freedom gave him courage to meet any contradiction, and intelligence enough to ignore it (408).

American freedom is, in short, suspension. In my terms American humor is suspension also, the quality of marking nothing exclusively. In this sense, and despite the severe censure Adams heaped on varieties of Americans, his view of "the true American" redeems all smaller criticisms.

Adams' commentary on Russia supported and clarified the reasons for the necessity for such suspension. Russia was pure inertia. She fell "into no line of evolution whatever, and was as wonderful to the student of Gothic architecture in the twelfth century, as to the student of the dynamo in the twentieth." That is, Russia, which "had nothing in common with any ancient or modern world that history knew" (408–409) confirmed Conservative Christian Anarchy and its largest synthesis which said "order and anarchy were one, but that the unity was chaos" (406). She completely spoiled any ordered attempt to triangulate the development of force. Russians looked to be people who "had lost the means of motion without acquiring the habit of permanence." Could they be changed? They never had changed. "Could inertia of race, on such a scale, be broken up, or take new form?" (409). The question allowed no answer for—once again Adams repeated his old refrain—"all opinion founded on fact must be error, because the facts can never be complete, and their relations must be always infinite" (410).

At this point I am reminded of the conclusion to Adams' *History* of a decade before, that series of questions so open-ended, so bleak in their implication of being unanswerable, yet so insistent a presence to the mind. At this point in the *Education* the canvas of speculation is but larger. No one could predict the speed of Russian acceleration. But it could not be left out of the problem of the twentieth-century world. Russia more than ever confused the helpless student in search of education. Traveling from Russia to Stockholm and far north to Hammerfest in Norway in 1901 Adams saw "the stupefying contrast with Russia, which more and more insisted on taking the first place in historical interest" (412). At distant Hammerfest he saw the triumph of telegraph and cable and electric light, which "upset for the moment his whole philosophy of conservative anarchy" (413) because the acceleration was so marvelous it seemed to be wholly in the lines of unity, not of chaos. But there was no way to measure it. He suspected that even more than coal, the power that controlled the world "From Hammerfest to Cherbourg . . . from Halifax to Norfolk," Russia was perhaps a surer power because it rested "on the eternal law of inertia" (415).

Chapter XXVIII, "The Height of Knowledge," turns out to be "the abyss of ignorance," the title of the following chapter. Adams declared again the task he had set himself:

Adams sought only instruction—wanted only to chart the international [universal?] channel for fifty years to come; to triangulate the future; to obtain his dimension, and fix the acceleration of movement in politics since the year 1200, as he was trying to fix it in philosophy and physics; in finance and force (423).

More fully than anywhere else Adams here set forth the fundamental goal behind his major works, *Mont-Saint-Michel and Chartres*, the *Education*, the *History* and the last essays. All these documents are pieces of this scheme. The chapter ends: "Probably this was the moment of highest knowledge that a scholar could ever reach." What did it amount to? After all, "Education could be carried no further" (424).

> Never had the proportions of his ignorance looked so appalling. He seemed to know nothing—to be groping in darkness—to be falling forever in space; and the worst depth consisted in the assurance, incredible as it seemed, that no one knew more (424–425).

What he insisted on throughout this section on force, this chapter confirms. The recognition of force itself threw him back to the beginnings of education. All must be begun over again—sequence, pattern, order, unity—all were missing: "no one knows," "ignorance is learning" (414), "history was a nursery tale" (412), "order and anarchy were one," "unity was chaos" (406). Yet chaos must not be *wholly* accepted as answer since suspension must operate.

If "The Height of Knowledge" is ignorance, "The Abyss of Ignorance" (Chapter XXIX) is no less. This chapter is a continued speculation on force. As he spent his summers in Paris these years studying and writing his *Mont-Saint-Michel and Chartres*, Adams found new lines of force increasingly replaced what he thought heretofore had existed—lines of will. His "mind stepped into the mechanical theory of the universe before knowing it." Again occurs the oft-repeated image that the mind of man is a mirror, in this time a "watery mirror at best," reflecting "the eternal mystery of Force—the sink of all science." Pascal had suggested man's *ennui* accounted for change—as reasonable an explanation as natural selection. But how account for the direction of change? Some kind of outside, attractive force may do it. Pascal had called it God (427). The Virgin at Chartres called it love and so did Thomas Aquinas. But love was a partial force, so on Thomas Aquinas' recommendation Adams turned to Christ and the schools who represented all other force. Helpless, Adams was tempted to do what the Church threatened—abolish everything intermediary "in order to look at God as actual; continuous movement, universal cause and interchangeable force" (428–429). Such a thought is Pantheism, but what difference can that make if the goal is to find ultimate energy? Thus here was an answer at last:

> Rid of man and his mind, the universe of Thomas Aquinas seemed rather more scientific than that of Haeckel or Ernst Mach. Contradiction for contradiction, Attraction for attraction, Energy for

energy, St. Thomas' ideal of God had merits. Modern science offered not a vestige of proof, or a theory of connection between its forces, or any scheme of reconciliation between thought and mechanics; while St. Thomas at least linked together the joints of his machine. As far as a superficial student could follow, the thirteenth century supposed mind to be a mode of force directly derived from the intelligent prime motor, and the cause of all form and sequence in the universe—therefore the only proof of unity. Without thought in the unit, there could be no unity; without unity no orderly sequence or ordered society. Thought alone was Form. Mind and Unity flourished or perished together.

Adams' sticking point was his usual one. He was trapped in logical explanations and, as Socrates had taught, logic is to be avoided above all other traps, for it is "the mirror of the mind" only (429). Again one is back at faith in ultimate unity of one kind or another. But "What was Unity? Why was one to be forced to affirm it?" (431). What happened when one denied unity? The history of philosophy showed no one ever did. The conclusion was always unity, "one Will"; or the "universe could be known only as motion of mind"; or "One could know it only as one's self; it was psychology" (432).

Exploring the last statement helped the student very little. The new psychology demonstrated that the single human mind was not a unity at all; the individual human mind was many-layered, and to push into it was to "fall into the sub-conscious chaos below" (433). The path of this new science only pointed to a frightful thing: "A dissolving mind." Before this Adams remarked:

His [man's] normal thought was dispersion, sleep, dream, inconsequence; the simultaneous action of different thought-centres without central control. His artificial balance was acquired habit. He was an acrobat, with a dwarf on his back, crossing a chasm on a slack-rope, and commonly breaking his neck.

Such imagery demonstrates the usual Adams suspicion of answers. He presented here a prelude to the final essays:

if history ever meant to correct the errors she made in detail, she must agree on a scale for the whole. . . . without it the historian would always remain a child in science (434).

165

"Scale" is not quite the same as "unity" but it implies as much.

Psychology helped to this extent: it suggested a unit of study, "the point of history when man held the highest idea of himself as a unit in a unified universe" (434–435). This was the century 1150–1250, expressed in "Amiens Cathedral and the Works of Thomas Aquinas" (435), the most extreme reach of the late medieval synthesis. So he projected two points on which to base his triangulation—a volume to be called "Mont-Saint-Michel and Chartres: a Study of Thirteenth-Century Unity," to be followed by a second, "The Education of Henry Adams: a Study of Twentieth-Century Multiplicity." From these points of relation he might be able to arrive at the third, the future.

Chapter XXX, "Vis Inertia (1903)," is an essay on the power of inert and mindless force, one the inert force of the Russian mass which moved uncontrollably (and was about to move over China, Adams thought in 1903), a force of race; the other the inert force of woman in maternity, reproduction, sex. The new woman, the American woman, was one who had failed to create a pleasing society and was bereft of lasting function for "at forty her task was over," left with only "the theatre or streets to decorate" (443). Yet she had moved into factories and offices, a new type but inarticulate and dissatisfied because "When closely watched, she seemed making a violent effort to follow the man, who had turned his mind and hand to mechanics" (445). She was diverted from her axis, "the cradle and the family," and as a result had become sexless. Only "the old energy of inertia" in sex was left "to carry on the race." Women seemed destined to become "machine-made, collectivist females" (446).

The future was ominous. Triangulation from the two points of twelfth-century woman and twentieth-century woman cast forward a line to a third point that dismayed. It could only lead "to extinguishing the race." Adams was moved to hope "that nothing ever changed—and that the woman would swim about the ocean of future time, as she had swum in the past, with the gar-fish and the shark, unable to change" (448). But what he observed and thought pointed forward otherwise.

Chapter XXXI, "The Grammar of Science (1903)," deals with "the shores of Multiplicity and Complexity" (449). Adams read Karl Pearson's "Grammar of Science." His mathematical ignorance prevented his understanding it fully, but he did see that Pearson had thrown into discard the nineteenth-century scientific efforts to prove unity. Pearson admitted the limitations of man's mind.

"Order and reason, beauty and benevolence, are characteristics and conceptions which we find solely associated with the mind of man. . . . Briefly chaos is all that science can logically assert of the supersensuous." . . . In plain words, Chaos was the law of nature; Order was the dream of man (450–451).

Not interested in the universal truth of such remarks, Adams as an historian "sought only their relative drift or direction." That is, he was seeking to triangulate still even though "since Bacon and Newton, English thought had gone on impatiently protesting that no one must try to know the unknowable at the same time that every one went on thinking about it." He was of course speaking for himself too and, like all previous speculators, he was forced "to enter supersensual chaos," reluctant as he was to do so.

Only the Church protested that "anarchy [chaos] was not order." Pythagoras, Bacon, Newton, Hegel (Hegel admitted every notion had its own negation, but ended with the "larger synthesis") (451), Darwin and Clerk Maxwell all had *assumed* the unity Tennyson expressed in the concluding lines of "In Memoriam":

"One God, one Law, one Element,
And one far-off, divine event,
To which the whole creation moves."

But Pearson exploded the comfortable dream, and Mme. Curie's radium was a "metaphysical bomb." "There remained no hole to hide in." What Pearson did was to leave "science adrift on a sensual raft in the midst of a supersensual chaos." Adams dramatically overstated it in a single one-line paragraph:

Suddenly, in 1900, science raised its head and denied.

Adams found the Copernican revolution of 1600 was a minor affair compared to this new thought. The year 1900 could be compared only to 310 when Constantine's Christian cross suddenly supplanted man-or-earth-directed belief: "When the *Civitas Dei* cut itself loose from the *Civitas Romae*, and the Cross took the place of the legions" (452). What was he to make of this, he, the "weary Titan of Unity"? He read M. Raymond Poincaré's "La Science et l'Hypothèse." Poincaré only showed, as best Adams could understand him, the simple under the complex, the complex beneath this, the simple again, *ad infinitum* (455). If happiness for the mathematician, it startled the historian "to the depths of his ignorance" (454) for it demonstrated the idiocy of assuming unity at all as the final end.

> To Thomas Aquinas, the universe was still a person; to Spinoza, a substance; to Kant, Truth was the essence of the "I"; an innate conviction; a categorical imperative; to Poincaré, it was a convenience; and to Karl Pearson, a medium of exchange (456).

Facts are not the essence. The *direction* of human thought is. Poincaré declared mathematics is but a system of symbols. It provides a continuity but seems to be a destructive "artistic measure" only (455) which I think means an artificial construct of the human mind. Mathematics points direction, perhaps, but it does not confirm an end. Is mathematics another dead end?

Facts cannot be of essence. As an historian Adams

> knew no more than a firefly about rays—or about race—or sex—or ennui—or a bar of music—or a pang of love—or a grain of musk —or of phosphorus—or conscience—or duty—or the force of Euclidean geometry—or non-Euclidean—or heat—or light—or osmosis—or electrolysis—or the magnet—or ether—or *vis inertiae* —or gravitation—or cohesion—or elasticity—or surface tension— or capillary attraction—or Brownian motion—or of some scores, or thousands, or millions of chemical attractions, repulsions or indifferences which were busy within and without him; or, in brief, of Force itself, which, he was credibly informed, bore some dozen definitions in the textbooks, mostly contradictory, and all, as he was assured, beyond his intelligence; but summed up in the dictum of the last and highest science, that Motion seems to be Matter and Matter seems to be Motion, yet "we are probably incapable of discovering" what either is (456).

This is the most unusual sentence in the *Education,* a compilation of ignorances the like of which never occurred to nineteenth-century minds. Ignorance was the explanation, "multiplicity baffling science." Adams found a new world. It portended helpless multiplicity in thought—a condition the human mind was not equipped to handle. In 1900, "the continuity snapped" (457). Until then historians had been comfortably aware of acceleration as in the year 310 and Constantine, of 1500 and Copernicus (or 1600 and Galileo) and Bacon. Adams preferred as always the eighteenth-century world when "God was a father and nature a mother, and all was for the best in a scientific universe" (458). But he could not adopt such a view any more. In 1900 there was a world where multiplicity was "truth." In this new land "where no one had ever penetrated before; where order was an accidental relation obnoxious to nature; artificial compulsion imposed on motion" (457) he was tossed back into ignorance. He was only a porpoise still, sporting in educational seas. At the end he found himself only "looking blankly into the void of death" (460). The "new avalanche of unknown forces" that fell on the mind in 1900 "required new mental powers to control."

> If this view was correct, the mind could gain nothing by flight or by fight; it must merge in its supersensual multiverse, or succumb to it (461).

In Chapter XXXII, "Vis Nova (1903–1904)," once again Adams contemplated the comparative force of the Virgin and the dynamo from another facet of approach. This time the "vis nova" was the St. Louis Exposition which he visited in the spring of 1904. It was not Chicago of 1893 or the Paris Exposition of 1900. This "new force" is suggestively named, probably with a double meaning, for a "nova" is also a sudden burst in a star which then sinks into relative obscurity. In one sense this was the Virgin's force. But she had created a world's fair in the thirteenth century "that turned Chicago and St. Louis pale" (469). She was by no means gone, though a dwindled and obscure power as "her fading away had been excessively slow" (470). No other equivalent to her existed or ever had.

During the summer of 1904 Adams studied the wealth of glass in French churches of the thirteenth, fourteenth, sixteenth centuries. While so engaged he learned of a new political assassination, that of M. Viatscheslaf de Plehve, the Russian Minister of the Interior. Suddenly drawn back by telegram from the sixteenth century, he found

> Martyrs, murderers, Caesars, saints and assassins—half in glass and half in telegram; chaos of time, place, morals, forces and motive—gave him vertigo. Had one sat all one's life on the steps of Ara Coeli for this? (471)

But Adams did not quit his thought, instead producing here the stoutest-hearted declaration he ever made about his life-long effort to find education:

> The effort for Unity could not be a partial success; even alternating Unity resolved itself into meaningless motion at last. To the tired student, the idea that he must give it up seemed sheer senility. As long as he could whisper, he would go on as he had begun, bluntly refusing to meet his creator with the admission that the creation had taught him nothing except that the square of the hypothenuse of a right-angled triangle might for convenience be taken as equal to something else. Every man with self-respect enough to become effective, if only as a machine, has had to account to himself for himself somehow, and to invent a formula of his own for his universe, if the standard formulas failed. There, whether finished or not, education stopped. The formula, once made, could be but verified.[34]

He sat down therefore once again to look for no extravagant or eccentric object, no absolute truth, but "only a spool on which to wind the thread of history without breaking it" (472). He "shut him up again in his garret . . . to shape after his own needs the values of a Dynamic Theory of History" (473). He could not really let go of his profession as an historian.

We are ready for the conclusion.

VII. Education as Inconclusion

Chapter XXXIII, "A Dynamic Theory of History," is one of the most difficult essay-chapters in the *Education*, leading to Adams' final incon-

clusion. It begins the sixth and last section of the book, the three chapters of which Adams meant to be the climax of it. Adams began by
saying that "A dynamic theory, like most theories, begins by begging
the question: it defines Progress as the development and economy of
Forces." That is, it is self-contradictory in that it deals with the limiting
(ordering) of force while at the same time it requires force to be
expanded. The dynamic theory "defines force as anything that does, or
helps to do work." Man begs the question again when he asserts that *he*
captures forces, for

> The sum of force attracts; the feeble atom or molecule called man is
> attracted; he suffers education or growth; he is the sum of the
> forces that attract him; his body and his thought are alike their
> product; the movement of the forces controls the progress of his
> mind, since he can know nothing but the motions which impinge on
> his senses, whose sum makes education (474).

The whole explanation is at first glance completely mechanical and de-
terministic. But *somehow* the surrounding universe that had formed
man "took shape in his mind as a reflection of his own unity, containing
all forces except himself." These surroundings were a congeries of forces
which taken as a whole man has called God, the unity. Man still thought
this way in 1904 even though after hundreds of thousands of years his
"science can no longer give to force a name." The development showed
that "certain lines of force" had gone on "mechanically selecting types
of race or sources of variation." What can "mechanically" possibly
mean? The same paragraph had begun:

> Man's function as a force of nature was to assimilate other forces
> as he assimilated food. He called it the love of power. He felt his
> own feebleness (475).

Nature created certain types to respond to the forces she likewise created. Adams went no farther in supplying explanation. The theory of
variation, of why the man-ape and not the monkey was chosen to respond, is not the affair of history but of "other science" (475–476).

Of all the forces that attracted man that of the highest energy was the
divine; this "science" he called religion which means "cultivation of

occult force whether in detail or mass." Philosophy and theology developed the pursuit of "Force as a unity," one in man himself, the other in the infinite. This meant introspection in the mind, "itself the subtlest of all known forces." Man "added nothing to his stock of known forces for a very long time," perhaps 4000 years (476). But until the year 300 the religious and super forces "were more apparently chaotic than ever" (477). What progress was made in Europe was in "economies of energy rather than in its development" (476). As such it was a nearly static process. Society learned to feel the vastness of nature but had not learned "economies in its methods of pursuit." Still in the fourth century civilization had achieved complete success. The Roman Empire had "solved the problems of Europe more completely than they have ever been solved since." It was as though this world harmonized with all dreams of any future world. What happened, then, to cause "the scandalous failure of civilization" at this very moment? For Adams the only acceptable explanation was "the economic theory of adverse exchanges and exhaustion of minerals." But this explanation was not sufficient, as Rome continued to develop resources and energies (477). Possibly the trouble was "the empire developed too much energy, and too fast" (France, England and Germany in northwestern Europe alone).

But the dynamic theory demanded that one assign values to the "forces of attraction that caused the trouble." Half the dynamic theory dealt with *development* of force; the other half with *economy*. In this case, it was further economy, for

> With the relentless logic that stamped Roman thought, the empire, which had established unity on earth, could not help establishing unity in heaven. It was induced by its dynamic necessities to economize the gods.

The result was the triumph of the Christian God as the only God.[35] Constantine admitted Christianity to the "Trust of State Religions" (478). He set up the Cross as a political tool, and no matter how much the Church denies that Christianity ruined the empire the facts show that to achieve economy of force Roman politicians let the Cross absorb "all the old occult or fetish-power."

The symbol represented the sum of nature—the Energy of modern science—and society believed it to be as real as X-rays; perhaps it was! The emperors used it like gun-powder in politics; the physicians used it like rays in medicine; the dying clung to it as the quintessence of force, to protect them from the forces of evil on their road to the next life.

The discussion of religion here is vastly different from that in *Mont-Saint-Michel and Chartres*. Impersonal, cool, even cold, Adams said the acceptance of the Cross was a money economy—for heathen incense cost too much (479). When Alaric finally sacked Rome in 410 he destroyed a system that was really incredibly poor in fact. Besides the fetish power of the Cross, Rome possessed "but one productive energy resembling a modern machine—the slave" (480). She was forced to expand each to the utmost. The slave system ended by consuming the empire; expansion of the fetish system was necessary to compensate for the loss. But the Cross (the Church) failed to save Rome from Alaric, and great outcry arose against it. St. Augustine saved it by convincingly substituting the *Civitas Dei* for the lost *Civitas Romae,* offering success in the next world for the mass of men who were horribly shocked to discover their failure in this one. Somehow the Cross came to possess the mind of the West— as the Crescent came to possess that of the East—with an increasing force that culminated in 1200 in Romanesque, then Gothic architecture. Again Adams declared that the meaning of this development is so unknown "history is inclined to avoid it altogether."

So little is known about the mind—whether social, racial, sexual or heritable; whether material or spiritual; whether animal, vegetable or mineral (481) —

but still one can admit for convenience that the mind does seem capable of storing force.

In any event, about 1200 two new forces suddenly erupted or dropped from the skies, the compass and gunpowder. At the very time Cross and Crescent "proclaimed the complete triumph of the *Civitas Dei*" and even for an overlapping time when they grew in strength to culminate in the grandeur of Gothic cathedrals and Scholastic theology, these two absolutely new mechanical forces appeared and changed the entire direction of the human mind, altering the whole dynamics of force. It was a revolution far more radical than that of 300. After all, Cross (and Crescent) represented the same force on men's minds as had the Pyramids of 3000 B.C., the "attraction of power in a future life" (482). During this whole immense period of history, under whatever varieties of form, men were fundamentally magnetized by a *Civitas Dei*.

No radical reaction to these new forces now at man's command appeared for several centuries. The activities of men in the West supported the *Civitas Dei*. Gutenberg, Columbus, Luther, Calvin, the Puritans in New England, the reformers of the Roman Church, the astronomers Bruno and Galileo all acted on the traditional belief in it.

> Neither Galileo nor Kepler, neither Spinoza nor Descartes, neither Leibnitz nor Newton, any more than Constantine the Great—if so much—doubted Unity.

All saw their work as a means "of magnifying God through his works; [but] a form of science which did their religion no credit" (484). Individual man "showed greater and greater insistence, without realizing what he was doing" on dealing with "the attractive mass of nature's energy" (483). But "Except as reflected in himself, man had no reason for assuming unity in the universe, or an ultimate substance, or a prime-motor." Finally Francis Bacon in 1600 tried to reverse the operating dynamics of western thought.

> He urged society to lay aside the idea of evolving the universe from a thought, and to try evolving thought from the universe. . . . As Galileo reversed the action of earth and sun, Bacon reversed the relation of thought to force. . . . unity must be left to shift for itself.

Following 1500 "the speed of progress so rapidly surpassed man's gait as to alarm every one" (484). The microscope, for example, "revealed a universe that defied the senses" and the entire past. Did man create it? Bacon said in effect, no, that nature did, but he did not explain how. Society resisted this new stream of thought for centuries, a resistance "often bloody, sometimes humorous, always constant." Only a few score men in Europe and America dared face it, men like Franklin who acted "as electric conductors of the new forces from nature to man." Finally, however, after 1800 the new forces "chemical and mechanical" increased sufficiently to substitute their attractions for the *Civitas Dei*. But still "Nature, not mind did the work. . . . Man depended more and more absolutely on forces other than his own" (485). "The mind should observe and register forces—take them apart and put them together— without assuming unity at all." Bacon had said "Nature, to be commanded, must be obeyed" (484). The new development actually lessened the power of man's mind while it served to increase the power of forces because mind did not change and grow while its recognition of new forces at work did. Bacon had foretold it, "Neither the naked hand nor the understanding, left to itself, can effect much. It is by instruments and helps that the work is done" (485).

"Non fingendum aut excogitandum sed inveniendum quid Natura faciat aut ferat."
(One must not imagine but one must find out what Nature is up to.)

It looked as though a "new variety of mind" appeared after Bacon. Newton, Franklin, Watt simply "held out their hands. . . . and great forces of nature stuck to them as though she were playing ball." But "The reaction of mind on the mass of nature was no greater than that of a comet on the sun"; which is to say not at all (486). The influx of new force was not only "nearly spontaneous," it was a "stupendous acceleration," and by 1900 had ended in "the appearance of the new class of supersensual forces, before which the man of science stood at first as bewildered and helpless, as in the fourth century, a priest of Isis before the Cross of Christ" (486–487).

The chapter ends. There are two energies: nature and man. The problem has always been the proportion between them. Purpose or unity or multiplicity in the ultimate is not the problem. The outside forces may be chaos or unity, and irresistibly the mind is drawn to them; it is a question whether to penetrate them will result in life or death, and it is on *this* question that religion, philosophy and science engage in battle. A further problem is the alarming acceleration of complexity as man discovers it or as it reveals itself to him. Can some "mechanical formula" be devised to explain it?

Chapter XXXIV, the next to the last chapter of the *Education,* is called "A Law of Acceleration (1904)." It opens:

> Images are not arguments, rarely even lead to proof, but the mind craves them, and, of late more than ever, the keenest experimenters find twenty images better than one, especially if contradictory; since the human mind has already learned to deal in contradictions (489).

Some of even the most elementary textbooks in 1904 asserted "science gets on only by adopting different theories, sometimes contradictory," and "science no longer ventures to explain causes" (497). Such a state of affairs hardly encouraged enthusiasm for the statement of any formula. Yet one could perhaps be offered, if "numerical correctness" (492) is not insisted on. Of course (Adams joked) any dynamic theory of history would begin by assuming a formula is possible if we knew the facts.

One image Adams used, one of his most successful ones, one to be developed more fully in the final essays, is the mind as a comet. It defies reasonable law as the comet does, that unknown substance that with accelerated speed wheels in its orbit so close to the sun it should be destroyed but instead speeds back on its path unharmed (489). The comet finally escapes. Can the human mind? The appalling fact of 1904 was that acceleration in the realization and use of new forces was so suddenly prodigious it was difficult to encompass; in fact, almost impossible for a nineteenth-century student seeking education, to say nothing of an eighteenth-century Henry Adams.

Another image represents all kinds of new forces and new complexity: the increase in the use of coal power. It had doubled every decade from 1840 to 1900. Applying a ten-year ratio to coal-power development and applying this ratio to the development of all forces man and society encountered, then counting backwards to check on the speed of acceleration, one finds that beyond 1400 "progress became so slight as to be hardly measurable" (492). Carried back to the stone arrowhead in "indefinite antiquity," "The motion at last became infinitely slight but cannot be proved to have stopped," like a comet at aphelion. (Or for

176

that matter, to have started, though like the backbone in the first verte-brate, the *Pteraspis*, it appeared.) To historians, the interest is not in the processes of evolution but "the single interest is the law of reaction between force and force—between mind and nature—the law of prog-ress."

Turgot and Comte had "first affirmed this law in its outlines by asserting the unity of progress" (493). It is here I think Adams' vast joke began, the one carried forward in the last essays. Unlike the many places where Adams emphasized the law of catastrophe, sudden leaps and jumps, the "unexplained appearance" of things like the *Pteraspis*, Cross, compass, gunpowder, or of "the sports of nature" like the new variety of mind that appeared in Newton (486), here he talks rigidly of "invariable law" as applying to acceleration in the release of new forces. What is man to do? Resistance or inertia "almost invariably has ended in tragedy" (493). For fifty years men had believed that power consumption would remain stationary and that "force would prove to be limited in supply." But radium appeared, revealing another fearful leap in the quantities of force. "Power leaped from every atom," and man found "Forces grasped his wrists and flung him about as though he had hold of a live wire or a runaway automobile." Adams concretizes the development with his old sanguinolence, saying that at that rate of progress, "bombs would double in force and number every ten years." In his own lifetime the tremendous attraction exercised by these new forces had engrossed minds in an increase of a "few scores or hundreds, in 1838, to many thousands in 1905" (494). The application of these forces to such things as railways caused a carnage that approached that of war; "an earthquake became almost a nervous relaxation." And "An immense volume of force had detached itself from the unknown universe of energy . . . attracting mankind with more compulsive course than all the Pontic Seas or Gods or Gold that ever existed, and feeling still less of retiring ebb" (495).

Clearly, the mind of man must somehow explode too, or reach new equilibrium like Newton's comet, to react with safety to the explosion of new forces that doubled and quadrupled in complexity every ten years. Otherwise, having entered so violent a field of attraction the mind would "suffer dissipation altogether, like meteoroids in the earth's atmosphere" (496). Adams had said far back at the beginning of his story of education, at the conclusion of Chapter III, "Washington," he thought in 1854 he had stood nearer the year 1 than the year 1900. Here at the end of the book he expanded this:

> At the rate of progress since 1800, every American who lived into the year 2000 would know how to control unlimited power. He would think in complexities unimaginable to an earlier mind. He would deal with problems altogether beyond the range of earlier society. To him the nineteenth century would stand on the same plane with the fourth—equally childlike—and he would only wonder how both of them, knowing so little, and so weak in force, should have done so much. Perhaps even he might go back, in 1964, to sit with Gibbon on the steps of Ara Coeli (496–497).

"Meanwhile he was getting education." What? He learned that a teacher of 1900 was more foolish than one of 1800 if he sought to educate an American for his future. Acceleration was too great.

> The teacher of 1900, if foolhardy, might stimulate; if foolish, might resist; if intelligent might balance; as wise and foolish have often tried to do from the beginning; but the forces would continue to educate, and the mind would continue to react (497).

". . . if intelligent might balance. . . ." And once again in this close-to-the-end account Adams indicates the necessity for suspension. To commit oneself or to give up altogether would end in disaster. It seemed "sheer senility" to do either (472).

The chapter ends on a definitive note that is deceptive—an exaggeration that fixes the development of Adams' thought throughout all the final chapters of *Education* on force and inconclusion. He spoke of unbroken sequence of development, but it was from unity to multiplicity and is accelerating so fast the assurance of such a kind of continuity is hardly comforting:

> The movement from unity into multiplicity, between 1200 and 1900, was unbroken in sequence, and rapid in acceleration. Prolonged one generation longer, it would require a new social mind. As though thought were common salt in indefinite solution, it must enter a new phase subject to new laws. Thus far, since five or ten

thousand years, the mind had successfully reacted, and nothing yet proved that it would fail to react—but it would need to jump (498).[36]

The final chapter of *The Education of Henry Adams* is called "Nunc Age (1905)," "Now Age or Act Now." [37] It begins with a reminiscence. Returning to America in November of 1904 Adams remembered his return with his family from seven years in England in 1868, nearly forty years before. The long introductory paragraph is full of an extravagant, frightening, alarming list of newnesses of the scene. He felt as though he might be now living in Rome under Diocletian, seeing the end of an era, unable to guess what would follow, but seeing "the two-thousand-years failure of Christianity . . . and no Constantine the Great was in sight" (500). A new type of man was needed (499). Where was he to come from? It looked as though he "could be only a child born of contact between the new and the old energies" (500) but he must be "either the child of the new forces or a chance sport of nature" (like Newton and Franklin of two centuries before). What would produce him? What would educate him? Man or nature? Mind or motion? And could he develop in time? Perhelion was due soon if there was any sense to this dynamic theory of history as acceleration. In any event—again a closing thought, an echo from the second preface to the book—"Therefore, dispute was idle, discussion was futile, and silence, next to good-temper, was the mark of sense." Such an attitude annoyed; but "If it was not itself education, it pointed out the economies necessary for the education of the new American" (501).

The end of the book is gentle, somber, tapering off into muted words, a coda for it all. Indian summer is mentioned once again, "a little sunny, and a little sad." Captain Scott had found "On the antarctic glacier, nearly five thousand feet above sea-level . . . carcasses of seals, where the animals had laboriously flopped up, to die in peace" (501–502). So by indirection Adams hinted he wanted to be viewed as an elderly man to be let alone by the pressure of thought and of theory, from the need to provide explanation and accountings, from the need for education.

At this later "Diocletian" time, Adams declared (with so heavy an undertone of distant echo and irony the conclusion dissipates at once) that thanks to John Hay's efforts, "For the first time in fifteen hundred years a true Roman *pax* was in sight." But Hay was nearly finished: "One walks with one's friends squarely up to the portal of life, and bids good-bye with a smile" (503). And thus it ended, and " 'The rest is silence' " (504). Hay died, and his death was for elderly Henry Adams "only the quiet summons to follow—the assent to dismissal. It was time to go." He was through. King was dead. Now Hay. As for his own life, he

> had no motive—no attraction—to carry it on after the others had gone. Education had ended for all three, and only beyond some remoter horizon could its values be fixed or renewed. Perhaps some day—say 1938, their centenary—they might be allowed to return together for a holiday, to see the mistakes of their own lives made clear in the light of the mistakes of their successors; and perhaps then, for the first time since man began his education among the carnivores, they would find a world that sensitive and timid natures could regard without a shudder (505).

And so the *Education* concluded on the most final of notes.

How then is one to account for the final two essays of four or five years later? I can do so only by referring once again to Adams' stout-hearted declaration at the end of Chapter XXXII, "Vis Nova," that "As long as he could whisper, he would go on as he had begun, bluntly refusing to meet his creator with the admission that the creation had taught him nothing." He had still "to account to himself for himself somehow" (472). It is one of the noble efforts of mankind, this persistence.

Chapter 4

The Scientist

I. "The Rule of Phase Applied to History"

Explanations and criticisms of the final "scientific" essays, "The Rule of Phase Applied to History" (1909) and "A Letter to American Teachers of History" (1910), nearly all agree that they are "pitched too high" and fail in their effect—that in them Henry Adams was being at best perverse and at worst dead wrong. He trifled with the grave. Newton Arvin went so far as to find Adams at the last guilty of "senile hysteria." [1]

The most complete, informative and scholarly study of Adams' science is William Jordy's *Henry Adams: Scientific Historian* (1952). Mr. Jordy's book is a penetrating analysis of Adams' science and a helpful presentation of the status of scientific thought generally during Adams' years of preoccupation with it. Mr. Jordy does not imply that Adams meant both the "Rule" and the "Letter" to be in large measure jokes. He does not of course view them as final examples of Adams' humor, which is to be expected since he does not operate on my interpretation of Adams' overall thought. Even so his book suffers from both seriousness and his own erudition, and his study is marred by his too-sharp criticisms of this "amateur of science," Henry Adams. To speak of Adams' "annotations defacing his copies of Stallo, Henri Poincaré, and Pearson" (233) or of Adams' "ridiculously attacking Pearson's statement that. . . ." (235) or of Adams writing "such nonsense" (207) and "More nonsense" (208) is to throw out of balance what is otherwise a useful work. I suggest that my point of view clears Adams of many of Jordy's charges of (what I think he accuses Adams of) limitations of mind. Jordy says in one place, after commenting on Adams' development during the course of writing his *History* and later,

> The mood of melancholy regret grew beside the intellectual conviction of man's helplessness before powers larger than himself until both mood and intellect merged on this point. The result was psychological paralysis, failure to arrive at decisive conclusion, a sense of drift (72).

Jordy reproaches Adams when he speaks of his "failure to arrive at decisive conclusion." I am suggesting, as I have repeatedly said, that decisive conclusion is exactly what Adams teaches us we cannot find, that this is the most fundamental result of the education he acquired. Jordy writes further:

> Dread of complexity yet repeated involvement with the very complexity he feared are among the major themes in both Adams' writing and his life. His passion for unity seduced him to his quest for a science of history, while no single element of the quest demonstrated better than this example of the physical ether the irrationality which his passion hid (241).

This is a reference to Adams' despair when he supposedly discovered that the concept of the ether was, by 1909, one that scientists recognized as no simple matter at all.

The whole view is to me out of focus. I see no "dread of complexity" but recognition of it; no fundamental "passion for unity" in the sense implied; no truly serious "quest for a science of history." As in *Mont-Saint-Michel and Chartres* fully definable facts are not what Adams wanted. I see no real disappointment either, only a hard "I told you so" when he found the ether theories had gotten mixed up. And finally I find no genuine irrationality anywhere except as joke and as realization of the mixed-up-ness of man's various characteristics of intellect, intuition, will, wish and instinct. Adams was a man of reason primarily, a man in what he himself called "the reflective, hesitating, relatively passive stage called Reason" ("Letter," 191). In addition he was a man with a high, imaginative artistry. Jordy's view is too literal and consequently too limited.

In sum, the "Rule" and the "Letter" are, I think, no more serious proposals about the application of physics to history, either the phase rule or the second law of thermodynamics, than the *Education* is autobiography, or than *Mont-Saint-Michel and Chartres* is history. I think we should take seriously what Adams wrote his brother Brooks about the "Rule" on February 10, 1909: "The paper is a mere intellectual plaything, like a puzzle. It is not meant to be taken too seriously" (Ford, II, 515, fn. 1). But this is not to say an elaborate image of the need for inconclusiveness, for an open mind, is not a serious matter. Further, Adams said more formally in the unpublished introductory letter to the "Rule" sent George Cabot Lodge in 1909, "I presume that no competent teacher now ventures to teach any doctrine or formula as true; he teaches it only as a provisional step to the next synthesis" (Cater, 783). As early as 1900 Adams wrote John Hay, "I can already see that the scientific theories and laws of our generation will, to the next, appear as antiquated as the Ptolemaic system" (Ford, II, 301). Considering such a firm statement it does not seem to me that we would be reading Adams rightly if we did not assume that his sense of inconclusion grew with the years. His firm declaration about the "dogma" of thermodynamics must be understood as a joke.

Yet a similar "misunderstanding" of Adams I think is revealed in J. C. Levenson's book (1957), another example of scholarly annoyance with Adams. In discussing the shift from the "Rule" to the "Letter," Levenson writes:

Within so short a time, the high humor of the "Rule" was changed into the bad joke of the *Letter*. Thinking that history would die if not irritated, he performed the service with such indecorous zeal that he could honestly say, "I don't know that I should see the joke myself if I were not its author." He thought that if his basic argument about the tendencies of modern history were correct, it should be convertible to any set of terms from modern science that he might try to use; but when he switched from Gibbs's rule of phases to Kelvin's second law of thermodynamics, something more than translation occurred. So much bitterness spilled forth in his exposition of entropy in history, that the despair of wasted energy was much more obviously a reflection of the author than a successful projection of mind into objective nature. Successful metaphors are never interchangeable, and Adams should have been artist enough to know that. The scientific figure he now elaborated had a tenor of its own which brought to expression the most desperate and perverse aspect of his personality. He gave in to intellectual waywardness (366).

Again here is a case of imaginative failure, I believe. Levenson scolds Adams in saying

> Had he cared less for his rhetoric, he might have cleaned out most of the defects of his amateur scientism, but he willfully chose to appall his audience rather than persuade them (373).

I cannot see that Adams had any intention to persuade his readers to anything; he sought to stimulate them to reaction and to irritate them by means of his rhetoric.

A final commentary is that of Ernest Samuels in the third volume of his monumental biography of Henry Adams (1964). It too is disapproving and ends by dismissing the final essay, the "Letter," as a failure or miscarriage:

> The artistic inspiration that produced the *Chartres* had spent its force and without that afflatus which gave the *Chartres* its matchless form, the *Letter* foundered in its own intellectual virtuosity (*The Major Phase*, 474).

Like his predecessors, I think Samuels misreads Adams' curious final work in not seeing that quite likely Adams meant his rhetoric to founder on purpose. It was the manner I think Adams employed to match his matter, a kind of grotesquerie.

Adams' own comment on the "Letter"—and it can equally well apply to the "Rule"—he made in a letter to John Franklin Jameson, April 3, 1910:

> I've not confided my last little volume to you, because I rather expected to get into trouble about it, with the geologists or physi-

cists or history-people. . . . As for me, they are all welcome to show that I'm a fool and a liar or an ignorant idiot. I know it already, and anyway it does not affect the question of what they are. My notion is that all the Universities and schools in America have not the energy now to react against any stimulous [*sic*] or irritant whatever; and they would prove me wrong if they were to show any reaction against me (Cater, 680).

The comment is pure Adams. It fits a recurrent pattern in his writing, first a declaration of mock fear, shown to be mockery when he patronizingly refers to his own professional colleagues as mere "history-people," then a full admission of *mea culpa* with a sudden reversal of the thrust into the ranks of the enemy, "you're another!" followed by a large blast with all his cannon, an absolute dogma wearily stated regarding not some, most, but all universities, which are absolutely without energy, and a final subtly enticing "come-on" where, his defenses down, he slyly asks to be blasted in turn if any of the enemy are still standing.[2]

The writing of these essays is splayed. It is obviously careless and obfuscated—too obviously, I think. The sentences and paragraphs lack clear sense in too many places, seeming to reveal a weakened control. Repetitiousness and sheer garrulousness annoy the reader. Large sections are quotations from the writings of various scientists or are fictional pseudo-quotations put in their mouths. Even the punctuation and capitalization are inconsistent. Unlike the orderly clarity in the *History*, or the smooth and lovely flow of *Chartres*, or the rigid organization and solid progression of the *Education* with its rich array of clever, saucy, sharp phrases and thoughts that so fascinate the reader and lead him on, in these final writings Adams seems to have labored hard, painstakingly and helplessly to convey ideas he did not understand. The reader who puzzles through to the end senses that the confusions, contradictions and paradoxes the world presented astonished and baffled Adams more than ever and had driven him into quite false positions as he apparently picked a jumble of examples at random that prove to be nonsense.

Yet, for all this, I suggest Adams was employing a definite method of which he was keenly aware. I contend that Adams sought to fit his manner to his matter. The prose style of *Chartres* reflects those qualities of smooth faith and great beauty in the period he chose to write about.

The gnarliness, complexities and involutions of the sentences in the *Education* best reveal those same qualities Adams found in the educational experiences of his own lifetime. I think the cumbersome tangle of the final essays, the cloudiness and muddiness of expression and organization, best show up those same qualities in the state of science in Adams' old age and in its relationship to humanitarian studies, especially history.

One needs to examine Adams' letters of this same period and afterward. They show no change of tone or quality or style from those of years before. And to read the last work, *The Life of George Cabot Lodge* published in 1911, shows a continued control of style. This proves to me that it is mistaken to accuse Adams too quickly of senility or of real failure of style. The style even more than the content is the real joke.

As early as 1894 Henry Adams had written a letter that shows his mind was working in the direction we have seen it follow from *Mont-Saint-Michel and Chartres* through the *Education* toward increasing speculation about "scientific history." 1894 was the year of "slack water," three years following the publication of his nine-volume *History*, a decade before the completion of *Chartres*, fifteen years before the final two essays that formally climaxed his thinking and his "education." He addressed the letter to the American Historical Association, calling it "The Tendency of History," and he mailed it from Guadá-c-jara (Guadalajara), Mexico, while he was out of the country.[3] As president of the association that year, he wrote his letter to be read before the body as his presidential address. The thesis he presented is very clear: the tendency of history was for historians to try to make history a science; that the effort "may fail is possible, and perhaps probable"; but "Historians will not, even if they would they can not, abandon the attempt. Science itself would admit its own failure if it admitted that man, the most important of all its subjects, could not be brought within its range" (124).[4] At the conclusion of the final volume of his *History* in 1891 Adams had written, implying a firm "of course it's true":

> No historian cared to hasten the coming of an epoch when man should study his own history in the same spirit and by the same methods with which he studied the formation of a crystal.

He then added, "Yet history had its scientific as well as its human side. . . . The interest of such a subject exceeded that of any other

branch of science, for it brought mankind within sight of its own end"
(IX, X, 224–225). One of the final, cool, sober and very provocative
eight questions Adams asked at the very end of the *History* was, "They
[the Americans] were scientific, and what control would their science
exercise over their destiny?" (IX, X, 242). Eight decades later it is for
us an even more sobering question.

Granting the grim possibility of failure to develop a science of history, but recognizing the compulsion to try to do so, where are we likely
to come out? Clearly, somewhere at a loss. In the letter accompanying
the copy of the "Rule" he sent George Cabot Lodge dated January 1,
1909, Adams concluded with one of his most succinct jokes:

> The human mind perpetuates its own multiplicity, and perhaps does
> well. Chaos may suit it best, and history tends to show that all its
> numerous efforts to think in Universals or Universities have failed.
> Even in that case the attempt to reduce universals to one general
> formula of physics is only a natural and appropriate mode of
> University education which connects closely with the theory and
> practise of the middle-ages; it is a return to first principles (Cater,
> 784).

What "attitude" is therefore possible? It must be despair, a retreat to
faith and hope (however ill-founded), or it must be suspended decision.
On the other hand (the other horn of the dilemma) a fixed science of
history would threaten "some prodigious interest" ("Tendency," 126).
The church: "science, by its definition, must exclude the idea of a
personal and active providence." The state: it would be hostile to "any
system or science that might not strengthen its arm." "Property" and
"labor" too would object. No science of history could possibly "lead
toward the interests of all the great social organizations. . . . Con-
ceivably, it might lead off in eccentric lines away from them all" (127).
Take one possibility: what if a science of history pointed to a socialistic
triumph? This would mean hostility to all existing institutions. Would
universities that depend on property interests be allowed freedom of
instruction in it (128)? Clearly, no. Take another: if a science of
history should compel us to announce the continued decline of civilization would society listen (128–129)? No. Take a third possibility:

> If, finally, the science should prove that society must at a given
> time revert to the church and recover its old foundation of absolute

faith in a personal providence and a revealed religion it commits suicide.

Still and all, "A science cannot be played with" (129), and if a science of history does develop no historian would dare do less than Galileo who though forced to recant his assertion that the earth moved around the sun still muttered "in secret if not in public, 'E pur si muove.'" Fortunately, Adams said quietly, the problem was not his but for the professors and historians of the future (130).[5]

The "Tendency" closed on a usual note. Admitting that "Beyond a doubt, silence is best," and denying that he expressed any opinion at all, "or, if I have expressed it, pray consider it as withdrawn," Adams mildly declared his remarks "are only casual and offered in the paradoxical spirit of private conversation." He concluded:

> I feel inclined to invite them [the members of the Association], as individuals, to consider the matter in a spirit that will enable us, should the crisis arise, to deal with it in a kindly temper, and a full understanding of its serious dangers and responsibilities (131).

I do not doubt Adams' seriousness in suggesting history can advance only if it adopts the methods of science. I do not doubt he was serious in pointing out the possible devastating results if it does. I do not doubt he clearsightedly saw a very troublesome dilemma. Nor do I doubt that he offered his remarks "in a paradoxical spirit" designed to upset historical apple carts that continued to plod to market with last year's crop of historical methods (what he was later to call lists of dates and editions of documents [the "Letter," 246]). Least of all do I doubt that, in view of all this, his recommendation of silence, first, and "kindly temper" finally, is his most sincere suggestion. In this case as in others before this "silence" means non-protest that is almost paradoxically full-scale protestantism; "kindly temper" is good temper.

Thus after presenting a perfectly logical forecast of the development of history, which whatever its future runs into very clear difficulties (he ignored the possibility of stagnation), Adams had the quiet gall to recommend silence and to call for good temper. In short, after raising alarms in every quarter, showing horror and worse in every direction, he concluded by withdrawing himself from the fray, leaving the mess behind him.

"The Tendency of History" appeared in 1894. Fifteen years elapsed before he returned formally to pure suggestions of historical theory presented in that letter, barring the final chapters in the *Education*, what I have called Section VI, "Education in Force." In the meantime he had himself set out to apply a kind of scientific principle to history in his attempt to triangulate into the future from the base points of the years 1200 and 1900 in his two best-known books. When once again he returned to the mode of 1894 he produced, first, the short essay of 1909, "The Rule of Phase Applied to History" (unpublished until 1919 when Brooks Adams put it in *The Degradation of the Democratic Dogma*) and the following year a more extended essay, "A Letter to American Teachers of History," consisting of two chapters, "The Problem" and "The Solutions." Adams printed the "Letter" privately and sent it out to a number of historians, scholars, libraries and friends.

These two essays are the most difficult pieces Henry Adams ever wrote, generally regarded as wrong-headed, ill-founded, and "only" irritating, as I have shown in citing Jordy's and Levenson's and Samuels' remarks. They cannot be readily paraphrased, summarized or otherwise reduced to clear and easy sense. This is true. But it does not follow that they are nonsense; it is in reading them seriously that they become that. Read as jokes they come to have great sense, and I think they are the final examples of Henry Adams' peculiar humor.[6]

Adams himself referred to the "Rule," the first of the two essays, as a supplement to the *Education* in a letter to Barrett Wendell on March 12, 1909. He made a usual remark indicating that no one ever read him and that he never received any criticism:

No echo whatever comes back. My favorite figure of the American author is that of a man who breeds a favorite dog, which he throws into the Mississippi River for the pleasure of making a splash. The river does not splash, but it drowns the dog.

My dispute, or rather my defense against self-criticism, is that our failures are really not due to ourselves alone. Society has a great share in it. When I read St. Augustine's *Confessions*, or Rousseau's, I feel certain that their faults, as literary artists, are worse than mine. We have all three undertaken to do what cannot be successfully done—mix narrative and didactic purpose and style. The charm of the effort is not in winning the game but in playing it. We all enjoy the failure. St. Augustine's narrative subsides at last into the dry sands of metaphysical theology. Rousseau's narrative fails wholly in didactic result; it subsides into still less artistic egoism. And I found that a narrative style was so incompatible with a didactic or scientific style, that I had to write a long supplementary chapter [45 pages] to explain in scientific terms what I could not put into narration without ruining the narrative. The game was singularly simple in that sense, but never played out successfully by any artist however great. Even allegory, as in Bunyan, remains only a relative success. The *Roman de la Rose* (the first part) is the best popular triumph ever won (Cater, 644–645).

In short, the *Education* insufficiently dealt with the science he wanted to write about.

Adams began the essay with the apology that Willard Gibbs' "Rule of Phase" was a chemical concept untranslatable into literary language (261). But phase meant, as Gibbs used it, equilibrium or a sort of stasis when a substance under different conditions remained the same in a "state of apparent rest" like ice, water and water-vapor. If new components were added to the substance, the phase of course differed; sea-water, for example, had different phases, equilibriums or stasis than ordinary water. The performance of the phase depended on the components—which might perhaps be infinite, and thus the number of phases possible in substances was likewise infinite.

In any event, a change of phase (in literature or in chemistry, be it remembered) meant "a change of equilibrium" (262) regardless of different components. Chemists and physicists had turned in recent years to the study of the relations between the different phases (263), away from the content of substances themselves, atoms and molecules. (Adams' own study of 1200 versus 1900 was a study of relations in which he sought to find sequences.) What if every phase could be dissolved into another? What would be the end? That was dependent on the law of solutions. Perhaps the only end would be dissolution of energy into "potential motion in absolute space" (264). Science could not help conceiving "something more universal behind or above it"—the final dissolve; thought (man?) could not help "behaving as though

sequence were probable until the contrary becomes still more probable."
But at the end of this process, "must all motion merge at last into
ultimate static energy existing only as potential force in absolute
space?" (265). (This end seemed to be Entropy, but Adams does not
here use the word itself. It does not appear until he wrote the "Letter"
the following year.) Was this then the "universal end"? Was this the
unity beneath the world? Was Entropy the "universal dissolve"? Cautious chemists and physicists did not go that far willingly. Still their
experiences dragged them there anyhow, into the "supersensual ocean
roughly called the ether" beyond which lay only "their own thought,—
which they positively refused to touch." [7]

At this point physicists were "helpless to escape the [next] step." They
must go forward only as mathematicians, not as experimenters (266),
and the minute they arrived at this point they were, so Adams said, in
the realm of metaphysics.

> No phase of hyper-substance more subtle than thought can ever be
> conceived, since it could exist only as his [the physicist's] own
> thought returning into itself. Possibly, in the inconceivable domains
> of abstraction, the ultimate substance may show other sides or
> extensions, but to man it can be known only as hyper-thought,—the
> region of pure mathematics and metaphysics,—the last and uni-
> versal solvent (267).

But the joke is that pure mathematical thought is an "artistic" construct,
a somehow imposed "unity" of "hyper-thought." All is in the mind of
God, whatever that is, and science, pretending empirical objectivity,
interested only in what and how and not in why, came circling back to
its ancient origin in metaphysical speculation, into a search for a unifying principle which is "why?" Adams pushed scientists into an uncomfortable corner, where stood Thomas Aquinas.[8]

Following this introduction Adams described the "hierarchy of
phases" of all substances all physicists accepted, a hierarchy he intended
to translate into historical theory. There are seven (268–270).

1. *Solids* (Ice changed by temperature.)
2. *Fluids* (Water changed by temperature.)
3. *Vapor* (Gas changed by new conditions affecting the atom and the
   molecule.)

4. *Electricity* (Magnetism. There is no indication how this changes into the next phase.)
5. *Ether* (The home of matter and mind alike; but an "inconceivable complex of possibilities"; it is solid and concrete compared to phase 6.)
6. *Space* (An even greater mystery, yet it is "almost the only concrete certainty of man's consciousness." But it is "That which is infinitely formless [and] must produce form."
7. Hyper-thought or pure mathematics. ("with the higher mathematics, metaphysics begins." [266–267]) (Curiously enough this "is the only phase that man can certainly know and about which he can be sure." [270])

Adams came full circle. Paradoxically the lowest and "simplest" step of the hierarchy, "solids," was the least intelligible; the highest, "Hyperthought or pure mathematics," was the only one man could grasp because it is a construct of his own self-consciousness. The dilemma of man's condition Adams demonstrated completely.

Each phase reached a critical point before change; the passage from one to the other could be expressed mathematically. This is not to say it was understood. Though in chemistry the rule of phase applied only to material substance, in physics the restriction did not exist. Electricity and ether were "as immaterial as thought itself." Radium only confirmed the notion of the impermanence of matter. So the mathematician-physicist could henceforward proceed to "the last thinkable stage of hyperthought and hyperspace which he knew as pure mathematics, and in which all motion, all relation, and all form, were merged" (271).[9]

But to back up a bit. Concentrating on Phase No. 5, *Ether:* granting it is as "undeniable as a granite rock" (a solid, by implication the most mysterious of all the phases) to understand it "requires new methods, perhaps new mind" (272). Did man have this new mind? At the end of Chapter XXXIV of the *Education*, "A Law of Acceleration," Adams had said that until 1900 the mind of man had successfully reacted to the accelerated movement from unity into multiplicity; but if it was to "enter a new phase subject to new laws . . . . it would need to jump" (498). Has it, we ask?

Yet the swifter scientific knowledge expands, the vaster are the areas of ignorance that seem to open . . . . presenting . . . "vast jumbles of new numbers, all with an insulting lack of obvious meaning" . . . . It may be science is on the threshold of a major breakthrough to a new unifying theory, like that of . . . Newton in his [day] . . . . But each time such a theory comes along, subsequent exceptions . . . prove its limitations.[10]

At this point Adams was only on Phase No. 5 of his series of seven. What happens when man moves on to No. 6, space, and further to No. 7, hyper-thought? By implication, by not speculating about the last two phases, Adams suggested that they are likely to be unsolvable. Mechanists had always been uneasy about omitting mind from their scheme of things. The "old laws of association formerly known as logic" (272) drove physicists and psychologists to concede to motion in its form as mind what it conceded to motion in its form as matter. After all, the problem of "direction" and "order" was conceived only by man's mind, whatever that is. Otherwise any mechanical system was as chaotic as the systems of any thousand nebulae. Vibration is not direction. They are as different as matter and mind. Or perhaps, I think Adams implied, as similar. Order, Adams said, citing Rudolph Goldscheid, is but "Direction regarded as stationary, like a frozen waterfall" (273). And direction is the most important "matter" of all.

The most irritating of all Adams' qualities was his raw insistence on repeatedly sounding basic questions. In the *Education* he had begun by asking "What was he?—where was he going?" (21). In these late essays of his November period, he repeated like elementary questions asking, "What is matter? What is mind? Where do they merge?" Far from foolishness, it is the essence of genius to worry the biggest questions of all. Henry Adams did not of course succeed in discovering answers, but he advanced the solutions to such questions by pointing up the necessity for good temper in handling them. This is a good deal. And as Roderick Seidenberg says in his *Posthistoric Man* (1950), Adams' analogy of history to phases in physics, "faulty as it may have been, had the minimum virtue, at least, of calling attention to this problem long before its general implications were widely appreciated. . . . But the virtue of Adams' analogy extends beyond its undeniable heuristic value." [11] Mr. Seidenberg does not explain this extension; "heuristic value" seems to me quite enough, especially when added to good temper.

Adams shifted now, beginning to apply all this scientific speculation to history. Considering the three important variables in physics, pressure, temperature and volume, that change the phases of equilibrium from one to another, from solids up to thought, he asserted that in history, attraction is the equivalent of pressure, acceleration of temperature, and volume remains volume (274–275). He declared man's thought is somehow history itself (274). And this rather thinly argued assertion is like the similar assertions about equivalent variables. But in suggesting that thought is analogous to water in passing through phases; and that "Among the score of figures that might be used to illustrate the idea, that of a current is perhaps the nearest"; and that this current is the solvent, Adams said,

> this ultimate motion which absorbs all other forms of motion is an ultimate equilibrium,—this ethereal current of Thought,—is conceived as existing, like ice on a mountain range, and trickling from every pore of rock, in innumerable rills, uniting always into larger channels, and always dissolving whatever it meets, until at last it reaches equilibrium in the ocean of ultimate solution (275).

Adams has tricked us in the space of two pages into seeing that applying the findings of physics to history results in showing history as well as science, because of pressure, temperature and volume—or attraction, acceleration and volume—ends in "equilibrium in the ocean of ultimate solution." This can only be Entropy.

Considering the current of thought, tracing it backwards, we can watch it historically for "only a brief time, at most ten thousand years," infer it for a hundred thousand, follow it back geologically for a hundred million; but "however long the time, the origin of consciousness is lost in the rocks before we can reach more than a fraction of its career." As man applies his thought, he discovers the world is one of phases of all kinds and that all the phases or equilibriums are unstable. (Man can barely calculate with mathematics the degree of instability [266–277] [12]). This world of phases is more astonishing than the explosion of rockets, and we can't stop every moment to ask what becomes of the salt we put in our soup, or the water we boil in our teapot, and we are apt to remain stupidly stolid when a bulb bursts into a tulip, or a worm turns into a butterfly (276).

The conclusion, Adams said, is almost self-evident. Unless historians proceed from an education in mathematical physics they must abandon their field to the physicists themselves, for "the future of Thought, and therefore of History" lies in their hands.

What will be the "possible term of the problem" for the new physicist-historian? Like an electric current thought obeys the laws of phase. One should then study thought as one does electric current and other immaterial substances (277). In history the advantage is that "a Law of Phase has been long established for the stages of human thought" (278). Fifty years before chemists began phase study Auguste Comte had laid down a precise enough law of phase for history. He had established three phases in the development of human thought, the theological, metaphysical and positive, which are analogous to the chemical phases of solid, liquid and gaseous. ("Once it was admitted that" human thought has passed through three phases, and then that they were analogous, is Adams' more cautious and more sly wording.) That Comte's three phases all exist together does not invalidate the law, for so do chemical phases coexist. The point is that each change of phase results in changes of the direction or the form of thought caused by "Acceleration, and increase of Volume or Concentration" (279–280).

To make any experimental study of historical phase the physicist-historian must start with a period everyone agrees broke "the continuity of Thought" (281) to produce a definite change in its direction or form. The Renaissance was such a period. It was a distinct change in the direction of thought, not mere acceleration; "it was an angle or tangent so considerable that the Church in vain tried to ignore it." The date of Galileo's enforced recantation (1633) Adams said is "altogether the most vital that history ever recorded" (282) because it marked a particularly singular change of phase, in which the "new lines of Force or Thought" obeyed the laws of mass (volume). As man proceeded to appropriate new forces, each "increased the attraction between the sum of nature's forces and the volume of human mind, by the usual law of squares, [and] the acceleration hurried society towards the critical point that marked the passage into a new phase as though it were heat impelling water to explode as steam" (283).

Thus the Renaissance period (1500–1700, say 1600) was the critical point of change (283–284). The old channel of thought, the phase of theology, had reached a maximum by then. The new Mechanical phase took over, to last until 1870, or 1900, when electricity took over in turn. (Curiously, the only seeming connection between the theological and the mechanical phases is that the latter grew to assume the qualities of a religion; that is, "The connection of Thought lay in the human reflection of itself in the universe" [284]). The clearest "fact" of all is that, in the mechanical phase, acceleration, the attraction of new forces to man or vice versa, advanced by "the old, familiar law of squares." This can be clearly measured by coal output alone. The physicist-historian is obliged to accept this method, "experimentally as a general law of history" (285). Why? Because mathematics like history "is obliged to assume . . . that something remains constant at last" though it be but a "fiction" (285–286). In this case, it "is likely to be the rule of geometrical progression." But though acceleration in the nineteenth century is observable and measurable, that before 1600 is a "far more difficult problem" (287).

During the phase of theology before 1600, one finds most historians admitting that the change from polytheism to monotheism occurred about the year 500 between the establishment of Christianity and Mohammedanism. This was a change in the form of thought (288) but not in direction: "the mind merely concentrated the image; it was an acceleration, not a direction, that was changed" (289).

At this point Adams shows his hand almost openly, for he equates science with religion by declaring they are both illusions. The thinnest of veils hides this momentous revelation of Adams' thinking, and it is quite important that his words be noted carefully in a passage buried in a thick discussion of the Religious phase:

The physicist, who affects psychology, will regard religion as the self-projection of mind into nature in one direction, as science is the projection of mind into nature in another. Both are illusions, as

196

the metaphysician conceives, and in neither case does—or can—the mind reach anything but a different reflection of its own features (288–289).

Again he reiterates his commonest image, the mirror, here to the clear disparagement of science. Only an insertion, the remark is too easily passed by. But it is there.

The religious phase of thought was enormously long, and the point of division between it and the preceding phase of instinct is lost in at least a hundred thousand years of time past. Even though "the critical point" of change in thought from the religious phase to the mechanical "seemed to be touched again and again,—by Greeks and Romans, in Athens, Alexandria, and Constantinople" (290), it did not come off, and the religious phase persisted. As for the phase of instinct in man, or in his ancestor the anthropoid ape, it has coexisted with later phases up to the present. When change of phase did occur it was probably a mutation that was caused "by some mechanism totally incomprehensible" (293). The anthropoid ape "felt no conscious need of mind. His phase had lasted unbroken for millions of years, and had produced an absolutely miraculous triumph of instinct" (292).

Somewhere, however, thought developed. Is there any equivalent to thought in any other substance? Adams again presented one of his most remarkable images in saying that "The nearest analogy would be that of a comet," which resembles thought in that, in the first place, "no one knows what it is" (294) for it too in some cases is immaterial, possessing no nucleus perhaps. It may be "an early condensation of the ether itself, as the human mind may be another, traversing the infinite without origin or end, and attracted by a sudden object of curiosity that lies by chance near its path." This object of curiosity may be accounted for by gravity; this may well be an explanation of mind too (295), and its attractions. Without any object of curiosity or attraction, without any deflecting power, it is likely that an equilibrium (a phase) would last forever (294). Seldom does this happen; change occurs, effected by temperature and pressure or their equivalents.

In 1843 a comet approached the sun. Coming from the most distant point on its course, aphelion, it reached perihelion and went flying back to space and aphelion again on lines parallel to its approach. At the critical point nearest the sun only twelve hours elapsed. At a speed of 350 miles a second it was unaffected by temperature, the basic variable that occasions a change of phase. It went from near nothing to 5000 degrees centigrade and back again (296). As for thought, 1800–1900 showed a speed of development that made the comet's a slow process indeed, so much so that "measured by electrical standards as in telegraphy, [it] approached infinity, and had annihilated both space and time. No law of material movement applied to it." In short though the closest analogy to the development of the phase of thought is the comet, certainly one of the fastest examples of accelerating motion possible to suggest, it is a weak comparison after all. In this same passage Adams jumped a step in speculation, asserting that "man's evolution had passed perihelion" already, and "that his movement was already retrograde."

The theory Adams advanced seems to break down here. He provided no argument of proof to support his conclusion. The analogy ended at this point between thought and the comet unless one follows Adams forward to see how retrogression is our future. But Adams was always cautious: "Nature is not so simple as to obey only one law, or to apply necessarily a law of material mass to immaterial substance," he says (297). All proved a comet is probably material while thought is less so. Thought must be gauged otherwise somehow. The figure of a comet only introduces the "problem." One can substitute electricity for comet. In any event, one studies the movement of current; and current undergoes a constant acceleration, measured by any scale, historical, geological or biological time. In the nineteenth century acceleration clearly was "far more rapid than before" (298). In fact, "the average motion of one phase is the square of that which precedes it" (299).

But if thought is past perihelion, won't it decelerate?

Pick a number. Square it forward, translate it into years, find its square root backwards and square it forward again. Well, take 6, 36, 1296. Assign 1296 to the mechanical phase of thought that lasted from 1600 to 1900 which is 300 years. Take the square of 300 years and you get a period of 90,000 years for the religious phase (299–300). Moving into the twentieth century and the electrical phase, squaring 1296 gives an acceleration of "what is equivalent to a straight line to infinity" (1,666,436) (299). The square root of 300 years would be 17.5 years. The electrical phase will thus be extremely short. Can the human mind "jump" fast enough to absorb it? Only a few minds had jumped sufficiently by 1870, when the dynamo was invented. The average man could no longer understand these accelerated developments (300). Ideas developed among Descartes, St. Augustine, Lord Bacon and Thomas Aquinas were intelligible—between the religious and the mechanical phases, that is. But "the idea of electro-magnetic-ether is not."

At any rate 1900 might prove to be as significant as the date of Galileo's denouncement in 1633. Nineteen hundred was the date of "the sharpest change of direction, taken at the highest rate of speed, ever effected by the human mind; a change from the material to the immaterial,—from the law of gravitation to the law of squares." In this year the discovery of radium caused quite as much consternation to chemists and physicists as Galileo caused the Church 300 years earlier (301).

Grant one's figures are off a hundred years; it matters little. Accepting them shows the electric phase would last only the square root of 300, or 17.5 years—to 1917. The next or ethereal phase, the square root of that, or four years, would "bring Thought to the limit of its possibilities in the year 1921."

> It may well be! Nothing whatever is beyond the range of possibility; but even if the life of the previous phase, 1600–1900, were extended another hundred years, the difference to the last term of the series would be negligible. In that case, the Ethereal Phase would last till about 2025.

But this develops through but five of Adams's suggested seven phases. Had he forgotten No. 6, space, and No. 7, hyper-thought or pure mathematics? If—not a likely chance—society should come to think in terms of ether or the higher mathematics then it would be thinking "in terms of itself," in pure mathematics and metaphysics (302). This might mean a long stationary period, mere consciousness, apparently a kind of Entropy. "In that case, the current would merely cease to flow." But if in the last phases, thought continued "to act as the universal solvent which it is," and reduced the forces of the atom, etc., "to that costless servitude to which it has reduced the old elements of earth and air, fire and water," and if more forces are set free, "the consequences may be as surprising as the change of water to vapor, of the worm to the butterfly, of radium to electrons." A quiet understatement.

Adams concluded, "Such seem to be . . . the lines on which any physical theory of the universe would affect the study of history, according to the latest direction of physics" (303). In short, adopting physics for method makes the traditional study of history nonsense: "the mind has always figured its motives as reflections of itself, and . . . this is as true in its conception of electricity as in its instinctive imitation of a God."

> Always and everywhere the mind creates its own universe, and pursues its own phantoms; but the force behind the image is always a reality,—the attractions of occult power.

Alchemy and astrology.

The joke is reached at last. Attractions to the mind must be assigned values; it is the physicist who must assign them. The figure chosen is of little consequence.

> . . . a physical theory of history is a mere matter of physical formula, no more complicated than the formulas of Willard Gibbs or Clerk Maxwell.

A mere matter indeed. We are indeed giddy in space now. If none of this is possible, we must then wait until the physicist-historian is "able to explain what Force is" (304). The final lines of this essay must be quoted in full:

> As yet he [the physicist-historian] knows almost as little of material as of immaterial substance. He is as perplexed before the phenomena of Heat, Light, Magnetism, Electricity, Gravitation, Attraction, Repulsion, Pressure, and the whole schedule of names used to indicate unknown elements, as before the common, infinitely familiar fluctuations of his own Thought whose action is so astounding on the direction of his energies. Probably the solution of any one of the problems will give the solution for them all.
> WASHINGTON, January 1, 1909. (304–305)

The reverse of hyperbole produced the conclusion here: understatement so great the mind of the reader reels as the thought of Henry Adams did also. "The Rule of Phase Applied to History" helps very little in solving an historical problem. Adams thrust History into a position no historian since his time has dared do. History remains antiquarian and antiquarianism.

II. "A Letter to American Teachers of History": The Problem

"A Letter to American Teachers of History" begins with a note addressed in 1910 to the president of the American Historical Association. Adams explained that fifteen years before he had presented a short address to the association "on the relations of the Historical Department to society" and he was now enlarging the address "to the dimensions of a Report" (133). He was extremely tentative and modest here. He planned not to publish the report. He wrote the volume as a letter to make it more colloquial and familiar than a usual scientific treatise would allow. He advised his correspondent it would probably be best to avoid discussion of the matter altogether, for elements controlling human affairs are not possible to know exactly, but "the need of determining these elements is all the greater on that account; and this volume is only a first experiment towards calculating these past, present and future values" (134).[13]

Chapter I of the two chapters, "The Problem," opens with an idea that had closed the "Rule" of the year before: "The mechanical theory of the universe governed physical science for three hundred years." It succeeded the theological scheme. Both schemes "affirmed or assumed" unity, one through the will of the Creator, the other founded on "the unity and indestructibility of Force or Energy" or the Law of the Conservation of Energy (136). But around 1850 a second law of dynamics appeared which said that though energy remained perhaps a constant sum, granting that the universe was a closed box from which nothing could escape (a fairly large grant), higher energies tended to fall to lower. This is the famous Second Law of Thermodynamics or the Law of Dissipation of Energy, asserted succinctly enough by William Thomson (Lord Kelvin) in England in 1852:

"Within a finite period of time past, the earth must have been, and within a finite period of time to come, the earth must again be,

unfit for the habitation of man as at present constituted, unless . . ."

And Adams produces a usual out, quoting Thomson still, providing a
protection against a too-definite declaration:

". . . unless operations have been, or are to be performed, which
are impossible under the laws to which the known operations going
on at present in the material world, are subject" (137–138).

Adams declared, letting go of his protective, modest "unless," that
Thomson here "tossed the universe into the ash-heap" in asserting absolutely this second law (138). The literary class continued to cling to the
Newtonian universe, and it was supported by the physicist John Tyndall
as late as 1862 when he defended the first law with an outburst of
eloquence: "To nature nothing can be added; from nature nothing can
be taken away" (140). Still one worry remained: if the earth inter-
cepted only $\frac{1}{2,300,000,000}$ of the sun's heat, what happened to the rest?
The new physicists had an answer; they flatly contradicted Tyndall,
claiming "that all nature's energies were slowly converting themselves
into heat and vanishing in space, until, at the last, nothing would be left
except a dead ocean of energy at its lowest possible level,—say of heat at
1° Centigrade, or −272° C. below freezing point of water."
    Which theory was most acceptable? An unscientific student sympa-
thized with Tyndall; and it did seem unreasonable that the universe
"could have gone on for eternity dissipating energy, and never restoring
it" (141). But the historian of human society least of all could "assert
or deny that energy could be created or could not be destroyed."
    In any event the historian dealt with social or human energy, which
he must either deny is energy or assert is energy independent of physical
laws. If he denied, he no longer had a function. He must therefore of
necessity believe that "Vital Energy was independent of mechanical law"
(142), holding the doctrine that the origin and phenomena of life were
produced by vital principles, immaterial force distinct from chemical
and physical force. "For human history the essential was to convince
itself that social energy, though a true energy, was governed by laws of
its own" (143). To nineteenth-century historians the problem was not

serious; to them history was not a science nor was society an organism. As geologists collected fossils historians happily collected facts, other fossils. "For them, it was a happy period, and literature profited by it." That is not to say history profited.

Unfortunately the problem was not simple. Energy came and went in mysterious phases of intensity. "Catastrophe was its law" (144). Solar energy fell on earth in some way, and part of it became vital energy which then "disappeared by a sudden and violent change of phase known as death." Vital energy must then be kin to *all* energy, not separate. Man always "flattered himself" that he was about to know "something that would make his own energy intelligible to itself, but he invariably found, on further inquiry, that the more he knew, the less he understood [Adams' old cry] . . . . he knew nothing at all!" The next paragraph begins, flatly and absolutely, "No one knew anything." Even so physicists increasingly insisted on an analogy between heat and vital energy (145). This can only mean that if the tendency of history is to ally with science, traditional history stands to be exploded. Adams' own nine-volume *History* of twenty years before was a study in "vital energy" or "social energy"; it contained a depth beyond its surface presentation of early U.S. politics and diplomacy. In concluding it so inconclusively Adams ended, I believe, by saying, "No one knew anything." One can add, "anything about vital energy or social energy as Force." *Chartres* was also a study of vital energy as a force, the most definitive one Henry Adams found possible to study, the only one that revealed any sort of measurable unity. And the *Education* as I have shown is a study of force also—in the multiple, twentieth-century sense.

In 1910 physicists seemed to be agreed society was an organism like any other in this serious respect: "It would die!" So it too would contribute to the increase of Entropy. Thus it is proved that history is a science since like other studies of the material world it deals with material subject to the same and final law, Entropy (146). So (Adams quoted Professor Andrew Gray of the University of Glasgow with his usual sanguinolent satisfaction) : "the inevitable death of all things will approach with headlong rapidity." And "It will be the height of imprudence to trust to the prospect, not infrequently referred to, at the present time, of drawing on the energy locked up in the atomic structure of matter" (147). To release the atom will but hasten dissipation. Adams quoted the German metaphysician Eduard von Hartmann to show that in the most advanced metaphysical thought the current conclusions were no different. Von Hartmann showed that society preferred to accept the first law of thermodynamics, the conservation of energy, because it proved endless continuity of life (148). If society accepted the second law, however, culmination, not continuity, would have to be faced.

Back in 1859, in presenting his theory of evolution, Darwin had contradicted *both* laws of thermodynamics in asserting (and letting his followers assert) not a constant in the emission of energy or a dissipation either; rather, he implied that evolution is from lower to higher, caused by "the spontaneous struggle of the organism for life." Darwin's great contribution was in showing *all* vital processes evolve, thus showing (Adams concludes this; he does not say Darwin did) that "all history [too] must be studied as a science." Naturally society picked up the hopeful theory of upward evolution (149). No one willingly chose to examine the prime problem, the sources of energy that produced the movement. Thus Darwin's theory came to mean to most that vital energy rose indefinitely "without the smallest apparent compensation" (150). But this cannot be. In biology, for example, though vegetables accumulate energies, the animal world in consuming the vegetables expends them "in the form of dissipated heat, to the cosmic space" (151).

Little by sly little, Adams showed that despite one's wish that John Tyndall be right, every area of science showed he was wrong. Society worked by degrading its energies. As much as anything the "Letter" is a devastating attack on nineteenth-century, optimistic, Darwinian evolution. Though evolutionists found firm support everywhere from almost everybody, "all striving to illustrate not the Descent but the Ascent of man," the degradationist, "the outlaw and the enemy" taught otherwise (153). Earlier, society had resisted the substitution of monotheism for the classic Gods and of Newtonian thought for scholastic philosophy. But the resistance or inertia gave way to the stronger "compulsory force."

> The acceleration of movement seems rapid, but the inertia, or resistance to deflection, may increase with the rapidity, so that society might pass through phase after phase of speed, like a comet, without noting deflection in its thought.

Only one field resisted the application of the Law of Degradation—the field of history (154). The resistance is indicated by the faith in evolution in the Victorian epoch; society had but to follow evolutionary science to

> Move upward, working out the beast,
>   And let the ape and tiger die. (155)
>   (Tennyson, "In Memoriam," CXVIII)

But throughout this period, increasingly scientists joined to show that not elevation but degradation of energies occurred:

> ". . . man has come late, when a beginning of physical decadence had struck the globe, his domain." ("Le Monde de Plantes," p. 109.) [Louis Saporta, *Le Mondes des Plantes avant l'Apparition de l'Homme*, Paris, 1879] (157).

Clearly, thoughts of uniform evolution from lower to higher violently contradicted the physicist (Kelvin) and the biologist (Saporta) (158) and the geologist (Lapparent) who taught degradation (158–160). If their thinking was true, Adams quietly suggested,

> In that case, man became the most advanced type of physical decadence, no longer at the top but at the bottom of the ladder, in face of accelerated extinction (162).

Since man's appearance no new species have appeared; rather "several forms have disappeared." There is the dodo, one can suggest, and the passenger pigeon.

The prospect presented is frightful in its fascination, yet one has the impression of reading an impersonal description of unspeakable horrors by someone not in the least involved. To ask, "Where is suspension here?" "Where is humor?" is to see that we are in its midst for, as this essay *reads*, Adams in his seventy-third year had achieved good temper by writing so cheerfully of the grim future his scientists foretold. He displays silence in the sense of non-protest, stoicism insofar as it is acceptance of what may be the unalterable circumstances of human life.

What can follow from this picture of mankind's accelerated extinction? Science seemed to indicate the only hope is that soul can free itself from the bonds of matter (164) as M. Lapparent, Adams' chosen geologist, 1906, suggested, but it appears the most slender straw. History must accede to the "lugubrious plan" science outlines unless the historian chooses to hold his tongue and remain in "the pleasant meadows of antiquarianism" of the nineteenth century (165). But if history does so remain, and if the historian chooses to look to Darwinism for help, he will find that

> the familiar, genial dispute over the origin of species has turned into a sinister and almost lurid battle over the extinction of species, for which the Darwinian theories of survival are declared inadequate to the point of childishness.

Adams continued to gloat. Some scientists, for one the palaeontologist Louis Dollo, explained that "the law of evolution" consisted of three sections: "1. Development has proceeded by leaps.—2. It is irreversible. —3. It is limited." Another authority, Edward Rosa, the American physicist, said, "every series of forms is destined to extinction according to the degree of its specialization" (166). Man, then, the most highly specialized, is nearest an end. Is this possible? "The mystery of man was then, and still remains, a scientific scandal which has inevitably roused bad temper, and sometimes bad manners, even in the centres of science itself" (167), and this of course Adams would see as quite bad sense. It would appear that man has evolved not from the anthropoid ape but from an eocene lemur, a creature less than a monkey, and from a source beyond him as distant as some "hypothetical lingula of archean time," from a kind of ancient bivalve mollusc (168). (One recalls the horseshoe crab or Limulus of Adams' Quincy seashore childhood mentioned in the *Education* [230].) But such an explanation of source has no value at all for human history ("Letter," 168). The lemur developed also into opossums and weasels and squirrels as vermin. He is a "grievance" to historians seeking a sure ancestry for man, and to accept him as an ancestor gives no foundation to any theory, "whether of conservation, elevation, or degradation, physical or moral." Besides there is no consecutive connection.

Thus the joke of human evolution gets either less and less humorous or more and more so, depending on the sources of one's sense of humor. For the man of suspension the latter must be true. What if one must accept the duckbilled platypus as a human ancestor (169) ? To seek for further sources might produce worse! For the historian the search was futile.

Man's much-vaunted superiorities of brain, hand, foot and vocal organs do not prove he has increased his vital energy (171). Man's brain is but slightly different from that of the higher monkeys. Even if one can prove man's increase in brain weight he cannot prove increase in usable force. If progress enlarges the brain, it may enfeeble the body. Weighing the seventeen heaviest brains known showed (Adams writes straightforwardly) seven lunatics and but three scientists "about whose degree of aberration no exact statistics can be reasonably expected (Topinard, 216)" (172). Four authorities declared further that the higher the degree of intellectual development in man, the higher the degree of man's physical degeneration. The higher man's development has been in such things as his "society" the more clearly it appears that he builds on sand. As all things develop perhaps the earth will in time only be a moon (174). What if dissipation of energies is unequal as M. Topinard suggested? This only accentuated the mystery. The second law of thermodynamics still operated absolutely; possible progress only produced "an inexplicable and unfortunate mystery."

Adams added with delighted sanguinolent and cataclysmic observation that whereas earlier astronomers and physicists had taken pains "to soften the harshness of their doom" by granting man some thousands or millions of years to adjust to his extinction, now their "pleasing thoughtfulness has vanished" (175). They now said

> The sun is ready to condense again at any moment, causing another violent disequilibrium, to be followed by another great outburst and waste of its expiring heat.

The next four paragraphs build up the possible horror: "physicists, astronomers, geologists, biologists, and sociological socialists" all, with humor, prophesied the end of the world. They warned with notes verging "on the grotesque"; they were "hysterically solemn; a little more, and it would sound like . . . a Salvation Army" (176). Adams continued by quoting M. Jacques de Morgan's saying that as man approached his end,

"revolutions will occur which the most fecund imagination cannot conceive,—disasters the more horrible because, while the population of the earth goes on increasing every day, and even the less favored districts little by little become inhabited, the different human groups, crowded back one on another, and finding no more space for existence, will be driven to internecine destruction" (177–178).

Adams built his case, quoting sanguinolent authorities redolent with doom. He did it on purpose, naturally. Not here did he employ his heretofore-usual "on the other hands" or "buts" unless they indicated something just as bad or worse. M. Camille Flammarion wrote in 1905 to the effect that as the world shrinks and gets colder, as the human race disappears progressively, as the ice creeps ever closer to the equator,

"The historian of nature would then be able to write:—'Here lies the entire humanity of a world which has lived! Here lie all the dreams of ambition, all the conquests of military glory, all the resounding affairs of finance, all the systems of an imperfect science, and also all oaths of mortals' love! Here lie all the beauties of the earth!'—But no mortuary stone will mark the spot where the poor planet shall have rendered its last sigh!"

M. Flammarion, said Adams, "goes on with a certain sombre exaltation" to show that apparently nature "regards her end as attained only when she has treated man as an enemy to be crushed" (179). Man— Adams—"the merest insect," may ask what then happens to such insects. Some scientists "are contented with freezing them," others suggest as did M. Lapparent, that "they will do better to become disembodied spirits." How this can be brought about no one knows, how to set up the "soul, freed from the bonds of matter" (180; also 164). In any event, degradation inexorably asserts all energies dissipate, and the more intense the energy, the quicker and more accelerated the dissipation. Vital energies will probably disappear the fastest (181).

The reader engrossed in these pages is caught down by the way Adams piled brick on brick on the grave of mankind. Even with

20,000,000 years to go, the inevitable end approached. Thus the scientific study of future history must be of Entropy. Society assumed progress to perfection but it gave every sign "of doubting its own health like a nervous invalid." If, Adams said, wickedly as usual, "the intended effect of intellectual education is . . . a habit of doubt, it is only in a very secondary sense a habit of timidity or despair."

> To a certain point, the more education, the more hesitation; but beyond that point, confidence should begin (182).

No evidence extant gave the student of education any reason for assuming that.

Suppose the American professor of history should advance his views in the university classroom that " 'a universal tendency to the dissipation of energy' and degradation of thought" existed (185–186). What would happen to him? He might not be burned like Giordano Bruno, but he could be made to recant like Galileo. "The University would have to protect itself by dismissing him" (186). But however true the laws of science are the historian's duty is to deal with them even though they condemn society to a lingering death.

Adams said this, in short:

1. Man as an animal is material and thus subject to the second law of thermodynamics; he tends toward Entropy.
2. Man as spirit or soul has his only chance to escape this doom.
3. Spirit—Soul—Reason—must be considered apart from body.
4. But Spirit, Soul and Reason cannot have come from a source different from that of other energies unless one grants a special act of creation that is totally contrary to all scientific law.

What differences are there between vital energy, will, entelechy, dominant, organic principle, trieb, strebung, intuition, instinct, spirit, soul, reason and force? All are terms used to describe that mysterious thing that gives "form" to other things, and which permits—or allows—or encourages—variations in the form. But any "branch which has lost the power of variation should be regarded as an example of enfeebled energy falling under the second law of thermodynamics" (190).

This is Adams' famous reversal of the cherished Darwinian hypothesis of evolution from lower to higher: the "Adams law" is simply that the highest developed species are the closest to extinction because of the second law of thermodynamics, simply that the most intense species will burn out the fastest. It follows that "the historian will have to define his profession as the science of human degradation" (191). Here follows an extension of Adams' theorizing that provokes thought as much as any he ever engaged in. In the *Education* he had laid down the line "physics stark mad in metaphysics," commenting on the wildly "immaterial" behavior of radium (382). Five years later, in the "Letter" he reversed the remark to say that the "strangest result is that of converting metaphysics into a branch of physics. Nothing in the history of philosophy is more distinctly marked than the effort of physics and metaphysics, since 1890, to approach each other" (192). The frontiers of modern physics approached the mysterious heights of age-old metaphysics. Turning to psychology in hope of finding an ally, to his despair he found no help, for psychologists had adopted tropism as the best explanation (Ostwald, Loeb) since organisms reacted to outside stimuli; will does not exist within any thing. Thus the belated historian who wanted to prove that will, force or energy was distinct from matter could find no help. It was all "really mechanical attraction" (193–195).

Purposely, Adams did not at this point try to account for the attraction. In demonstrating an almost complete mechanical and materialistic explanation for will (force, energy, instinct and intuition) as tropism, he moved onto another stage of speculation. Thought may be electricity, an equally unknown thing; will may be chemical affinity. If so all "fall at once under the second law of thermodynamics as one of the energies which most easily degrades itself, and, if not carefully guarded, returns bodily to the cheaper form called Heat." The sad conclusion is that "Of all possible theories, this is likely to prove the most fatal to Professors of History" (195). Adams fingered always the sorest edges, only to rocket off from time to time to possible distant hills from which he could, with safety, view the antics of thought. Yet another psychologist, Dr. Hanna Thomson, declared that the "Will, which lies within and behind the brain . . . 'is not natural, but supernatural, both in its powers and in its creations.' " Adams draws the worrisome point:

Of course the supernatural character of the Will is the whole point in dispute, and the usual doctrine of the modern psychologist substitutes the word Nature for the word Supernatural (196).

To summarize the theories, will is

1. A physico-chemical reaction; or
2. An organic function; or
3. A supernatural force (197).

Adams continued to pick sores, to worry the problem where it hurt, of material as opposed to immaterial, of flesh versus spirit, of matter against mind, of a universe or a multiverse. And the final mystery of all for physicists, chemists, psychologists, and historians, the meaning of "Nature" (198).[14]

Adams' method here—the most advanced writing style he had yet shown in one sense—was to repeat and repeat his emphatic point. All recent accelerated developments in thought had accelerated what students of intellectual education had known for half a century: the development of physics and of other fields only emphasized to excruciating frontiers the question, *Where does materiality meet the supernatural?* The historian's dilemma "remains untouched" (199). He quoted the physicist Lord Kelvin:

"We are absolutely forced by science to admit and to believe with absolute confidence in a directive power" (198).

But no directive power is defined.

One who is far along down the evolutionary path because he thinks is what Jean Jacques Rousseau called long ago, "a depraved animal." "In him the degradation of vital energy is flagrant." Or as André Lalande said in 1899, "Thought comes as the result of helplessness" (199). Henri Bergson admitted this in his *Creative Evolution* only to add (probably a hopeful borrowing of optimistic Darwinism) that the independence of human thought could counteract the impact of physics by somehow showing the continuing existence of that separate force, human will, presumably the life force. Then Adams quoted Bergson:

"From our point of view, life appears globally as an immense wave which starts from a centre to propagate itself outward" (200).

What is the centre? Only in man, said Bergson, had the liberty of development progressed to consciousness. It has become what we call intelligence, but at the expense of an earlier power, intuition, which only flickered now. So proud are we of our intelligence we are left with intelligence only (200–201).[15]

Adams begins the following paragraph with this topic sentence:

If this is the best that physiology and metaphysics can do to help the historian of man, the outlook is far from cheerful (201).

As the sentence goes, it is typical Henry Adams—borrowing on the preceding paragraph, assuming an assimilation of what had been said earlier, demanding something to follow, one can expect what follows in the paragraph to be instructive. It is not. The historian cannot assume from all this that he can prove triumphs of material thought as the rose is known to produce beauty, the peacock its tail. Still the historian must show somehow that

Thought . . . not Instinct but Intellect is the highest power of a supernatural Will;—an ultimate, independent, self-producing, self-sustaining, incorruptible solvent of all earlier or lower energies, and incapable of degradation or dissolution (202).

In the same paragraph Adams raised the unsettling question of whether "the plant exists to produce the flower, or to produce the leaf" (202). If intellect is the flower, is it developed or degraded instinct? He slyly showed it is probably degraded.

Was there no hopeful solution? It looked as if—no.

Intellect he compared to the sun, instinct to a gaseous nebula. Man had alternately been "insane with his own pride of intellect, and shuddering with horror at its bloody consequences" (202–203). If intellect led society to abandon its primitive claim to be supernatural, this proved "the universal truth of the second thermodynamic law." The chief theme of history had always shown man's mind was "the highest energy of nature," society's sole claim to special identity. Historians had always dealt with vital energy as their subject. But as they moved into "mathematical expression"—into statistics (203)—they only demonstrated a decline of vigor. Abandoning the position that man's mind is a separate form of energy, historians proved degradation (204).

This first half of the essay ended with the calm presentation of a paradox and some grim new realizations. The Church preached unity; it also preached the independence of the human soul. All other schools taught hostility to any form of energy claiming independence, yet they seemed to recognize multiplicity. The teacher had to realize and teach that reason is an instrument of will. Will is like any other energy and thus subject to the same laws. Further, all energy converted from higher to lower forms. In the case of history, its tendency to become scientific was another indication of the accelerated movement toward total Entropy, the final unity, hardly a unity of heart's desire.

III. "A Letter to American Teachers of History": The Solutions

The final fifty-five pages of the "Letter," Chapter II with the sanguine title "The Solutions," conclude Adams' speculation begun with "The Tendency of History" in 1893–1894. He found the solutions to follow the steps I have already shown:

1. The tendency of history was to convert itself into a science.
2. Science found its only unity in admitting the operation of the second law of thermodynamics.
3. But history could not admit the full force of this fact if it claimed man is a separate energy, not accountable under scientific laws, and so exempt from the second law.
4. Yet it was not likely physicists would give way to historians who wanted a field of work—a field that treated mankind and society as separate entities.
5. And yet man could not escape the nagging sense that he was a universe separate from other universes; and the historian dared not assume otherwise or he would lose his field and his function.

There is no final solution yet. After all, man sees himself as apart from all other things; he can continue to oscillate. And he had better do so.

But those historians who would continue to collect facts and figures and dates avoid the fundamental question of the "function of history," remaining antiquarians, taxonomists and romantics, playing cat's cradle with their subject. Adams pinpointed the disturbing problem facing historians in a letter to Henry Bumstead dated February 1, 1910. He wrote that he intended his "Letter" not "to amuse or annoy physicists, but only in order to worry historians." He meant to ask his brother historians, he wrote in a second letter a week later, *"Have you the smallest idea what you are teaching?"* (Cater, 677, 678, my italics.)

Yet physicists too are not free of fault. If they pursued their investigations on the basis of pure "objectivity" they engaged in but half a goal since their interest was only in "how" not at all in "why." At the end of the *History* in 1891 Adams had set up the problem more quietly but just as distinctly. I quote the passage again—

> No historian cared to hasten the coming of an epoch when man should study his own history in the same spirit and by the same methods with which he studied the formation of a crystal. Yet history had its scientific as well as its human side, and in American history the scientific interest was greater than the human (IX, I, 224–225).

Such controlled thinking pushed farther as it was in the final essays has caused scientists to laugh at him and historians to scorn him. Ferdinand Schevill, who praised the *History of the United States* so highly, in the same essay expresses the annoyance best when he writes:

> The failure has become increasingly manifest since his death and turns on his attempted betrayal of the ancient and honorable department of literature called history by stripping it of its independence and depressing it to a branch of the natural sciences. While his attempt ended in a universally admitted failure, it points to some flaw of mind or character about which agreement will not be easy to attain ("Henry Adams: Achievement and Defeat" 187–88).

To call physicists (scientists) half useful and historians foolish is not a winning game. But Adams presents his own best defense for any claim one might make for him as a serious speculator in the letter of introduction to his "Rule" essay sent to George Cabot Lodge in 1909, stressing one of the principal ideas he was working with, acceleration; he wrote:

> The most pressing concern of science, as well as of history, law and legislation, is to ascertain what effect such an acceleration will have on the ion of mind (Cater, 783).

This is not a joke. The humor comes in Adams' treatment of the problem and the attitude he took toward it, especially as shown in this last half of his "Letter."

But to a closer analysis.

The drift of educational energy had passed to scientists in the first decade of the twentieth century. They accepted the law of Entropy, applicable to "Gods and men as well as universes" (205) (a rather arbitrary overstatement, as Jordy has painstakingly shown). Historians —teachers of history in the universities—naturally resisted this shift, for it emasculated them (205–206). The ordinary mind also was repelled by the idea of universal degradation. While "Notoriously civilization and education enfeeble personal energy" (207), it was observable that society did work the individual could not do. One may be comforted to learn of the strict economy of nature who locks up so much energy in atoms; yet (the comfort vanishes) she wastes it extravagantly in the glow-worm (208). But individual instances like the atom and the glow-worm hardly spoil the fact that dissipation of energy occurs in the mass.

One hope remained: "further knowledge may—and probably will— overthrow much of the experience of physics" (208); "new scientific horizons will open to him [the Darwinian, the Elevationist]" (209). (The reader must remember that at the beginning of the "Letter" after citing William Thomson's definition of the second law Adams had added immediately that the law applied unless new laws governing the material world are discovered [138]. He had then dropped this corrective to emphasize the fuller implications of the second law.) Thus despite the state of affairs in 1910 that so crushingly showed the complete dominance of the second law everywhere, Adams, because of his reluctance to accept, because of his own hard-earned suspension, provided a future for mankind and was at least tentatively hopeful at last. But he was tentative; he but faintly hoped; and the clear implication is that the wise man can only maintain suspension of mind by refusing any final commitment and seek to cultivate good temper.

These new scientific horizons were puzzles. Adams had in his first chapter quoted M. Topinard, the leading anthropologist of France who, though a thorough-going degradationist, realized the inequalities of intensity at work and permitted a situation that allowed progress is still possible, permitted elevation. But Topinard bewailed the fact as an "inexplicable and unfortunate mystery" (175) because it demonstrated cross-purposes at work. Here Adams seemed to say explanation lay in this: history became

a record of successive phases of contraction, divided by periods of explosion, tending always towards an ultimate equilibrium in the form of a volume of human molecules of equal intensity, without coordination (209).

But the "evolutionist," a term Adams used synonymously with "elevationist," one who believed in progress, could not finally admit degradation of energy. He had to insist on two points:

1. That organic life has the exclusive power of economizing nature's waste.—2. That man alone enjoys the supernatural power of consciously reversing nature's process, by raising her dissipated energies, including his own, to higher intensities.

He rephrased these remarks, saying

That is to say, men must possess the exclusive power of reversing the process of extinction inherent in other activities of nature (210).

The physicist could only deny these contentions. He pointed out that all kinds of inorganic life stored energy better than organic life; for example the storage power of an atom of radium. Even the evolutionist complained "man does more to dissipate and waste nature's economies than all the rest of animal or vegetable life has ever done to save them."

And to the physicist he seemed to have no other function than to burn up coal, oil, gas, trees, zinc and oxygen (Kelvin suggested enough oxygen was left for four or five centuries) in armaments, alcohol and fireworks (212–213). The little that man did restore to higher intensities was trifling in the form of heat-rays, water-power and wind-power which he instantly degraded and dissipated again for some momentary use (213–214). The sun wasted all but $\frac{1}{2,300,000,000}$ of its heat as far as it benefited man, as Adams had said earlier, but in comparison "man is a bottomless sink of waste unparalleled in the cosmos" (214). The evolutionist could only claim that through all this combustion man created a more intense form of energy called thought which could be stored in libraries and drawn upon "without limit," because "In literary language, Thought was God" (215), and in setting its hand on anything it "impresses the result with FORM," and thus its act was divine (216).

But for the physicist the fact remained that, whatever its higher power, as a product of other energies thought was not supernatural but subject to the same laws as those other energies, meaning of course subject to eventual degradation. The evolutionist could not admit this because if he conceded that like the sun thought or vital energy maintained its energy through contraction, then he totally surrendered his claim. Again Adams sounded his theme: "The mind either was an independent energy, or it was not" (217). If the evolutionist asked for time to prove his case, physicists could give as much of it as the evolutionist would like. But what good would it do? Increased tension, not time, is wanted, an increase in power to raise the level of vital energy. Adams piles up a series of examples, as if one could find them anywhere. He has an imagined physicist say:

> "A watch-spring stores elasticity better than the mind stores thought. Any chance bit of obsidian or crystal can set forests afire, without calling itself intelligent. A fall of one degree in temperature gives form to an icicle, without claiming to be divine. A summer shower develops electricity at a tension sufficient to reverse the energy of as many minds as get in its way, without asserting the smallest pretension to reverse natural laws."

In any case, infinite variety of forms, directions, intensities and complexeties existed in nature before the least sign of man or vital energy "ever stirred!" Should the evolutionist still insist his mind was "the highest possible intensity of energy on account of its consciousness" (219) then the degradationist must reply that consciousness is only a sign of weakened will. The scorpion, the butterfly, the orchid all displayed more intensity of vital energy than man ever had.[16] One found the highest intensities of nature in the atom and molecule, the earliest on the scale (220). No new creative energies were known to be at work any more, "unless it be the radiating activities. Mere heat creates nothing . . . nor does motion account for direction" (221). Specialization of species is more likely the result of less intensity, not more, and of a steady dissipation of energy.

Adams produced closet drama for pages (217–226). He gave the stage to a hypothetical Physicist-Degradationist who pretended to give a humanitarian (Evolutionist-Elevationist) his innings, but he stacked the deck. The latter got brief opportunity to assert his claim that "Yes, physics is right—except when it denies man his claim to special and separate Force." Adams even denied that man could express much in the way of artistic production for some plants or butterflies or birds did better. Besides, what gifts man had in this direction were probably inheritances "from an earlier, more gifted, animal" (225). Now Adams punned to create a paradox of manner as well as of matter in a sentence that is as typical of Adams grotesquerie as any in all the pages of the final essays. The degradationist speaks:

"So far as his *reason* acts as an energy at all, it is a miraculous invention for this purpose [to accelerate the second law of thermodynamics], which inspires wonder and almost worship, but in strictness and *reason* does not work,—it is only a mechanism;—nature's energy, which we have agreed to call Will, that lies behind *reason*, does the work—and degrades the energy in doing it!" (226, my italics).

Possibly both theories can operate at once. Man is a mysterious result of dissipation of energy; and the ascending line may equally as well be a descending line or can be superimposed on the line of degradation or dissipation. Adams' point was that evolutionists preferred to see elevation, but they had no proof.

I think these pages from 217–226 do create confusion—a confusion

Yvor Winters charged Adams with generally—but the confusion was a conscious construct. (Adams said of the contradiction between the two opposed forces, "Of course the contradiction has been slightly exaggerated to make it clear" [226].) Man's instinct automatically rejected any physical theory that put him in the class of all other energies subject to "a thermodynamic mechanism" (226–227). Man had always assumed he was the lord of creation until Galileo and Newton deposed him. The nineteenth-century doctrine of evolution seemed to have reinstated him to a position wherein he could think of himself "as child and heir to the

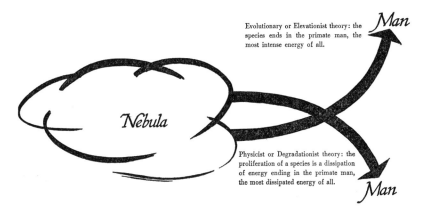

Evolutionary or Elevationist theory: the species ends in the primate man, the most intense energy of all.

Nebula

Man

Physicist or Degradationist theory: the proliferation of a species is a dissipation of energy ending in the primate man, the most dissipated energy of all.

Man

infinite" (227). But a catastrophe as crucial as that provided by Newton occurred with the promulgation of the second law of thermodynamics as absolute at the middle of the nineteenth century, before Darwin himself had published.

Still the old dilemma remained, the old row over free will. A professor of history after 1830 could show that "man's progress in mental energy is measured by his [tremendously accelerated?] capture of physical forces" (229). But the physicist-degradationists could "impale their antagonist on the reversed horn" of the dilemma by simply suggesting man's mind or reason had not won control over physical forces; rather, the physical forces absorbed both. (See the *Education:* "Forces grasped his wrists" [494; also see 484].) So the ocean dissolves a crystal of salt (230–231).

One extension of this theory leads, I think, to an explanation of the overall title of this book, *The Degradation of the Democratic Dogma,* a title given it by Brooks Adams when he published the last two essays in

1919, a title in large part a misnomer, but one still appropriate as an indication of a further application of Henry's theories had he carried them forward to man's supreme political invention. The professor of history as a humanitarian was interested in quality, not quantity; the latter was the preserve of the scientist. But the historian saw that an increase in quantity or volume did affect quality. As mechanical energies increased in volume, society somehow dissolved into a single mixture, a result called by a new word, "panmixia." Concretely, as mechanical energy took over manufacturing towns, "nervous energy" in the population weakened; "great masses of people under uniform conditions tend to a mechanical uniformity of mind, as in agricultural districts" (231). This implies degradation of human energy, of mind and reason, along those very lines. Ortega y Gassett was to write of this years later in his *The Revolt of the Masses* (1930). In the phrase of Joseph Wood Krutch even later (1954), the common man is much too common.[17] Leveling is therefore downward, accounted for by noting that forces absorb the human mind. But man thinks he dominates the forces. Where is the solution to this dilemma? Adams wrote at this point, as I quoted him at the beginning of this essay, a passage fully representative of his humor, one of both form and substance, sanguinolent, sharp, suspended, uncommitted, yet definite:

> The most ardent lover of paradox,—the most inveterate humorist, —would hardly think it worth his while to follow a train of reasoning which would surely immolate physics and metaphysics together. Such amusements seem to be reserved for astronomers.

But is it true that some developments of science have "been made at the cost of man's—and of woman's—vitality" (232)? Has not the motor car enfeebled man's power to walk? Historians could not admit the truth of this. If they did, "the Universities as well as the technical schools would alike close their doors without waiting for the sun to grow cold." The historian has continued to assert man's separate independence from the operation of the second law of thermodynamics. Yet at the same time if he wishes to "contest the ground with the teacher of physics, he must become a physicist himself, and learn to use laboratory methods" (233).

As Adams presented his point the physicist was hardly more sure of himself nor more respectable than the withered humanitarian-historian. Adams delightedly thrust forth the other horn of his dilemma: scientists like Lord Kelvin had no firm faith in their own laws. Kelvin in fact died thinking himself a failure in his "long effort to reduce his physical energies to a single term," leaving "unity, duality, or multiplicity of energies as much disputed as ever." Origins were so far lost in time as to be transcendental (234–235).

If biologists either asserted or accepted "an act of creation," they committed "logical suicide" by in essence giving up a search for cause. If they admitted multiple cause they denied a unity for creation, admitting mystery, transcendentalism and lost origins for what they saw existed. And physicists did the same. Far from solving any paradox or providing solution for any dilemma Adams thus, this close to the end of his speculation, managed to retie the knots of contrariety. What could provide us all with some sort of unified explanation of "monism" (236)? After all, unity's appeal to the human mind is equal to the appeal of matter to gravitation. It "survives the idea of God or of Universe; it is innate and intuitive. Thought floats much more easily towards than against it." But

> when heat, or electricity, or thought, or any other form or symbol or medium of energy, was likened to a falling substance tending to an ultimate ocean of Entropy. . . . Astronomy, geology, palaeontology, biology, psychology, could all move majestically down the decline.

Reason resulted from a development of nervous systems "when dynamically ill-nourished," just as a worried tree develops a very complex series of roots when deprived of moisture (238). Thus "Thought then appears in nature as an arrested,—in other words, as a degraded,—physical action." The physicist, despite any degradationist theories he might have, was safe from attack "so long as he can still promise expansion of power, or relief from pain." But a professor of history, not being able to promise either, but thinking history showed "with headlong rapidity" degradation toward "inevitable death" still "would not think it suited to the interests of the students or of the University" to teach it as such (239).

European universities never "preached upward evolution at all," it is true, and historians never taught the superiority of "the tombs and temples of Berlin" to the "childlike inferiority" of Egyptian pyramids (240). And historians considered new races as "so much fresh fuel, or oxygen, flung on the burnt-out energies of empire." Furthermore, Adams cheerfully pointed out, "the greatest historical work in the English language is called 'The Decline and Fall,' " and despite the assertion the moderns made 200 years ago that they are superior to ancients, Swift's denial of this in "Battle of the Books" remains better known.

Dealing with the "dogma of Degradation," the universities presented a worse record than in preaching upward evolution (241). Before 1500 the Church in control of the schools had preached "eternal degradation" for all except those rare ones to whom God showed pity. But afterward the universities, freer of church control, still looked back for standards of excellence "among the Greeks, or the Romans, or the Jews, when it was not carried back to the Garden of Eden." Today astronomers, geologists, physicists and anthropologists all teach "exhaustion" and "steady degradation" (242). Only the historian "for respect of youth" cannot discuss the problem that "was serious before schools began," because history is a course in the humanities; it is therefore not a science. And it touches man and society too close to home. Science got and gets forgiveness by virtue of its prime strengths, impersonality and objectivity. Or, I would add, its interest is in *what* and *how*, not in *why*.

Society, one presumes, has a "silent, half-conscious, intuitive faith" that eventually a stable equilibrium will be reached (243). But should this occur historians would have nothing to record (244)—an interesting if ironic possibility to point out to teachers of history. Universities insisted that historians treat man "as a creature habitually striving to attain imaginary ideals always contrary to law." To them man was outside natural law, full of will and intution, though "history" showed no clear evidence that will and intuition operated as forces separate from other force. An historian "compiling tables of dates" (246) solved no essential problem. His dilemma remained. If the law of Entropy applied to man, a universe separate from the universe, man was not then separate.[18] And the enfeeblement of his will increases:

the statistics show that in 1809 there was one lunatic in every 418 of the total population of England and Wales; in 1909, there was one in every 278; so that in three hundred years one half the population should be insane or idiotic. "These are the facts!" continues Dr. Forbes Winslow; "they cannot be in any way challenged" (250).

Man was at the reverse end of the evolutionary scale in a world that "is unceasingly wearing itself out" (251) though "the appearance on earth of living beings more and more elevated . . . undoubtedly give[s] the impression of a progress and a gain" (252).

In this final essay, as I have perhaps over-demonstrated in summarizing his material, Adams garrulously repeated himself to make the basic point that is both the culmination as well as the basic theme of all this years of thought and of all his literary work: the dilemma persisted, the two horns of which remained a paradox of faith against reason (*Esther*), of mystery and fact (the *History*), unity and multiplicity (*Chartres* and the *Education*), elevation and degradation (the "Rule" and the "Letter"), of "man against the universe." A creature called man thought of himself as a special creature moving ever upward; but in thinking so he boosted himself into direct contradiction to the fact that like all else he is subject to the physical law of degradation which is reality. Therefore man's view of himself is illusion. In 1200 he found himself a mighty cog in God's machinery as Adams showed in *Chartres*. By 1910 he had to face the fact he was only a portion, and perhaps a small portion, of a multiplicity (fully described in *Education*) that is God's "universe." Man is the creature, not the creator, of it.

The "problem" Henry Adams presented in the "Letter" in 1910 can now be said thus: How can the teacher of history reconcile the second law of thermodynamics with his teaching of man's progress? Beyond this image of the problem, Adams asked, how can man, a separate unity, be reconciled with unity itself? Adams concluded his final essay mildly enough, presenting as the "solution" a quiet call for an "arrangement" that once achieved would be the most satisfactory juncture we can dream of because it would disappear:

If the physicists and physico-chemists can at last find their way to an arrangement that would satisfy the sociologists and historians, the problem would be wholly solved.

223

And then Adams ends on a final note of inconclusion, jerking out the words like a sob or like stifled laughter:

> Such a complete solution seems not impossible; but at present,—for the moment,—as the stream runs,—it also seems, to an impartial bystander, to call for the aid of another Newton (259).

Epilogue

Mabel La Farge quotes a letter Henry Adams wrote to a "young person on painting" in which he said:

> There is nothing new to say—at least not in our formulas. Everything has been said many—many—many times. The pleasure is in saying it over to ourselves in a whisper, so that nobody will hear, and so that neither vanity, nor money can get in as much as a lisp. I admit that this unfits one for one's time and life, but one must make some sort of running arrangement on every railroad and even in every school.[19]

Should one turn the burning glass of his observations on the many facets of this brief passage he can see much, much more than advice on painting. The least it shows is that Adams strove to avoid meretriciousness. He strove for learning.

I have a strong final impression that Adams came, finally, as late perhaps as 1900, past the age of sixty, to the realization of his true goal: the production of a new literature. He had spent long years in fermentation. Only late in life did he come to the full realization that art is long while life is short; that—in his terms, I think—thought as revealed in a carefully formed style is what will always remain.

As the years pass Henry Adams comes to appear as important an Adams as any one of his illustrious ancestors or as any one of his more widely known contemporaries. I think he well knew the involved men like Hay, King, Roosevelt and Charles Francis Adams the railroad magnate would, in being men of commitment and action, dissolve into oblivion because their action limited them to a temporal theater. I think Henry Adams is one of America's great writers because he touched so sharply and so well the themes that most press on man's thought. He flatly denied cycles and circles and answers though he set up many for consideration, and though in a curious way he ended with an anti-circle; that is to say, he denied that history repeats itself but that history does not seem to be getting anywhere. His matter is a long declining trajectory as he penetrated down and deep into perpetual problems. But his manner, his artistry, leads his readers up to knowing more. The figure his art makes is thus a paradox finally.

The only "final" explanation of Henry Adams lies in an examination of his style, of the intricate manner with which he treated his complex matter, of his artistry. This is final because artistry is infinite.

Notes

Chapter 1

1. *The Education of Henry Adams: An Autobiography,* Boston, Houghton Mifflin
   Company, 1918 (reprinted as *The Education of Henry Adams,* New York, Modern Library, 1931, and as *The Education of Henry Adams: An Autobiography,*
   Boston, Houghton Mifflin Company, Sentry Edition, 1961, same page numbering),
   389. The basic texts I have used in this work in addition to the *Education* are:
   > 1. *History of the United States of America,* 9 vols., New York, Charles Scrib-
   > ner's Sons, 1921.
   > 2. *Mont-Saint-Michel and Chartres,* Boston, Houghton Mifflin Company, 1912,
   > 1933, 1963 (Sentry Edition).
   > 3. "A Letter to American Teachers of History" and "The Rule of Phase Ap-
   > plied to History" in Henry Adams, *The Degradation of the Democratic Dogma,*
   > with an Introduction by Brooks Adams, New York, Macmillan Company,
   > 1919 (reprinted, New York, Capricorn Books, G. P. Putnam's Sons, 1958).
   The number in parentheses that follows any quotation or remark in my text
   refers to the page number of the work cited. I will refer to the *History* by vol.
   and chapter number as well.
2. Worthington Chauncey Ford, ed., *Letters of Henry Adams (1858–1891),* Boston
   and New York, Houghton Mifflin Company, 1930, 262. This is the first of two
   volumes of Adams' letters Ford edited. The second is entitled *Letters of Henry
   Adams (1892–1918),* same publisher, 1938. I will refer to these books as "Ford,
   I" and "Ford, II" respectively in my text with page number citations.
3. In the *Education* Adams remarked more sharply, "Critics who know ultimate
   truth will pronounce judgment on history" (105).
4. *In Defense of Reason,* Denver, Alan Swallow, 1947. After some thirty pages of attack Winters roundly declared, "I have been tracing the disintegration of a mind"

(405). He claims Adams' high point of achievement was the *History* and thereafter his writing and his thought got worse. Mr. Winters objected that Adams
found no position.

5. "The Easy Chair," *Harper's Magazine*, 195, 1171 (December, 1947), 516.

6. "Introduction," *The Selected Letters of Henry Adams*, New York, Farrar, Straus
and Young, Inc., 1951, xxx.

7. Lynn White, Jr., "Dynamo and Virgin Reconsidered," *The American Scholar*, 27,
2 (Spring, 1958), 193–194.

8. In a letter to Homer Saint-Gaudens in 1908 Adams wrote of the statue, "Your
father meant it to ask a question, not to give an answer." (*Henry Adams and
His Friends: A Collection of His Unpublished Letters*, compiled with a Biographical Introduction by Harold Dean Cater, Boston, Houghton Mifflin Company, The
Riverside Press Cambridge, 1947, 610. Hereafter this book will be referred to
as "Cater.") Ernest Samuels explains that having been given his instructions by
Adams, in executing the figure St. Gaudens "moved with surer instinct back to
a figure he had designed a dozen years before, the 'Silence,' in which, avoiding
the suggestion of any particular mode, Greek, Roman, or Egyptian, he created
his own 'Style Libre.'" (*Henry Adams: The Middle Years*, The Belknap
Press of the Harvard University Press, Cambridge, Massachusetts, 1958, 336.)

9. "Adams Goes to School: I. The Problem Laid Out," *Kenyon Review*, XVII, 4
(Autumn, 1955), 604.

10. In great measure the later works of Henry Adams are essays in imagery as I
will seek to show. Unless one sees his thought thus he will miss Adams' most
fruitful contribution to contemporary thinking.

11. "The Expense of Greatness: Three Emphases on Henry Adams," *The Expense
of Greatness*, New York, Arrow Editions, c1940, 254. Dealing with quite another
thinker, Eugene O'Neill, Doris Falk shows in the very title of her work that
O'Neill had a mindset very like Adams'. She says the very fact of man's lost-
ness is the key to his humanity (this is Sartrian existentialism): if man is not
conscious of it, if he is, "harmonized," he is a vegetable. She explains Jung in
this connection also, saying that according to him (she used O'Neill's *The Great
God Brown* as an example), "Individuation takes place only when the opposites
of self—both the Dion [mother] and the Brown [father]—can be combined in
the individual in a sort of harmonious compromise, when the tension between
opposites is not resolved, but accepted as the inevitable condition of all growth
and change." The "only unity is to be found in disunity. . . . Integration or the
discovery of an absolute other than change and process is death." (*Eugene
O'Neill and the Tragic Tension*, New Brunswick, New Jersey, Rutgers University
Press, 1958, 34, 108, 111.)

12. B. F. Skinner in his *Verbal Behavior* says, "It is generally assumed, in line
with traditional conceptions of verbal behavor, that there are only two elements
in a literary work—form and meaning." He adds, "But there is obviously something more in good writing—something not far from wit or verbal play. This
has been argued to be a subtle connection between form and meaning, but a
more likely possibility is that it has to do with how a reader's behavior is
prepared and released by a text" (New York, Appleton-Century-Crofts, Inc.,
1957, 284–285). Thus, if I understand Skinner, there is a distinct third element.
I grant this in part. Still, too much emphasis on a distinct, third element that is

"concrete" too easily blurs the fact that the juncture is puzzlingly abstract, thus mysterious, thus permanently problematical.

13. "Some Remarks on Humor," in *The Second Tree from the Corner*, New York, Harper & Brothers Publishers, 1954, 173.

14. In "Laughter" (1920), *And Even Now*, New York, E. P. Dutton & Co., 1921, 304.

15. R. P. Blackmur refined this simplex explanation of mine very helpfully when he wrote, "in reconciling two points of view into one it [irony and skepticism, of preferring Montaigne to a fly or a beetle] manages to imply the possibility of a third and quite unadjusted point of view." He added, "Increasingly as he grew older, Adams was able to feel his own complexity as unity only in the form of a fable or a riddle. He could no longer, if indeed he ever did, feel the complexity as resolvable into a single energy." ("Henry Adams: Three Late Moments," *Kenyon Review*, II, 1 [Winter, 1940], 28–29).

16. To read Ecclesiastes without humor is profoundly discouraging. When the Preacher repeatedly asserts that both the righteous man and the sinner stand to gain the same final reward or punishment, that *all* is vanity, then the only protection man can have is to cultivate good temper.

17. *An Essay on Comedy and the Uses of the Comic Spirit*, New York, Charles Scribner's Sons (c1897), 1923, 81.

18. Louis I. Bredvold, Alan D. McKillop, Lois Whitney, eds., *Eighteenth Century Poetry & Prose*, New York, The Ronald Press Company, 1939, xxi.

19. Edgar Johnson, "The Nature and Value of Satire," *A Treasury of Satire*, New York, Simon and Schuster, c1945, 8–9.

20. Perry Miller produces this apposite comment in explaining much of Jonathan Edwards' thinking: To Edwards, "sensationally and environmentally conditioned man . . . . takes his stand, his last stand, upon the conviction that persons who have a true knowledge of God have their minds greatly enlightened 'in the knowledge of divine things in general.' Is this illusion? Must the only remaining stronghold of sanity be surrendered, and shall an utter chaos of partial and conflicting systems of secondary virtue engulf us?" (*Jonathan Edwards*, the American Men of Letters Series, New York, William Sloan Associates, 1949, 297). Adams' God was not Edwards'.

21. Robert A. Hume is one of the few Adams scholars who looks in my direction. He writes, "Interfused with the wisdom of his later books, especially, and inseparable from it, is an ironic lightness, a tongue-in-cheek aptness for contrast and paradox, that marks the consummate humorist in the truest sense." (*Runaway Star: An Appreciation of Henry Adams*, Ithaca, New York, Cornell University Press, 1951, 232.) Samuel McChord Crothers also showed some appreciation of Adams as a humorist. In 1920 he wrote: "I find here [in the *Education*] a delightful work of humor. It is humor in the old English sense. We see a really solid mind displaying itself capriciously and with a whimsical willfulness. The author might have taken as a Shakespearean motto Nym's pugnacious declaration, 'I have a humor to knock you indifferently well.'" ("Education in Pursuit of Henry Adams," *The Dame School of Experience*, Boston and New York, Houghton Mifflin Company, The Riverside Press Cambridge, 1920, 187.)

22. Max Eastman, *The Sense of Humor*, New York, Charles Scribner's Sons, 1922, 24. Eastman said, more elaborately, "He [the mystic] declares that all the failures

and imperfections in the bitter current of time's reality are a part of God's eternal perfection, and so he makes himself happy to suffer them. The humorist declares that they are funny, and he accomplishes the same thing. . . . And so it is not surprising that the mystics should seem wanting in the sacred gift of humor, and that humorists should be not often of a prayerful turn."

23. Emerson uses a term that helps clarify my meaning. He refers to humor as "halfness": "The essence of all jokes, of all comedy, seems to be an honest or well-intended halfness; a non-performance of what is pretended to be performed, at the same time that one is giving loud pledges of performance." ("The Comic," *Letters and Social Aims*, Vol. VIII, Emerson's Complete Works, Riverside Edition, Boston and New York, Houghton, Mifflin and Company, The Riverside Press, Cambridge 1890, 151)

24. One would expect that a book entitled *American Humor* would be helpful in clarifying the term. However, Constance Rourke's book with that title, valuable otherwise, is curious in that reading it does not show one much humor in the ordinary sense. She explains American jokes as bravura and brag founded on fear of the new world. She shows they are not really "funny." Miss Rourke does not demonstrate Americans have much sense of humor. But she does, indirectly, show that what passes for it is a sense of inconclusion, nervousness and uncertainty. Without saying why or how she implies that good temper was lacking. (*American Humor: A Study of the National Character*, New York, Harcourt Brace and Company, Inc., 1931.)

25. Cater, xcii. Ernest Samuels says Adams' income at the death of his father in 1887 may "have reached as much as $50,000 a year, of which he habitually reinvested half" (*The Middle Years*, 317). At his death he left an estate worth $800,000. Samuels further says Adams' investments in 1900 earned an income of fifty or sixty thousand dollars on a million dollar fortune. (*Henry Adams: The Major Phase*, Cambridge, Massachusetts, The Belknap Press, of Harvard University Press, 1964, 364.)

Chapter 2

1. *Historical Essays*, New York, Charles Scribner's Sons, 1891, 371. A single example from the first volume of the *History* shows how common the pattern is: "If their theory was sound, when the day of competition should arrive, Europe might choose between American and Chinese institutions, but there could be no middle path; she might become a confederated democracy, or a wreck" (I, VI, 163).

2. Philadelphia, Lippincott and Company, 1879. The *Gallatin* still, however, is regarded as a fine piece of scholarship, though it has been superseded. Commenting on its style, Ernest Samuels says, "the book was studded with bravura passages of a somewhat old-fashioned eloquence, massive periodic sentences artfully wrought and sustained, often ending in an exuberant flourish." This was the result, Samuels says, of Adams' "habit to re-read his Macaulay to 'whet' his style." (*The Middle Years*, 61) J. C. Levenson in his *The Mind and Art of Henry Adams* (Boston, Houghton Mifflin Company, The Riverside Press Cambridge 1957) indicates something of the "undeveloped" style of Adams as shown in

this work. In writing his novel *Democracy* (1880), "he now worked to develop a more supple prose. Despite conscious struggles with [the literary style of] the *Gallatin*, he had loaded that biography with thirty-line chains of semicolon clauses, all too appropriate to the heavy weight of his scholarship" (96).

3. Boston and New York, Houghton Mifflin Company, The Riverside Press Cambridge, 1882, 1898.

4. Samuels says, "The *Randolph* was no hack work, boiled up for the occasion, but a return to materials which he had already studied with great care, first for his Harvard lectures, then reconsidered in the light of his painstaking work on the *Gallatin*" (*The Middle Years*, 186). Unfortunately the volume reveals no special care in its writing.

5. "Henry Adams: Achievement and Defeat," *Six Historians*, Chicago, University of Chicago Press, 1956, 169.

6. Levenson, 168. The four parts of the work as published in New York by Charles Scribner's Sons each had different titles as follows:

History of the United States of America during the First Administration of Thomas Jefferson, 2 vols. (1889)

History of the United States of America during the Second Administration of Thomas Jefferson, 2 vols., (1890)

History of the United States of America during the First Administration of James Madison, 2 vols., (1890)

History of the United States of America during the Second Administration of James Madison, 3 vols., (1890)

When the whole nine volumes were published in 1891 as a set by G. P. Putnam's Sons in London, the title given was simply *History of the United States of America*.

7. "Introduction," *Henry Adams: History of the United States of America During the Administration of Thomas Jefferson*, New York, Albert and Charles Boni, 1930, Books I and II, xv.

8. *The Middle Years*, 409–410. Quotation from New York *Critic*, December 7, 1889.

9. Housatonic [William Henry Smith, in New York Public Library copy], "A Case of Hereditary Bias: Henry Adams as an Historian: Some Strictures on the 'History of the United States of America'," *New York Tribune*, September 10 and December 15, 1890; Washington, no publisher shown, 1891, 33.

10. As early as 1870 in his "The New York Gold Conspiracy" published in the *Westminster Review*, Adams employed sanguinolence. In a lively attack on those rascals James Fiske and Jay Gould, he wrote, "For weeks the nation writhed and quivered under the torture of this modern rack" (*Historical Essays*, 333–334). Horror, terror, and sanguinolence characterize so much of Adams' writing, reading him often is a bloody experience. But he usually means to make jokes. I find this consistent with his humor, but some would not. Stephen Leacock, for example, in commenting on "cruel" jokes wrote, "But let those find this humor who can. . . . It lacks the element of kindliness essential to real humor and passes into the hideous mockery into which humor may degenerate" (*Humor: Its Theory and Technique*, New York, Dodd, Mead & Company, 1935, 218). Few can claim that "the element of kindliness" is any essential of Adams' humor.

Leacock is better when he says, "And so humor rests, as all high humor does, on a real basis of thought" (141).

11. *Henry Adams: A Biography,* New York, Macmillan Company, 1956, 242. And Robert F. Spiller concludes his article on Adams in *Literary History of the United States* (New York, Macmillan Company, 1948, 1963, vol. II):

> In his style, Adams came nearer to a classic restraint, but here too he indulged in extravagance when the pen became willful. His revisions of his historical essays when he collected them show a peeling off of the superfluous phrase, a stripping down to clear and explicit statement. When he turned from direct to imaginative writing, he deliberately created an *alter ego* and from an oblique angle surveyed himself together with other phenomena, past and present. The direct style would no longer do and he deliberately cultivated, even in his personal letters, the irony which had always been his. A careful reading of Pascal, Montaigne, and Voltaire helped in this study. In his final testament of futility and affirmation, his vein was comic in spite of the tragic intensity of his feelings. Wit alone could bear the burden (1103).

12. Adams had little reverence for great men. He was Tolstoyan, finally, not Carlylean. William Jordy says, "Neither the hero nor the heroic held much interest for Adams" (*Henry Adams: Scientific Historian,* New Haven, Yale University Press, c1952, 20). This led to a fundamental attitude toward history. In a letter to Samuel Jones Tilden in 1883 he wrote: "My own conclusion is that history is simply social development along the lines of weakest resistance, and that in most cases the line of weakest resistance is found as unconsciously by society as by water" (Cater, 126). Levenson quotes from the *History* to show the same thing: "The scientific interest of American history centred in national character, and in the workings of a society destined to become vast, in which individuals were important chiefly as types" (124; *History,* IX, X, 222). No remark in any of Adams' works shows the contrary. He speaks, to be sure, of "my beloved Gibbon," but hardly more. In fact, in discussing his great friend Hay toward the end of the *Education* he exhibits if not malice at least doubt. Edmund Wilson says Adams intimated to a would-be biographer of Hay that "he had constantly betrayed this purpose [to provide a suitable memorial for him] by intimating in backhanded but unmistakable fashion his conviction that Hay was a mediocre person." (Introduction to Henry Adams, *The Life of George Cabot Lodge* [1911] in *The Shock of Recognition,* New York, Doubleday, Doran & Company, Inc., 1943, 744.)

13. Charles A. Beard wrote (1933) that three broad conceptions underlie history: (1) history as total actuality is chaos; (2) history as actuality is part of some order of nature and moves in cycles; and (3) history shows movement upward to more ideal order ("Written History as an Act of Faith," *American Historical Review,* XXXIX, 2 [January, 1934], 225–226). If "(1)" is true, one can only write *on* history, as Beard says. I think Henry Adams came to this position while writing his nine volumes.

14. Jacob E. Cooke, "Chats with Henry Adams," *American Heritage,* VII, 1 (December, 1955), 43. In a letter to Charles Milnes Gaskell in 1908 Adams made the same statement: "I cannot even rewrite a chapter without greatly changing it, and I think I never have written a chapter less than five times over, unless it

were from sheer collapse. If I went on forever, I should always do it differently, and of course each version is a correction" (Ford, II, 501).

15. Gaetano Salvemini begins his *Historian and Scientist: An Essay on the Nature of History and the Social Sciences* (Cambridge, Massachusetts, Harvard University Press, 1939) by saying, "Let us take as the starting point of our discussion of history and the social sciences the Aristotelian doctrine according to which intellectual activity is either scientific—if it aims at the ascertainment of truth; or aesthetic—if it has as its goal poetical creation; or practical—if it is directed toward action" (3). In this sense, Adams' *History* is "scientific" while *Chartres* is "aesthetic," for "poetry" is its impact. The *Education* may be considered "practical" though it is directed "indirectly" toward inaction.

16. Samuels says the initial draft of the book was finished in the fall of 1900, rewritten by April of 1902 (*The Major Phase*, 224, 254). Adams had worked on its materials since perhaps 1895 (Levenson, 235). It was completed by March 15, 1903, according to a letter Adams wrote to Elizabeth Cameron on that date: "My great work on the Virgin is complete even to the paging, and I've no occupation" (Ford, II, fn. 1, 403). It was not printed until 1904 and then only in a hundred copies. In 1912 at a request from Ralph Adams Cram of the American Institute of Architects, Adams allowed it to be printed for public circulation. It was rewritten in parts between these years.

The book dealt with a second choice of materials in a sense. Adams wrote Albert Stanburrough Cook in August of 1910, "The Chartres volume was the second in the series, and intended to fix a starting-point, since I could not get enough material to illustrate primitive society, or the society of the seventh century B. C., as I would have liked" ("Six Letters of Henry Adams," ed. A. S. Cook, *Yale Review*, X, 1 [October, 1920], 134). Or, as he said in another letter to Frederick Bliss Luquiens in July of 1910, "The next esoteric doctrine [to the twelfth century], as I feel it, belongs to Pythagoras and the Greeks, seven hundred years before Christ. I know of no other period which approached the same charm." (F. B. Luquiens, ed., "Seventeen Letters of Henry Adams," *Yale Review*, X, 1 [October, 1920], 113)

17. "The Skepticism at the House of Adams." *Main Currents in American Thought*, New York, Harcourt, Brace and Company, c1927, 1930, III, 221.

18. R. P. Blackmur has written, "For Henry, facts as such were nothing; the value they illustrated, the meaning they illuminated, everything" ("Henry and Brooks Adams: Parallels to Two Generations," *Southern Review*, V, 2 [Autumn, 1939], 309). Adams himself wrote to Henry Osborn Taylor in 1905, contrasting the purposes of his *Chartres* and Taylor's *The Medieval Mind*:

Your work is of a totally different kind. I have no object but a superficial one, as far as history is concerned. To me, accuracy is relative. I care very little whether my details are exact, if only my *ensemble* is in scale. You need to be thorough in your study and accurate in your statements. Your middle-ages exist for their own sake, not for ours. To me, who stand in gaping wonder before this preposterous spectacle of thought, and who can see nothing in all nature so iconoclastic, miraculous and anarchistic as Shakespeare, the middle-ages present a picture that has somehow to be brought into relation with ourselves. To you, there is no difficulty in transferring ourselves into the middle-ages. You require serious and complete study, and careful attention to details. Our two paths run in a manner parallel in reverse directions, but I can run and jump along mine, while you must employ a powerful engine to drag your load. I am glad to know that your engine is powerful enough (Cater, 559–560).

19. Adams had described a parallel to this episode in his 1891 poem "Buddha and Brahma" in which the Buddha when asked for final answers had merely raised the lotus in his hand, wordlessly.

20. Maurice DeWulf in his *Philosophy and Civilization in the Middle Ages* (Princeton University Press, c1922; New York, Dover Publications, Inc., c1953) says medieval thought produced the notion of individual feelings (55–56). If this is true, the medieval man must have been torn when he considered the possibility of Unity while also considering his own separate identity.

21. William Jordy notes that "To laugh and wonder why he laughed, such was Adams' fate. Hence the ambiguity in his historical speculations between the serious and the ironical" (162). I suggest Adams' purpose was to point up ambiguity.

22. In 1908, in writing to William James of *Chartres*, Adams said, "the last chapter is the only thing I ever wrote that I almost think good" (Ford, II, 490). He recognized, I think, the superior worth of his whole *Chartres*. His niece Mabel La Farge later printed a letter to her dated September 15, 1908. For a man so much given to exaggerated belittling of himself, it is a rare boast. He said, "I was at Chartres yesterday to see whether I myself had changed. The day was gorgeous, and the sun too strong for the glass. I saw nothing to correct. After some ten years of reflection, it seems to me I got it pretty right." (*Letters to a Niece and Prayer to the Virgin of Chartres by Henry Adams With A Niece's Memories*, Boston and New York, Houghton Mifflin Company, The Riverside Press Cambridge, 1920, 121)

23. Adams described Theodore Roosevelt in the *Education* as pure act also, a man without thought, and therefore by implication intellectually contemptible (417).

24. Bertrand Russell has written, "Aquinas' temperament is ratiocinative rather than mystical" (*A History of Western Philosophy*, New York, Simon and Schuster, 1945, 460). Etienne Gilson wrote in his *The Spirit of Mediaeval Philosophy* (Gifford Lectures, 1931–1932; New York, Charles Scribner's Sons, 1936, 1940):

> How far indeed in Thomist doctrine does God seem to recede from man and the world! The thirteenth century Augustinians felt it keenly, and that explains their often rather lively reactions against St. Thomas. However, St. Augustine's God does nothing that St. Thomas' God does not, and the Thomist creature can do more without God's aid than the Augustinian creature can. In both doctrines God produces all things, and creatures produce what they produce; the difference is that the Thomist God shows Himself more generous than St. Augustine's. Let us say, rather, since it comes to the same thing, that however great is God's generosity towards the world in Augustinianism, it is greater still in the philosophy of St. Thomas Aquinas. He has created an intellect which lacks nothing that it needs, and in particular lacks nothing needed for the exercise of its proper function: namely to know the truth (140–141).

25. II. Corinthians, 3, 18: "But we all, with open face beholding as in a glass

the glory of the Lord, are changed into the same image from glory to glory, even as by the Spirit of the Lord."

26. In 1895 Adams wrote his brother Brooks, "The Gothic always looks to me a little theatrical and false, like its roofs. The Gothic church, both in doctrine and in expression, is not my idea of a thoroughly happy illusion. It is always restless, grasping and speculative; it exploits the world, and makes profits; it is the legitimate parent of Lombard Street; the legitimate child of the Jews. The pointed arch is cheap. Still, it had very great beauties in its best time, and, as an artistic form of illusion, it gives me a sense of reflecting my own ideals and limitations. It is human . . ." (Ford, II, 80).

27. In the *Education* Adams also wrote, "To Adams she [the Virgin] became more than ever a channel of force; to St. Gaudens she remained as before a channel of taste" (387). In *Chartres* Adams emphasized "taste" and "sympathy." In the last section of the *Education*—the last two sections—his emphasis was on force. Reason and taste are human. Force is outside. It is a paradox still.

28. Thus the remark of a Catholic who read *Chartres* before going to see the cathedral; he warns readers against accepting the book as a reliable guide to it: "the Virgin Adams loved was not the Virgin of the Catholic Church. It was the synthetic Virgin of anti-Catholic prejudice, such a Virgin as was never known in Catholic devotion." The writer says Adams could not find the real Blessed Virgin because he had "never found her Son. He had no love of Christianity." He "takes a perverse delight in setting her as high above her Son as he can." The whole book "leaves us gasping at its blasphemy" (Hugh F. Blunt, "The Mal-Education of Henry Adams," *Catholic World*, 145 [April, 1937], 47, 49, 51).

29. Gilson says:

The Middle Ages that first appeared over the historical horizon was the Middle Ages of the romantics, a stirring, picturesque and brightly coloured world where saints and sinners jostled familiarly in the crowd, a world which expressed its deepest aspirations in architecture, sculpture and poetry. And that, too, is the Middle Ages of symbolism, where realities dissolved into the mystical meanings with which they were charged by artists and thinkers, so that the book of nature became a sort of Bible with things for words. Bestiaries, Mirrors of the World, stained glass, cathedral porches, each in its own way expressed a symbolic universe in which things, taken in their very essences, are merely so many expressions of God. But by a very natural reaction the study of the classical systems of the thirteenth century led historians to oppose to this poetical vision of the mediaeval world, the scientific and rational conception that presented itself in the writings of Robert Grosseteste, Roger Bacon and St. Thomas Aquinas. And this was entirely justifiable, in this sense at least, that from the thirteenth century onwards the universe of science begins to interpose between ourselves and the symbolic universe of the early Middle Ages; but it would be wrong to suppose that it suppressed it or even tended to suppress it. What really then took place was this: first, things, instead of being nothing more than symbols, became concrete beings which, above and beyond their own proper nature, were still charged with symbolic significances; and then, next, the analogy of the world to God, instead of being expressed only on the plane of imagery and feeling, was now formulated in precise laws and definite metaphysical conceptions. God in fact penetrated more deeply into nature as the depths of nature became better known. For a Bonaventure, for instance, there is no joy like the joy of contemplation of God as mirrored in the analogical structure of beings; and even the more sober mind of St. Thomas expresses, nevertheless, the same philosophy of nature when he reduces the efficacy of second causes to nothing but an analogical participation in the divine efficiency. Physical causality is to the act of creation what beings are to Being, and time to eternity. Thus, under whatever aspect we consider it, there exists in reality but one mediaeval vision of the world, whether it expresses itself now in works of art or now in defined philosophical concepts: that, namely, which St. Augustine drew with a master-hand in his *De Trinitate*, and which is directly referable to the words of the Book of Wisdom (xi, 21): *omnia in mensura, et numero, et pondere disposuisti*" (100–101).

30. See Perry Miller, "The New England Conscience," *American Scholar*, 28, 1 (Winter, 1958–1959). Miller says the *Education* "is another of these Puritan introversions, written under the compulsion of a conscience that can never rest until it exhausts its victim" (53).

31. Henry Osborn Taylor wrote in *The Atlantic Monthly* in October of 1918 (" 'The Education of Henry Adams,' " CXXII), "There was never a touch of cynicism or disillusionment in anything he [Adams] had to say of symbolical or dead women, any more than in his conversation with their living daughters" (486–487). Such a remark has been followed ever since by every writer on Adams, all of whom say Adams "worshipped woman." But as early as his "The Great Secession Winter of 1860–61" Adams made an anti-female remark: "He [Rep. Winter Davis of Maryland] was persecuted in every way that even female ingenuity could invent" (*The Great Secession Winter of 1860–61 and other Essays*, ed. George Hochfield, New York, Sagamore Press Inc., 1958, 17). This may be only a young man's remark. But Adams continued to say things of this sort.

32. In his "Primitive Rights of Women" (1876) Adams had said, speaking of Homer's Penelope, "The whole story both of the Iliad and the Odyssey is little more than a running commentary on the Greek law of marriage" (*Historical Essays*, 17). And further he declared that Penelope though urged by her brothers, father and son to wed again, "paid no attention to the opinions or wishes of any one. . . . She was perfectly independent" (23). Though Adams meant to emphasize the strong legal position Penelope held in Greek society as a woman, he also indicated that serene disregard for the views and desires of men that he later showed characterized the Virgin Mary, a female quality of a "peculiar" sort.

A pertinent comment on this Virgin Mary that Adams presented is made by Henry Miller:

> There are few among us today who are able to view the immediate future with anything but fear and apprehension. If there is one book among all those I have recently read which I might signal as containing words of comfort, peace, inspiration and sublimity, it is Henry Adams' *Mont-Saint-Michel and Chartres*. Particularly the chapters dealing with Chartres and the cult of the Virgin Mary. Every reference to the "Queen" is exalted and commanding. Let me quote a passage.

("Preface," *The Books in My Life*, Norfolk, Connecticut, [London, Peter Owens,

Limited, 1952, 1961], 20) Had Miller read *Chartres* as I do, the "words of comfort, peace, inspiration and sublimity" might well have turned sour.

33. In the "Primitive Rights of Woman" Adams said the Church had to disfavor the woman because of her corruption in the late Roman Empire. It inculcated duties in women, not rights. It made them more and more dependent on the Church. It set up as a standard not the Hallgerdas, Brunhildas, Fredegundas, but the patient Griseldas (*Historical Essays*, 36–38).

34. In a letter to Elizabeth Cameron February 18, 1901, he said he would send her the poem presently (Ford, II, 317). It was published in 1920 by Mabel La Farge in her *Letters to a Niece and Prayer to the Virgin of Chartres*, pp. 125–134.

35. The book was published as *Esther: A Novel* with the pseudonym Francis Snow Compton on the title page by Henry Holt & Company in 1884 (reprinted with an Introduction by Robert E. Spiller, New York, Scholars' Facsimiles and Reprints, 1938). The actual authorship was not revealed until Henry Holt told of it in his autobiography in 1923, *Garrulities of an Octogenarian Editor* (Boston and New York, Houghton Mifflin Company, 1923, 138).

Adams' choice of the name "Esther Dudley" is a puzzle. R. P. Blackmur declared Adams wrote *Esther* as his version of the old Nathaniel Hawthorne story of Esther Dudley that appeared in "Legends of the Province House." Hawthorne depicted an old spinster who preserved the Province House in Boston, the seat of the English colonial governors, long after the Revolutionary War, hoping for their return. As Hawthorne's old Esther waited for someone to bring back the old "faith" in the reign of English imperialists, so Adams showed that his Esther wished to restore the conventional faith represented by her suitor, Stephen Hazard. ("The Novels of Henry Adams," *Sewanee Review*, LI, 2 [April–June, 1943], 297–299). J. C. Levenson says much the same thing, that Adams' Esther is like Hawthorne's, a "spinster defender of an integrity passing out of fashion" (200). I am not satisfied with these explanations, but I can suggest no other much more acceptable unless it is that Adams means the name to be ironic as the names of Strong and Hazard are. Perhaps a memory of the Biblical Esther helps sense.

36. Strong is one of those nineteenth-century minds which "refuses to be interested in what it cannot understand; a violent reaction from the thirteenth century which cared little to comprehend anything except the incomprehensible" (*Chartres*, 109).

37. His niece Mabel La Farge discovered it there and sent it to his family, "who," Adams wrote Elizabeth Cameron, "only said: *'Tiens! il se croit poëte!'* which he don't, but the fun must be in the fact that they never saw the Chartres or heard of the Saint Vierge. I honestly believe they never read a word of me either." (Letter to Elizabeth Cameron, December 18, 1915, Ford, II, 632.) The full reference for the poem is *Yale Review*, V, I (October, 1915), 82–89.

38. That it does, I think, serve to show with astonishing fullness his private explanation of the death of his wife and his own reaction to the event, is not relevant to my present study. See my "The Lotus of Henry Adams," *The New England Quarterly*, XXVII, 1 (March, 1954), 75–95.

39. See Edward J. Thomas, "Buddha and Buddhism," *Encyclopaedia Britannica* (1949 edition), IV, 326.

40. In a Buddhistic sense the lotus has this symbolic meaning, as one writer

explains it: "In the Samyutta Nikaya and elsewhere a comparison occurs between the Buddha and the flowers: as the lotus grows up in the water from which it is born, rises above it, and ceases to be sullied by it, thus the Buddha grows above the world and is no longer defiled by it." (A. Berriedale Keith, "Buddhist Mythology in India and Tibet," in Louis H. Gray, *The Mythology of All the Races*, Boston, Marshall Jones Co., 1917, VI, 191.)

41. Alfred North Whitehead in *Science and the Modern World* (1925) makes a curiously parallel statement: "An unflinching determination to take the whole evidence into account is the only preservation against the fluctuating extremes of fashionable opinion. This advice seems so easy, and is in fact so difficult to follow." He then added the revealing and Adams-like statement, "One reason for this difficulty is that we cannot think first and act afterwards" (New York, Macmillan Company; reprinted, New York, Mentor Books, New American Library of World Literature, Inc., 1948, 186).

Chapter 3

1. A letter to Lodge dated March 1, 1915, shows Adams wrote the Preface and attached Lodge's name (Cater, 770).
2. Cater, 646. "The last three chapters of each [the *Education* and *Chartres*] make one didactic work in disguise."
3. *The Degradation of the Democratic Dogma*, 6.
4. Letter to Margaret Chanler, September 9, 1909 (Ford, II, 524).
5. *Ibid.*, 445. See other letters containing expressions of this idea: to John Hay in January, 1891 (Cater, 235); to Brooks Adams in June, 1895 (Ford, II, 70); to Mabel Hooper La Farge in January, 1896 (Cater, 358); and again to Brooks Adams in August, 1899 (Cater, 475).
6. Henry Adams was a good deal smaller than his brothers, shorter by "two or three inches in height" (*Education*, 6). It interests me to ponder the effects on his mental growth of his scarlet fever at the age of nearly four (December, 1841), a disease that seems to have dwarfed him though it hardly shortened his life. At the beginning of the *Education* he said, "As a means of variation from a normal type, sickness in childhood ought to have a certain value not to be classed under any fitness or unfitness of natural selection; and especially scarlet fever affected boys seriously, both physically and in character, though they might through life puzzle themselves to decide whether it had fitted or unfitted them for success" (*Ibid.*). Because of this lag in his start, he says the result made him not the typical New England character but the variation.
7. To call the figure Henry Adams depicted picaresque goes too far, but the word does suggest one characteristic the picaresque hero has that Adams reveals, and that is a figure to whom things happen, a victim of destiny more than one who manages it.
8. Adams does not agree with me in words. In *Chartres* he said, "nothing proves that the greatest artists who ever lived have, in a logical sense, understood!" (159). Elsewhere he indicates that artists do not "know" what they are up to. The catch is of course the phrase "logical sense" which is not to say the artist did not understand, that their minds were not in operation. No one "understands." Logic is a limited tool.

9. R. P. Blackmur, speaking both of Henry Adams' *Education* and of Henry James' *Notes of a Son and Brother,* says, "Both men were concerned with experience as education, and to both the judgment of education called for a specialized form of autobiography in which the individual was suppressed in the act only to be caught in the style." Blackmur concludes with saying, "Our ends resort to their means; constantly the pattern, like character, of which it is the inert form, reasserts itself, until in the end nothing but pattern is left—and character only its last sophistication" ("Henry Adams: Three Late Moments," 16, 29).

10. In the letter to William James in 1908 Adams wrote that "St. Augustine alone has an idea of literary form,—a notion of writing a story with an end and object, not for the sake of the object, but for the form, like a romance. I have worked ten years to satisfy myself that the thing cannot be done today. The world does not furnish the contrasts or the emotion. If you will read my *Chartres,*—the last chapter is the only thing I ever wrote that I almost think good,—you will see why I knew my *Education* to be rotten" (Ford, II, 490). Levenson comments, "In short, art took precedence over autobiography in his personal narrative. If Rousseau was an admitted model of his form, he was also the anti-model of his didactic content" (306). Whatever Levenson meant by the last part of his comment, the first sentence is sound enough.

11. So, Adams discovered, did the members of his 1858 Harvard class: "They were pleasant to live with . . . chiefly because each individual appeared satisfied to stand alone. It seemed a sign of force; yet to stand alone is quite natural when one has no passions; still easier when one has no pains" (*Education,* 56).

12. *Webster's New Collegiate Dictionary* and *The Shorter Oxford English Dictionary.*

13. Much earlier, in his 1876 "Primitive Rights of Women," Adams had been much more conventional and perhaps more Marxian. "All new discoveries in the record of human development point to the familiar facts that the most powerful instincts in man are his affections and his love of property" (*Historical Essays,* 40).

14. In the unpublished introductory letter that accompanied the copy of "The Rule of Phase Applied to History" which he sent to George Cabot Lodge, dated January 1, 1909, Adams wrote very plainly, in a manner not employed in the *Education,* "the lay-figure, the manikin, had no education, since the Universities of his time were a hundred years behind the level of his needs, and the technical schools at least fifty; but . . . the technical schools had the advantage of unity and energy of purpose." He continued in a manner much more like that of the *Education* and even more like the seeming giddiness of the "Rule" and the "Letter": "After illustrating this statement in a great variety of ways, through some four hundred pages, the book closes by a belabored effort to state the problem, for its special domain of history, in a scientific formula, which affects the terms of astronomy merely because every child is supposed to know the so-called law, as well as the fact, of gravitation" (Cater, 782). What relation astronomy has to gravitation one must apparently ask every child. Adults do not know.

15. To Margaret Chanler in 1909 Adams wrote, "I like best Bergson's frank surrender to the superiority of Instinct over Intellect. You know how I have

preached that principle, and how I have studied the facts of it. In fact I wrote once a whole volume—called my *Education* . . . in order to recall how Education may be shown to consist in following the intuitions of instinct. Loeb calls it *Tropism*, I believe; which means that a mother likes to nurse her own child" (Ford, II, 524).

16. Adams wrote, "The boy might ignore, as a mere historical puzzle, the question how to deduce George Washington from the sum of all wickedness, but he had himself helped to deduce Charles Sumner from the sum of political corruption" (50). Still Sumner was like most others in Adams' experience: he shifted and dwindled; (See also, *Education*, 76 and 275).

17. This is a more abstract statement than one occurring in Chapter VIII: "patience was the last resource of fools as well as of sages" (*Ibid.*, 117).

18. As early as 1890 a reviewer in *The Atlantic Monthly* of Adams' first two volumes of his *History* declared, "He seems to like to express the truth through negatives, and he makes his chief object the furnishing antidotes to the somewhat exaggerated praises of which other writers have been undoubtedly over-liberal" ("Recent Books on American History" LXV, 338 [February, 1890], 275).

19. In a suggestive article entitled "Henry Adams and Lincoln Steffens" published in 1949, John Lydenberg says that both Adams and Steffens are naturalists in the fundamental sense. They had "a feeling that the conventional dogmas had failed as explanations of the life and society of the time." Thus they presented to readers amoral descriptions of an immoral world, though it is one that they and other naturalists don't like any more than other people. He explained that Adams, as well as other naturalists, though amoral, dealt with moral problems basically in broad ethical concepts. As naturalistic novels boiled over into muckraking and reform novels, so naturalistic investigations such as those of Adams and Steffens "led them to seek a new way of life, a new faith. The naturalist philosophy was one of transition and readjustment, a way station between the unacceptable old and the uncharted new." Such men are negative in form but not in basic intent. "Naturalism was an expression of the moral bewilderment of people facing a world for which they were not prepared" (*South Atlantic Quarterly*, 48 [January, 1949], 43, 47, 61–62, 64).

20. But who is genius? Kipling perhaps. It could be that recognition of genius accounted for Adams' sense of being apart. "Perhaps, after all, it was only that genius soars," he said later; then he added stoutly, "but this theory, too, had its dark corners." Adams never easily admitted genius.

In speaking of Kipling, Adams produced the only sentence in the *Education* that falters:

> Rudyard Kipling, on his wedding trip to America, thanks to the mediation of Henry James, dashed over the passenger his exuberant fountain of gaiety and wit—as though playing a garden hose on a thirsty and faded begonia (319).

The remarkable fact is that this funny sentence is the only such I have found —unwitting humor of an ordinary kind. (But what if it were true that Henry James helped Kipling so and did not just introduce Adams to Kipling?) Some others have noticed this odd sentence too: Robert A. Hume, "The Style and Literary Background of Henry Adams: With Attention to *The Education of Henry Adams*," *American Literature*, 16 (1945), 307 (but he does not see the inserted Henry James phrase as odd) ; Joseph Mindell, "The Uses of Metaphor: Henry Adams and the Symbols of Science," *Journal of the History of Ideas,* XXVI, 1 (January–March, 1965), 93, fn. 9.

21. Charles Francis Adams, Henry's oldest brother, after the Civil War engaged himself in railroading, becoming president of the Union Pacific Railroad. His *Autobiography,* however, published in 1916, shows the dismal fact that it was a thin experience, for his conclusion was "a less interesting crowd [his big business associates] I do not care to encounter . . . . they were essentially unattractive and uninteresting." (*An Autobiography 1835–1915,* Boston & New York, Houghton Mifflin Company, Riverside Press Cambridge, 1916, 190).

22. Jordy says "This interest in public morality remained throughout [his] life" (65). Adams' interest in Randolph, Burr and Napoleon were three studies in public morality. Jordy adds a bit later, "The nine volumes [of the *History*] remain the greatest moral history ever produced in America" (67). Jordy seems to say Adams deplored immorality, but he does not say what proper morality was to Adams.

23. The scientist Edgar Zilsel wrote in 1941, "the more incomplete our knowledge of the initial conditions is, the more difficult is discovery of laws. We shall be very modest, therefore, in our expectations regarding historical laws" ("Physics and the Problem of Historico-sociological Laws," *Philosophy of Science,* 8, 4 [October, 1941], 568). Mr. Zilsel is a good deal more modest in his ambition than Henry Adams was. Adams was deeply distressed by this situation. As Paul Elmer More wrote in 1920, "By education Adams meant not at all the mere accumulation of knowledge, of which, nevertheless, he had abundance, but that insight into the nature of things which should enable a man to know what the world is and what he himself is, and so to adjust his life to the forces that play upon it" (*Commemorative Tribute to Henry Adams,* New York, American Academy of Arts and Letters, 1922, 5.

24. This is a case of underplay. Adams taught by contradiction: Henry Cabot Lodge noted later in commenting on Adams' teaching at Harvard, "He had the power not only of exciting interest, but he awakened opposition to his own views, and that is one great secret of success in teaching" (*Early Memories,* New York, Charles Scribner's Sons, c1913, 1925, 187). The success of *Mont-Saint-Michel and Chartres* and of the *Education,* to say nothing of the "Rule" and the "Letter" is largely dependent on an "awakened opposition," I think.

25. Thurman Wilkins, *Clarence King: A Biography* (New York, Macmillan, 1958).

26. In a letter to James Ford Rhodes in 1908, Adams described the *Education* as a "centipede" that crawled twenty sections downhill and fifteen sections up a little for the view (Levenson, 326, from a letter in the Library of the Massachusetts Historical Society). As I see it, the first twenty chapters go downhill as they accumulate failures of education; the final fifteen go up as they retreat into more and more abstract theory.

27. "The St. Gaudens Monument at Rock Creek Cemetery," *The Atlantic Monthly,* CXX (November, 1917), 607.

28. William Roscoe Thayer, *The Life and Letters of John Hay* (Boston and New York, Houghton Mifflin Company, c1908, 1915), II, 61.

29. Letter to Elizabeth Cameron, April 19, 1903, in Ford, II, 407.

30. Homer Saint-Gaudens reproduced a poem on the figure by Hildegard Haw-

thorne in his *Reminiscences of Augustus Saint-Gaudens* (New York, The Century Co., 1913, I, 363). It was admired by his father, Homer Saint-Gaudens said:

NIRVANA

Yea, I have lived! Pass on
And trouble me with questions nevermore.
I suffered. I have won
A solemn peace—my peace forevermore.
Leave me in silence here.
I have no hope, no care,
I know no fear:
For I have borne—but now no longer bear.

Deep-hid Sorrow calls me kin,
But my calm she cannot break.
I know not good—I know not sin—
No love, nor hate can me awake.

Though I have sought, I care not now to find.
If I have asked, I wait for no reply.
My eyes, from too much seeing, are grown blind.
I am not dead, yet do not need to die.
Pass on. Ye cannot reach me any more.
Pass on—for all is past!
Hush—Silence settled ever more and more,
Silence and night at last!

31. Ernst Scheyer, the art historian, says of it, "it is plurasign, not monosign and has therefore not one meaning but many" ("The Adams Memorial by Augustus Saint-Gaudens," *Art Quarterly*, XIX, 2 [Summer, 1956], 195).

32. Maurice F. Neufeld supplies one explanation for this remark, saying Adams meant that with William Dean Howells he "saw the Fair of 1893 as a great landmark in the history of the decline of *laissez-faire* as the dominant American philosophy and as a landmark in the beginning of a planned civilization in the United States." The White City was "planned and administered to the last detail" ("The Crisis in Prospect: Henry Adams and the White City," *American Scholar*, 4, 4 [Autumn, 1935,] 397). I doubt this political or economic view is the limited one Adams had in mind.

33. Alfred North Whitehead has written, "The Gospel of Force is incompatible with a social life. By *force*, I mean *antagonism* in its most general sense" (*Science and the Modern World*, 207). What he means is only vaguely clear to me.

34. A few commentators and critics of Henry Adams have in a sense met Adams on these terms, seeing the genuine "quality" behind the commonly-seen fooling. One is James Stone who wrote in 1941:

The nearest he came to a personal solution was sincere humility before what he did not know, and a determined and persistent effort to play what he, like Melville and the pragmatists, conceived to be the human game—to keep acting and searching. . . . But to keep searching [though blocked by Mystery] was a human fate which was an expression itself of the energetic restlessness of force beyond; to succumb was to acknowledge a sort of intellectual adolescence which sought to comfort itself in the fond belief that it knew all.

("Henry Adams's Philosophy of History," *New England Quarterly*, XIV, 3 [September, 1941], 547). Stuart P. Sherman, writing in 1923, says also in his "Evolution in the Adams Family" that Adams' real lesson is that his refusal to settle anywhere is balanced by his realization that he would not find his lofty answer; that (the message Sherman drew from the St. Gaudens statue in Washington) "Man is the animal that destiny cannot break" (*Americans*, New York, Charles Scribner's Sons, 1923, 315). A more direct and, I think, convincing episode is related by Owen Wister who, in talking with Adams in 1912, reports that he told Adams he refused to see the future as black as Adams did. Adams suddenly softened, "and in a voice quite changed" said, "Keep the faith!" Wister commented, "I am not sure what he meant; but he had wholly dropped his pose, and was for the moment a different Henry Adams, perhaps the real Henry Adams." (*Roosevelt: The Story of a Friendship, 1880–1919*, New York, Macmillan Company, 1930, 152–153)

35. Havelock Ellis in his essay on Nietzsche wrote, "He held that polytheism had played an important part in the evolution of culture. Gods, heroes, supernatural beings generally, were inestimable schoolmasters to bring us to the sovereignty of the individual. . . . But it has not been so with monotheism. The doctrine of a single God, in whose presence all others were false gods, favours stagnation and unity of type; monotheism has thus perhaps constituted 'the greatest danger which humanity has had to meet in past ages.' Nor are we yet freed from its influence" (*Affirmations* [1898], Boston and New York, Houghton Mifflin Company, 1922, 53–54). It seems to me Adams hinted at the same notion. And thus he created yet another paradox of thought, for here unity would seem decadence and degradation whereas multiplicity would be a superior state.

36. Three and a half decades before, John Fiske in a long review article called "The Laws of History" had said that man's mind had successfully reacted to new force. He was hopeful, confident, comforting. He wrote to show that "progress has been on the whole the most prominent feature of the history of a considerable and important portion of mankind," that "The advance to higher forms of life consists in the orderly establishment of internal relations of sequence answering to external relations of coexistence and sequence, that are continually more heterogeneous, more remote in space and in time, and at once more general and more special; until at last we reach civilized man, whose intelligence responds to every variety of external stimulus, whose most ordinary needs are supplied by apparatus of amazing complexity, and whose mental sequences are often determined by circumstances as different as the Milky Way, and as ancient as the birth of the solar system." He added, "The history of scientific progress is in like manner [increased ability of society to adapt itself to emergencies which beset it] the history of an advance toward complete correspondence between our conceptions and outward realities." He concluded his essay by saying that the social life of man as it grew higher and more complex at the same time

freed the individual more and more. This is all consistent with the "harmony of the world" (*North American Review*, CIX [1869], 199, 219, 221–222, 229–230). What is lacking in Fiske's view is any notion of vast acceleration or of sudden leaps in the release of force or "external stimulus." His faith is in "immutable law" and "orderly sequence."

37. Frederick I. Carpenter suggests three puns might be intended for "Nunc Age": "Thus his punning use of 'AGE' first implied 'old age'; second, ironically, 'act'; but third, seriously, 'learn to "react" to the new age'" ("Three AGE's of Henry Adams," *College English*, 15, 3 [December, 1953], 149). Any one or all possibilities of meaning are credible, most probably all.

Chapter 4

1. *The Selected Letters of Henry Adams*, xxx.

2. (And Henry Adams was only five feet three inches tall.) In Adams' favor it can be said mildly enough that more than a half century's progress since Adams wrote his absurd essays shows no evidence historians and scientists have either one approached a solution to the problem he raised, nor have they moved much closer towards making an arrangement with one another. C. P. Snow's *The Two Cultures: And A Second Look* (New York, The New American Library, a Mentor Book, 1959, 1963) only emphasizes the split.

3. "The Tendency of History" was published with the "Rule" and the "Letter" by Brooks Adams in *The Degradation of the Democratic Dogma* in 1919.

4. Edgar Zilsel says, "History . . . must never be compared to laboratory physics. It compares only to geophysics, i.e., to physics of earthquakes and sea-currents, to volcanology and meteorology." But he adds a question that Adams would find support in I think: "What would scientists think of a geophysicist who gives up the search for geophysical laws because of their inexactness?" (570)

5. Alfred North Whitehead in his *Science and the Modern World* (1925) wrote,
   There is, however, a Nemesis which waits upon those who deliberately avoid avenues of knowledge. Oliver Cromwell's cry echoes down the ages, "My brethren, by the bowels of Christ I beseech you, bethink you that you may be mistaken."
   The progress of science has now reached a turning point. The stable foundations of physics have broken up: also for the first time physiology is asserting itself as an effective body of knowledge, as distinct from a scrap-heap. The old foundations of scientific thought are becoming unintelligible. Time, space, matter, material, ether, electricity, mechanism, organism, con-figuration, structure, pattern, function, all require reinterpretation. What is the sense of talking about mechanical explanation when you do not know what you mean by mechanics? (17–18). (Cf., *Education*, 456.)

6. The remarks of several writers are apropos here. William James on his re-ceipt of a copy of the "Letter" in 1910 revealed a disapproval only developed by Jordy, Levenson and Samuels. He wrote to Adams (a remark frequently quoted to Adams' disadvantage), "it doesn't impress me at all, save by its wit and erudition; and I ask you whether an old man soon about to meet his Maker can hope to save himself from the consequences of his life by pointing to the wit and learning he has shown in treating a tragic subject. No, sir, you

can't do it, can't impress God in that way" (*Letters of William James,* ed. Henry James, Boston, Atlantic Monthly Press, 1920, II, 344).

Some other writers do in varying degrees support my interpretation. One is Roy F. Nichols who in his article "The Dynamic Interpretation of History" published in 1935 presented an excellent summation of the state of scientific thought of that year. He said Adams' challenge to seek a dynamic interpretation, a law for history, still stands, but his own formula must be discarded: biology and psychology, not physics, will help the most (*The New England Quarterly,* VIII, 2 [June, 1935], 163–178). Adams, however, did not neglect to mention these other sciences and their possible contribution to a science of history though he did emphasize physics principally. Considering its current prominence he did well to put the burden on it, perhaps.

Robert A. Hume stated in 1951 that Adams' "dynamic theory of history was, as will be seen, a logical failure in its violent (and deliberate) misapplication of the rules of physics to human affairs; but artistically it was a metaphorical triumph. . . . The fitness of the result poetically redeems the daring illogic of the method" (*Runaway Star: An Appreciation of Henry Adams,* 37).

Howard M. Munford in 1959 wrote, "Re-reading *The Tendency . . . A Letter . . .* and *The Rule . . .* in the light of these hints helps to bring into focus the grim humor and the elaborate irony which are not only their particular traits but perhaps their chief point" ("Henry Adams and the Tendency of History," *The New England Quarterly,* XXXII, 1 [March, 1959], 80).

Joseph Mindel in 1965 wrote that Adams' approach to his public was "through the metamorphic link between history and science," and that "for his purpose, he knew enough science." He further explains his interpretation, saying, "The metaphor should be seen in its most inclusive, most general form: as the laws of science provide unifying principles for understanding and explaining the natural universe, so historical laws can be discovered to rationalize the social universe" (100–102).

7. In the *Education* Adams spoke of Karl Pearson's having cut "science adrift on a sensual raft in the midst of a supersensual chaos" (452). I assume he thought of "chaos" and "ether" as synonymous in this regard.

8. It is doubtful that (pure) mathematicians enjoyed being classed with metaphysicians, yet in our day many do admit the close relationship. (And there are the older examples of Russell and Whitehead.) Both fields of study engage in abstractions; both fields deal with actual immeasurables. Do both also found themselves as they seem to on a firm faith in their own validity? Adams meant, I think, to point up the endless persistence of man's desire for unity. In *Chartres* he had said, "Man is an imperceptible atom always trying to become one with God," and he continued, "If ever modern science achieves a definition of energy, possibly it may borrow the figure: Energy is the inherent effort of every multiplicity to become unity" (328). In the *Education* and the final essays he declared the exact opposite in many places—unless even in 1904 he meant the unity would end as Entropy.

Oppenheimer wrote in 1959, "There is a lot of relation in this world of science. It has structure, and refers to a beautifully ordered world." But he also said the specialist finds it increasingly difficult to communicate to the layman—that, for example, the biologist may shortly understand "What is life?" but only the few will see it. It is sad to think that the "beautifully ordered world" will be understood only by a few. In Adams' attempts sixty years ago to understand the relatively simpler science of his day he found that as a layman, even then, he came up with baffled misunderstanding (Robert Oppenheimer, "Tradition and Discovery," *ACLS Newsletter*, X, 8 [October, 1959], 12, 13).

9. Oppenheimer wrote also, "Today, it can hardly be doubted . . . that every ten years or so we know twice as much of such knowledge as we did ten years earlier" (*Ibid.*, 10). But what, one asks today, of Einstein's pure mathematical formula "$E = MC^2$"? It provided a recipe for the atom bomb. The point is that wrong as Adams may have been in his facts (as Jordy and others clearly show), these facts are *images* that in general reflect Adams' realization of the need for inconclusion, for suspension, for humor.

10. The passage reads like Adams but is from an editorial in *Life* in 1957 called "A Crisis in Science" (42, 4 [January 28], 28). The phrase "vast jumbles of new numbers, all with an insulting lack of obvious meaning" is Robert Oppenheimer's.

11. Chapel Hill, University of North Carolina Press, 122.

12. Whitehead presented a very different attitude towards the developments in science in 1925. He wrote:

> Faith in reason is the trust that the ultimate natures of things lie together in a harmony which excludes mere arbitrariness. It is the faith that at the base of things we shall not find mere arbitrary mystery. The faith in the order of nature which has made possible the growth of science is a particular example of a deeper faith. This faith cannot be justified by any inductive generalisation. It springs from direct inspection of the nature of things as disclosed in our own immediate present experience. There is no parting from your own shadow. To experience this faith is to know that in being ourselves we are more than ourselves: to know that our experience, dim and fragmentary as it is, yet sounds the utmost depths of reality: to know that detached details merely in order to be themselves demand that they should find themselves in a system of things: to know that this system includes the harmony of logical rationality, and the harmony of aesthetic achievement: to know that, while the harmony of logic lies upon the universe as an iron necessity, the aesthetic harmony stands before it as a living ideal moulding the general flux in its broken progress towards finer, subtler issues (*Science and the Modern World*, 19–20).

I think that in view of Adams' thought this is shallow, although Whitehead's suggestion of a possible "harmony of aesthetic achievement" would have won Adams' artistic approval. But Adams' reliance on reason was not a faith in it; as far as his thinking progressed, ultimate harmony, if there is any, pointed to entropy. His reaction to Whitehead's comforting and somewhat smug faith in the "harmony of logical rationality" would have been skepticism. It is not surprising to see such a faith as Whitehead describes must be the stimulus for scientific growth.

13. As late as 1937 Charles A. Beard and Alfred Vagts wrote that historiography must discard words borrowed from other fields like optics, civil engineering,

etc., and "employ a terminology appropriate to, corresponding to, its own subject matter. . . . This operation will dispose of a number of projects that have loomed large in recent historical thought. It will consign to the realm of curiosities Henry Adams' 'Letter to American Teachers of History' (1910) on the 'rule of phase' applied to history, in which he sought to apply a theory of general physics to history as actuality" ("Currents of Thought in Historiography," *American Historical Review*, XLII, 3 [April, 1937], 478). Beard and Vagts in this instance are like Mr. Jordy too literal; and they have mistaken the "Letter" for the separate 1909 essay, the "Rule."

14. Adams' well-known dismissal of Emerson's thought, his "less aggressive protest" as "*naif*" (*Education*, 35), is nowhere more clearly explained than here. In his initial book *Nature* (1836) Emerson had introduced his subject with the simple definition of nature as the "not me." Adams and the twentieth century are quick to raise the obvious doubt about the distinction between the "me" and the "not me." One strong and solid effect of Adams' *Education* and his final essays is to show how science has increasingly magnified the not me at the expense of the me.

15. In a letter of August 6, 1910, Adams wrote, "In other words, I am a creature of poor old Calvinist, St. Augustinian fathers, and am not afraid to carry out my logic to the rigorous end of regarding our present society, its ideals and purposes, as dregs and fragments of some primitive, essential instinct now nearly lost. If you are curious to see the theory stated as official instruction, you have only to look over Bergson's 'Evolution Créatrice.' (pp. 228, 289)" (Cook, ed., "Six Letters of Henry Adams," 134).

16. This is a twist on Adams' old dictum that man should act, not think, for thought prevents and paralyzes action. It is Theodore Roosevelt again, or Napoleon, Garibaldi, or Grant perhaps. In Adams' terms thought does weaken will because reflection produces hesitation.

17. Joseph Wood Krutch, "Is the Common Man Too Common?" in book of the same title, Norman, University of Oklahoma Press, c1954.

18. In a letter to Henry Osborn Taylor, January 17, 1905, Adams made a comment that ends on the usual shock note: "I am trying to work out the formula of anarchism; the law of expansion from unity, simplicity, morality, to multiplicity, contradiction, police" (Cater, 558).

19. *Letters to a Niece and Prayer to the Virgin of Chartres*, 18.

Bibliography

The following bibliography of books and articles lists only those items directly referred to in the text or cited in the footnotes. No complete bibliography on Henry Adams has yet been compiled. For additional references the reader may most helpfully consult those bibliographies provided in their respective books by Hume (1951), Jordy (1952), Stevenson (1956), Levenson (1957) and Samuels (1948, 1958, 1964).

Adams, Brooks, *The Law of Civilization and Decay: An Essay on History,* London, 1895; New York, The Macmillan Company, c1896, 1897.

Adams, Charles Francis, Jr., *An Autobiography 1835–1915,* Boston and New York, Houghton Mifflin Company, The Riverside Press, Cambridge, 1916.

Adams, Henry, "Buddha and Brahma," *Yale Review,* V, 1 (October 1915), 82–89.

——, *The Degradation of the Democratic Dogma,* with an Introduction by Brooks Adams, New York, The Macmillan Company, 1919; reprinted, New York, G. P. Putnam's Sons, Capricorn Books, 1958.

—— (anonymous), *Democracy: An American Novel,* New York, Henry Holt and Company, 1880, 1933.

——, *The Education of Henry Adams: An Autobiography,* Boston, Houghton Mifflin Company, 1918; reprinted as *The Education of Henry Adams,* New York, Modern Library, 1931; as *The Education of Henry Adams: An Autobiography,* Houghton Mifflin Company, Sentry Edition, 1961.

—— (Frances Snow Compton), *Esther: A Novel* (New York, Henry Holt and Company, 1884); reprinted with an Introduction by Robert E. Spiller, New York, Scholars' Facsimiles & Reprints, 1938.

——, "The Great Secession Winter of 1860–61" (first published in the *Proceedings* of the Massachusetts Historical Society, 1909–1910, 43, 660–687), *The Great*

Bibliography

Secession Winter of 1860–61 and Other Essays, ed. George Hochfield, New York, Sagamore Press Inc., 1958, 3–33.

——, *Henry Adams and His Friends: A Collection of His Unpublished Letters*, compiled, with a Biographical Introduction by Harold Dean Cater, Boston, Houghton Mifflin Company, The Riverside Press Cambridge, 1947.

——, *Historical Essays*, New York, Charles Scribner's Sons, 1891.

——, *History of the United States of America*, 9 vols, London, G. P. Putnam's Sons, 1890–1891, 1920; New York, Charles Scribner's Sons, 1921.

——, *John Randolph*, Boston and New York, Houghton Mifflin Company, The Riverside Press Cambridge, 1882, 1898.

——, *Letters of Henry Adams (1858–1891)*, ed., Worthington Chauncey Ford, Boston and New York, Houghton Mifflin Company, 1930.

——, *Letters of Henry Adams (1892–1918)*, ed., Worthington Chauncey Ford, Boston and New York, Houghton Mifflin Company, 1938.

——, *The Life of Albert Gallatin*, Philadelphia, Lippincott and Company, 1879.

——, *The Life of George Cabot Lodge* (1911), in Edmund Wilson, ed. *The Shock of Recognition: The Development of Literature in the United States Recorded by the Men Who Made It*, New York, Doubleday, Doran & Company Inc., 1943; New York, Farrar, Straus and Cudahy, 1955, 747–852.

——, *Mont-Saint-Michel and Chartres*, Boston, Houghton Mifflin Company, The Riverside Press Cambridge, 1912, 1933, 1963 (Sentry Edition).

——, *The Selected Letters of Henry Adams*, ed. with an Introduction by Newton Arvin, New York, Farrar, Straus and Young, Inc., c1951.

——, "Seventeen Letters of Henry Adams," ed., Frederick Bliss Luquiens, *Yale Review*, X, 1 (October 1920), 111–130.

——, "Six Letters of Henry Adams," ed., Arthur Stanburrough Cook, *Yale Review*, X, 1 (October 1920), 131–140.

Beard, Charles A., "Written History As an Act of Faith," *American Historical Review*, XXXIX, 2 (January 1934), 219–229.

—— and Alfred Vagts, "Currents of Thought in Historiography," *American Historical Review*, XLII, 3 (April 1937), 460–483.

Beerbohm, Max, "Laughter (1920)," *And Even Now*, New York, E. P. Dutton & Co., 1921, 303–320.

Blackmur, R. P., "Adams Goes to School: I. The Problem Laid Out," *Kenyon Review*, XVII, 4 (Autumn 1955), 597–623.

——, "The Expense of Greatness: Three Emphases on Henry Adams," *The Expense of Greatness*, New York, Arrow Editions, c1940, 253–276.

——, "Henry Adams: Three Late Moments," *Kenyon Review*, II, 1 (Winter 1940), 7–29.

——, "Henry and Brooks Adams: Parallels to Two Generations," *Southern Review*, V, 2 (Autumn 1939), 308–334.

——, "The Novels of Henry Adams," *Sewanee Review*, LI, 2 (April–June 1943), 281–304.

Blunt, Hugh F., "The Mal-Education of Henry Adams," *Catholic World*, 145 (April 1937), 46–52.

Bredvold, Louis I, Alan D. McKillop, Lois Whitney, eds., *Eighteenth Century Poetry and Prose*, New York, The Ronald Press Company, c1939.

Carpenter, Frederick I., "Three AGE's of Henry Adams," *College English*, 15, 3 (December 1953), 148–155.

Bibliography

Commager, Henry Steele, "Introduction," Henry Adams, *History of the United States of America during the Administration of Thomas Jefferson*, New York, Albert and Charles Boni, 1930, Books I and II, vii–xviii.

Cooke, Jacob E., "Chats with Henry Adams," *American Heritage*, VII, 1 (December 1955), 42–45.

"A Crisis in Science," *Life*, 42, 4 (January 28, 1957), 28.

Crothers, Samuel McChord, "Education in Pursuit of Henry Adams," *The Dame School of Experience*, Boston and New York, Houghton Mifflin Company, The Riverside Press Cambridge, 1920, 186–213.

DeVoto, Bernard, "The Easy Chair," *Harper's Magazine*, 195, 1171 (December 1947), 515–518.

DeWulf, Maurice, *Philosophy and Civilization in the Middle Ages*, Princeton University Press, c1922; New York, Dover Publications, Inc., c1953.

Eastman, Max, *The Sense of Humor*, New York, Charles Scribner's Sons, 1922.

Ellis, Havelock, "Nietzsche," *Affirmations* (1898), Boston and New York, Houghton Mifflin Company, 1922, 1–85.

Emerson, Ralph Waldo, "The Comic," *Letters and Social Aims*, Emerson's Complete Works, Riverside Edition, Boston and New York, Houghton, Mifflin and Company, The Riverside Press Cambridge, 1890, VIII, 151–166.

Falk, Doris, *Eugene O'Neill and the Tragic Tension: An Interpretive Study of The Plays*, New Brunswick, New Jersey, Rutgers University Press, 1958.

Fiske, John, "The Laws of History," *North American Review*, CIX (July, 1869), 197–230.

Gassett, José Ortega y, *The Revolt of the Masses* (Spanish original: *La Rebelión de las Masas*, 1930), New York, Mentor Books, The New American Library of World Literature, Inc., 1950.

Gilson, Etienne, *The Spirit of Mediaeval Philosophy* (Gifford Lectures, 1931–1932), tr. A. H. C. Downes, New York, Charles Scribner's Sons, 1936, 1940.

Hawthorne, Hildegard, "Nirvana," *The Reminiscences of Augustus Saint-Gaudens*, ed. and amplified by Homer Saint-Gaudens, New York, The Century Co., 1913, I 363.

Holt, Henry, *Garrulities of an Octogenarian Editor*, Boston and New York, Houghton Mifflin Company, 1923.

Housatonic [William Henry Smith in New York Public Library copy], "A Case of Hereditary Bias. Henry Adams as an Historian: Some Strictures on the 'History of the United States of America,'" *New York Tribune* [originally], September 10 and December 15, 1890; Washington, no publisher shown, 1891.

Hume, Robert A., *Runaway Star: An Appreciation of Henry Adams*, Ithaca, New York, Cornell University Press, 1951.

——, "The Style and Literary Background of Henry Adams: With Attention to *The Education of Henry Adams*," *American Literature*, 16 (1945), 296–315.

James, William, *Letters of William James*. ed., Henry James, Boston, The Atlantic Monthly Press, 1920, II.

Johnson, Edgar, "The Nature and Value of Satire," *A Treasury of Satire*, New York, Simon and Schuster, c1945, 3–37.

Jordy, William H., *Henry Adams: Scientific Historian*, New Haven, Yale University Press, c1952.

Keith, A. Berriedale, "Buddhist Mythology in India and Tibet," in Louis H. Gray, *The Mythology of All the Races*, Boston, Marshall Jones Co., 1917, VI, 187–219.

Bibliography

Krutch, Joseph Wood, "Is the Common Man Too Common?" *Is the Common Man Too Common?* Norman, Oklahoma, University of Oklahoma Press, c1954.

La Farge, Mabel, *Letters to a Niece and Prayer to the Virgin of Chartres by Henry Adams with a Niece's Memories*, Boston and New York, Houghton Mifflin Company, The Riverside Press Cambridge, 1920.

Leacock, Stephen, *Humor: Its Theory and Technique*, Dodd, Mead & Company, 1935.

Levenson, J. C., *The Mind and Art of Henry Adams*, Boston, Houghton Mifflin Company, The Riverside Press Cambridge, 1957; reissued Stanford, California, Stanford Univ. Press, 1968.

Lodge, Henry Cabot, *Early Memories*, New York, Charles Scribner's Sons, c1913, 1925.

Lydenberg, John, "Henry Adams and Lincoln Steffens," *The South Atlantic Quarterly*, XLVIII (January, 1949), 42–64.

Meredith, George, *An Essay on Comedy and the Uses of the Comic Spirit* (c1897), New York, Charles Scribner's Sons, 1923.

Miller, Henry, "Preface," *The Books in My Life*, London, Peter Owens Limited, 1952, 1961.

Miller, Perry, *Jonathan Edwards*, The American Men of Letters Series, New York, William Sloan Associates, 1949.

——, "The New England Conscience," *The American Scholar*, 28, 1 (Winter 1958–1959), 49–58.

Mindel, Joseph, "The Uses of Metaphor: Henry Adams and the Symbols of Science," *Journal of the History of Ideas*, XXVI, 1 (January–March 1965), 89–102.

More, Paul Elmer, *Commemorative Tribute to Henry Adams*, prepared for the American Academy of Arts and Letters, 1920, New York, American Academy of Arts and Letters, 1922.

Munford, Howard M., "Henry Adams and the Tendency of History," *The New England Quarterly*, XXXII, 1 (March 1959), 79–90.

Neufeld, Maurice F., "The Crisis in Prospect: Henry Adams and the White City," *The American Scholar*, 4, 4 (Autumn 1935), 397–408.

Nichols, Roy F., "The Dynamic Interpretation of History," *The New England Quarterly*, VIII, 2 (June 1935), 163–178.

Oppenheimer, Robert, "Tradition and Discovery," *ACLS Newsletter*, X, 8 (October, 1959), 3–19.

Parrington, Vernon Louis, "The Skepticism of the House of Adams," *Main Currents in American Thought: An Interpretation of American Literature from the Beginnings to 1920*, New York, Harcourt, Brace and Company, c1927, 1930, III, 212–236.

"Recent Books on American History," *Atlantic Monthly*, LXV, 388 (February 1890), 274–280.

Rourke, Constance, *American Humor: A Study of the National Character*, New York, Harcourt, Brace and Company, Inc., 1931; reprinted, Doubleday Anchor Books, Garden City, New York, Doubleday & Company, Inc., 1953.

Russell, Bertrand, *A History of Western Philosophy*, New York, Simon and Schuster, 1945.

Salvemini, Gaetano, *Historian and Scientist: An Essay on the Nature of History and the Social Sciences,* Cambridge, Massachusetts, Harvard University Press, 1939.

Samuels, Ernest, *Henry Adams: The Major Phase,* Cambridge, Massachusetts, The Belknap Press of Harvard University Press, 1964.

——, *Henry Adams: The Middle Years,* Cambridge, Massachusetts, The Belknap Press of Harvard University Press, 1958.

——, *The Young Henry Adams,* Cambridge, Massachusetts, The Belknap Press of Harvard University Press, 1948.

Schevill, Ferdinand, "Henry Adams: Achievement and Defeat," *Six Historians,* Chicago, University of Chicago Press, 1956, 157–190.

Scheyer, Ernst, "The Adams Memorial by Augustus Saint-Gaudens," *The Art Quarterly,* XIX, 2 (Summer 1956), 178–197.

Seidenberg, Roderick, *Posthistoric Man: An Inquiry,* Chapel Hill, University of North Carolina Press, c1950.

Sherman, Stuart P. "Evolution in the Adams Family," *Americans,* New York, Charles Scribner's Sons, 1923, 288–315.

Skinner, B. F., *Verbal Behavior,* New York, Appleton-Century-Crofts, Inc., 1957.

Snow, C. P., *The Two Cultures: And A Second Look,* New York, The New American Library, a Mentor Book, 1959, 1963.

Spiller, Robert E., "Henry Adams," *Literary History of the United States,* ed. Robert E. Spiller, Willard Thorp, Thomas H. Johnson, Henry Seidel Canby, New York, The Macmillan Company, 1948, 1963, II, 1080–1103.

Spring Rice, Cecil, "The St. Gaudens Monument at Rock Creek Cemetery," *Atlantic Monthly,* CXX (November 1917), 607–608.

Stevenson, Elizabeth, *Henry Adams: A Biography,* New York, The Macmillan Company, 1956.

Stone, James, "Henry Adams' Philosophy of History," *The New England Quarterly,* XIV, 3 (September 1941), 538–548.

Taylor, Henry Osborn, " 'The Education of Henry Adams,' " *Atlantic Monthly,* CXXII (October 1918), 484–491.

Thayer, William Roscoe, *The Life and Letters of John Hay,* Boston and New York, Houghton Mifflin Company, c1908, 1915, II.

Thomas, Edward J., "Buddha and Buddhism," *Encyclopaedia Britannica,* 1949 ed., IV, 325–327.

Wagner, Vern, "The Lotus of Henry Adams," *The New England Quarterly,* XXVII, 1 (March 1954), 75–94.

White, E. B., "Some Remarks on Humor," *The Second Tree from the Corner,* New York, Harper & Brothers Publishers, 1954, 173–181.

White, Lynn, Jr., "Dynamo and Virgin Reconsidered," *The American Scholar,* 27, 2 (Spring 1958), 183–194.

Whitehead, Alfred North, *Science and the Modern World* (Lowell Lectures, 1925), New York, The Macmillan Company, 1925; reprinted, New York, Mentor Books, The New American Library of World Literature, Inc., 1948.

Wilkins, Thurman, *Clarence King: A Biography,* New York, The Macmillan Company, 1958.

Winters, Yvor, "Henry Adams, or the Creation of Confusion," *The Anatomy of Nonsense,* Norfolk, Connecticut, New Directions, 1943, 23–87; reprinted in *In Defense of Reason,* Denver, Alan Swallow, 1947, 374–430.

Bibliography

Wister, Owen, *Roosevelt: The Story of a Friendship, 1880–1919*, New York, The Macmillan Company, 1930.

Zilsel, Edgar, "Physics and the Problem of Historico-sociological Laws," *Philosophy of Science*, 8, 4 (October 1941), 567–579.

Index

Abélard, 46

"The Abyss of Ignorance," Ch. XXIX of *Education*, 164-166

Acceleration, 163, 169, 196; as new force, 151; and Russia, 163; after 1500, 174; stupendous by 1900, 175; by 1904, 176; coal power as image of, 176; as invariable law, 177; from unity to multiplicity, 178; causes changes of phase, 195; in thought seen in comet, 198; constant in current, 198; of extinction of man, 205-206; on most intense energies, 208; on mind, 215

Accident, order as, 169

Adams, Abigail (Mrs. John Adams), 104-105

Adams, Brooks, 89, 153; *The Law of Civilization and Decay*, 53; quoted, 88

Adams, Charles Francis (Sr.), 22, 119, 121, 123, 124, 126; as education, 95-97, 98; as negative educational force, 96

Adams, Charles Francis, Jr., Ch.3 n21, 226; unsuccessful education of, 115

Adams, Henry Brooks, 1874 letter on style, 10, 31; mind set of, 13, 15; schooling, 22-23; as student in Ger-

many, 22-23; travels, 23, 24, 153; income of, 24, Ch.1 n25; as paradox, 25; summation of main characteristics, 25; four major works of, 26; 1879 letter on variety in sentence style, 29; chiarascuro in style of, 35; letters on rewriting of *History*, 41, Ch.2 n14; letters on choice of materials for *Chartres*, Ch.2 n16; 1905 letter on purpose of *Chartres*, Ch.2 n18; letters on his evaluation of *Chartres*, Ch.2 n22; sympathy for Thomas Aquinas' mental processes, 61; 1895 letter on Gothic as false, Ch.2 n26; and God of Truth, 66; anti-female attitude exposed, Ch.2 n31; 1908 letter on *Education* as literary experiment, 85; successes in active life, 88; his meaning of failure, 88-89; letters quoted on silence, 89; as Lilliputian, 92, Ch.3 n6; as a picaro, Ch.3 n7; as image of nineteenth-century education, 94; 1908 letter on literary form, Ch.3 n10; 1908 letter on autobiography, 94; his education as stamp of Puritan generation, 98; 1909 letter on content of *Education*, Ch.3 n14; end of education in youth as inconclusion, 114; on

Index

Index

Force, of Virgin Mary, 45; as leit motif of *Education*, 105; uses of word in Ch. I of *Education*, 105-106; as key word in *Education*, 113; as sink of science, 164; contradictions in definitions of, 168; and nature, 171; absorbs mind, 220; new ones in 1900, 169

Form, in writing never arbitrary, 9; material in, 9-10; in artistry, 86; as thought, 165, 217

Fortieth Parallel Survey, 143

France, Anatole, as humorist, 19

Francis of Assisi, Saint, as disbeliever in reason, 20, 61; and love, 45, 55, 78; and unity, 45; as naive, 46; represents Virgin Mary, 51; and transition architecture, 52; abandoned man for God, 60; and Mario in *The Last Puritan*, 67

Franco-Prussian War, 139, 140

Franklin, Benjamin, 25, 179; as humorist, 19; open to new thought, 175

"Free Fight," Ch. XVIII of *Education*, 136

Freud, Sigmund, 21; on jokes, 14

Frost, Robert, as humorist, 20

Futilitarian silence, 153

Galileo, 169, 174, 209, 219; recantation of, 188, 195; denouncement of in 1633, 199

Gallatin, Albert, 150

Garfield, James A., 136, 137

Garibaldi, 23, 119, 129, Ch.4 n16

Garden of Eden, 222

Gaskell, Milnes, 131

Gassett, Ortega y, 220

Gautama Buddha, 78-83 *passim*

German junior high school, 22

Gibbon, Edward, 30, Ch.2 n12, 37, 92, 93, 178

Gibbs, Josiah Willard, 183, 190, 200

"Le Gieus de Robin et de Marion," 72

The Gilded Age, 88

Gilson, Etienne, on Thomist doctrine, Ch.2 n24; appraisal of mediaeval world, Ch.2 n29

Gladstone, William Ewart, 121, 122, 123

"Gnarliness," in *History*, 31; in *Education*, 91, 186

Godkin, E. L., 150

Goldscheid, Rudolph, 193

Gold Standard, as unity, 152

Good temper, 12, 18, 62, 89, 133, 137 152, 194, 216, 134; as sense of humor, 14; as wisdom, 15; as attitude, 16; and silence, 44, 61, 114, 147, 179, 188, 205; of Saint Francis, 51; and in-conclusion, 56; missing in two poems and *Esther*, 73; cost of in George Strong, 76; missing in Esther Dudley, 78; as beyond silence, 83; encouraged in *Education*, 92; in "Tendency," 188; needed in asking difficult questions, 193

Gothic arch, as harmony, 46; as inconclusiveness, 46; as Transition, 46; two weak points of, 65; as broken, 66

Gothic architecture (late or full), as statement of beauty, 48; in Amiens cathedral, 49; Aquinas as, 49; *Education* as, 49; as tendency to vulgarity, 59

Gould, Jay, 137

"The Grammar of Science," Ch. XXXI of *Education*, 166-169

Grant, President Ulysses S., 27, 135, 136, 150, Ch.4 n16

Grant Administration, 137

Gravity, and magnet as contradiction, 160

Gray, Prof. Andrew, quoted, 203

"The Great Barbecue," 138

"Grief." *See* "Silence" statue

Grotesque, as figure of Adams in *Education*, 93

Grotesquerie, in Adams' final essays, 13, 184; in *Education*, 145; example of, 218

Guadalajara, Mexico, 186

Gunpowder, as new force, 173-174

Gutenberg, Johann, 174

Haeckel, Ernst Heinrich, 164

Hallgerda, in Icelandic *Njalsaga*, 28

Harte, Bret, 158

Hartmann, Eduard von, 204

Harvard, 138, 140; class of 1858, 22, Ch.3 n11; Adams' honorary degree from, 88; worth of degree from, 134, 142; professor at, 134

"Harvard College," Ch. IV of *Education*, 114

Hawthorne, Hildegarde, poem "Nirvana," Ch.3 n30

Index

Index

McKillop, Alan D., on satire, 17
Magnet, and gravity as contradiction, 160
Man, as one of two energies, 175; mind of in danger of dissipation, 177; his vaunted superiorities, 207; his development as degeneration, 207; his constitution summarized, 209; reason and soul in, 209; exempt from degradation by evolutionists, 216; against the universe, 223; at reverse end of evolutionary scale, 223; his view of self as illusion, 223; creature, not creator, 223; as unity, 223
"Mandalay," 147
Marx, Karl, 21
Marxism, 132
Mary. *See* Virgin Mary
Mary of Champagne, 71
Materialism, 47
Mathematics, as artificial construct, 168; as entropy, 199; as metaphysics, 191, Ch.4 n8
Maxwell, James Clerk, 167, 200
Mechanical phase (1600–1900), 196, 201
The Medieval Mind, Ch.2 n18
Medieval period, details of misery, 60
Medievalism, 111
Melville, Herman, as humorist, 19
Mencken, H. L., 109
Meredith, George, 15; comic spirit of, 16, 17
Metaphysics, mathematics as, 191, Ch.4 n8; science as, 191; as entrophy, 199; approached physics after 1890, 210
Michael, Saint, as logic, 51-52
Miller, Henry, on Adams' exaltation of Mary, Ch.2 n32
Miller, Perry, Jonathan Edwards and chaos, Ch.1 n20; *Education* as Puritan, Ch.2 n30
Milnes, Richard Monckton, Lord Houghton, 126-127, 128; as ideal of educated man, 126
Mind, as unity, 165; little known about, 173; new variety after Bacon, 175; in danger of dissipation, 177; suited to chaos, 187; new one needed after 1900, 192; and gravity, 197; question of its independence, 217; absorbed by force, 220
Mindel, Joseph, on Adams' metaphoric link of science and history, Ch.4 n6

Mirror image, 62, 92, 148, 164, 165, 197
Moby Dick, 9
Mockery, 158; in style of *Education*, 106-108
Mohammedanism, establishment of in 500, 196
La Mondes des Plantes avant l'Apparition de l'Homme, quoted, 205
Money, as education, 152
Monotheism, 204; from polytheism in 500, 196
Mont Blanc, 139
Mont-Saint-Michel, as masculine, 45, 64, 65; its architecture as statement of fact, 48; as justice, 50; and simple faith, 55; represents God of fact, 66; as unity of God, 66
Mont-Saint-Michel and Chartres, 90, 156, 157, 160, 164, 186, Ch.4 n8, 223; as history, 9; as art appreciation, 9; on general style of, 10, 185; satire in, 18; subject matter of, 24; as incertitude, 42; as aesthetic, Ch.2 n15; dates of composition, Ch.2 n16; choice of materials, Ch. 2 n16; appraisal of tone, 43-44; Parrington on, 43-44; as inconclusion, 44, 56; as opposition of three ideas, 44-45; hyperbole of meaning, 45; as feeling and poetry, 45; Adams' purpose in, Ch.2 n18; as historical reality, 46, 183; sequel to *History*, 48; an examination of transition, 48; as balance between *History* and *Education*, 49; hyperbole in, 55; Thomas Aquinas as main subject, 57; as blasphemy, Ch.2 n28; as tribute to love, 73; last three chapters of, 86; Adams' pride in last chapter of, Ch.3 n10; as triangulation of twelfth century, 154; as antiquarian study, 154; as study of thirteenth-century unity, 166; facts in, 182; Ernest Samuels on, 184; smooth flow in, 185; as study of vital energy, 203; paradox of unity and multiplicity, 223
Morality, politics as, 124-125, 150
More, Paul Elmer, appraisal of Adams' goal, Ch.3 n23
Morgan, M. Jacques de, quoted on overpopulation, 208
Multiplicity, joined to unity by Thomas Aquinas, 58; bridge to unity, 46; in George Strong, 78; eccentricity as, 130; Adams' growing conviction of,

263

Vern Wagner took his Ph.D. degree at the University of Washington. Author of various articles in professional journals, he was a professor of English at Nebraska State Teachers College at Chadron before going to Wayne State University where he is an associate professor of English.

The book was edited and prepared for publication by Ralph Busick. The book was designed by Richard Kinney. The type face for the text is Bodoni Book design by Giambattista Bodoni in the Eighteenth Century; and the display face is also Bodoni Book.

The book is printed on S. D. Warren's Olde Style Antique paper and bound in Columbia Mills' Atlantic Linen over binders board. Manufactured in the United States of America.

124821